The
PLAIN
SENSE of
THINGS

The
PLAIN
SENSE of
THINGS

The Fate of Religion
in an Age of Normal Nihilism

James C. Edwards

The Pennsylvania State University Press
University Park, Pennsylvania

"The Plain Sense of Things" from *Collected Poems* by Wallace Stevens, Copyright 1952 by Wallace Stevens, is reprinted by permission of Alfred A. Knopf Inc. and Faber and Faber Ltd.

Library of Congress Cataloging-in-Publication Data

Edwards, James C., 1943–
    The plain sense of things : the fate of religion in an age of normal nihilism / James C. Edwards.

        p.   cm.
    Includes bibliographical references and index.
    ISBN 0-271-01677-9 (cloth : alk. paper)
    ISBN 0-271-01678-7 (pbk. : alk. paper)
    1. Religion—Philosophy.   2. Nihilism (Philosophy).   3. Philosophy, Modern—20th century.   I. Title.
    BD573.E38   1997
    210—dc21   96-48047
                                                                        CIP

Copyright © 1997 The Pennsylvania State University
All rights reserved
Printed in the United States of America
Published by The Pennsylvania State University Press,
University Park, PA 16802-1003

It is the policy of The Pennsylvania State University Press to use acid-free paper for the first printing of all clothbound books. Publications on uncoated stock satisfy the minimum requirements of American National Standard for Information Sciences—Permanence of Paper for Printed Library Materials, ANSI Z39.48-1992.

*This book is for Jane S. Chew, for Emily Edwards,
and for Creighton Edwards*

CONTENTS

PREFACE

This book is no apology for any form of religious belief; far from it. But it does suggest that we need, and luckily still have available to us, practices that can contain, concentrate, and transmit the sacramental energies—energies for limitation in the face of hubris and for transformation in the face of complacency—that used to be bound up in the stories of the gods. If the distinction were not both too crude and too familiar, one might say that the book is about what it might mean for us to be religious without explicit religion.

The first chapter tells the story (or *one* of the stories, to be precise) of how we got to be who we are. It is a story made popular by Heidegger, a story about how the philosophical Ground beneath our feet has shifted from a divine order of craft and might, through a Platonic order of formal perfection, to the Cartesian ego-subject in its solitary and self-possessed splendor, and then to the centerless and fluid Nietzschean will to value. My account is the schoolchild version of this tale, accurate (I hope) but deliberately schematic. It is intended mostly to set the problem for the chapters to come.

That problem is the loss of religion's traditional power in a culture of (what I call) normal nihilism. When every system of belief is recognized only to be a set of values posited by the will to power in its attempt to preserve and enhance itself, or—shifting from Nietzsche's grandiose idiom to Rorty's more circumspect one—when every illuminating vocabulary is recognized only to be contingently useful, then how can any cultural symbol retain sufficient power to check our well-documented (and contrary) tendencies both to addictive, individualist self-magnification and to (equally addictive) totalitarian, fundamentalist rigidity? In other words, what any more can help us to resist the temptation either to go mad with unlimited self-fashioning or to sink helplessly into an imprisoning and soothing normality? "Values" are either too strong or too weak for the job. As the term is used by conservatives, values—the *right* ones, at least—enforce ahistorical ways of life from which there is no proper escape. But in the radical (and derivatively Nietzschean) lexicon, values are just the always already ossified provocations to an endless self-invention. One may, of course, find one of these glosses more attractive than the other. (As an atheist, historicist liberal, I certainly do.) But one may also hope to sidestep the choice altogether.

The remaining chapters explore that possibility of escape from values, first by looking in Chapter 2 at Kierkegaard's attempt (a failed attempt, I argue) to cut Christianity loose from Western metaphysics, and thus from the normal nihilism that is its fate; and then by looking at the work of Heidegger. In Chapter 3 I examine *Being and Time,* finding there a brilliant rewriting of Nietzschean *amor fati* that sharpens rather than ameliorates the sting of the problem I have posed. In Chapter 4 I offer a reading of some later Heidegger essays that represent, I believe, his own best response to the matter. In his notion of "poetic dwelling on the earth as a mortal" one finds a description of linguistic and behavioral practices—practices of "building dwelling thinking," as he puts it—that preserve and extend the dialectical energies for liberation and limitation formerly comprised in religion. Chapter 5 illustrates these practices in *Walden,* in Norman Maclean's *Young Men and Fire,* and by reference to Wallace Stevens's poem, "The Plain Sense of Things."

Having finished a book there are long moments when it seems a cheat to sign it only with one's own name, so essential are the contributions made by various others. These moments are inevitably succeeded by those when one knows it would be unfair, and perhaps insulting, to lumber one's friends with responsibility for stilted sentences and gassy ideas. The conventional compromise is a set of general acknowledgments. In these paragraphs one's collaborators, even though named, are offered a decent cover in which to hide, if they wish to; none can be held accountable for anything in particular in what follows. But what one wishes is that one could adequately convey, without maudlin sentiment and without an occasion of embarrassment to the other, a sense of what is truly owed.

The first and easiest thing to say is that the book couldn't have been written without the help of Furman University. A complete—but not final—draft was finished during a sabbatical leave for the winter and spring terms of 1994, but work on it was begun four years earlier. One summer's effort was supported by a grant funded by the Knight Foundation and awarded by Furman's Committee on Research and Professional Growth. I am especially grateful to John H. Crabtree Jr., now retired, but for a decade or so my dean. His support for scholarly work at Furman was exemplary. I am grateful as well to the members of my department, and particularly to my good friend Douglas M. MacDonald. An important part of Furman's contribution to the book goes back thirty years, in the person of my own first philosophy teacher there, James H. Hall, for many years now a teacher at the University of Richmond. I am grateful for his encouragement and example. Some of the texts discussed in the book have been assigned over the years to my students in classes in philosophy of religion, and their reactions—frequently surprising and always thoughtful—have been instrumental in shaping my own responses. In many ways this book has been written with these students in mind.

Although he may not be able to see it, this book continues to be a reflection of my large philosophical and personal debts to Richard Rorty. Much of it shows the beneficent influence of Thomas B. Turner, my intellectual companion and friend since 1972. Stanley Hauerwas thinks I'm wrong about most of the stuff that matters in life, but his encouragement and aid have been indispensable to this book. I'm also grateful to Jim Peterman for his friendship and his insightful philosophical mind.

For four consecutive summers I was lucky enough to have research assistants funded by the Furman Advantage program. Rob Sica, Sebastian Lurie, and Taylor Trussell each made significant contributions to this book. To Sebastian Lurie I am particularly indebted for help with Chapter 1, where he saved me from a serious error in judgment; and several of my conversations with Taylor Trussell about Kierkegaard were a source of both delight and instruction. Each of the two made innumerable other suggestions that have improved my efforts. About Sica's contribution, I can only (and inadequately) say here that most of the consequential ideas of the book were worked out in hundreds and hundreds of hours of intense conversation with him over two or three years. My various debts to him, as I trust he knows, are enormous, complicated, and continuing. Every philosopher should have, even if only for a time, a brilliant friend who knows the terror of a lee shore.

Sanford G. Thatcher, director of Penn State Press, was everything a writer could hope for in an editor: honest, encouraging, an insightful reader.

Finally, I thank those to whom the book is dedicated: my wife, Jane Chew, and my parents, Emily and Creighton Edwards. In many and cunning ways they have been trying, sometimes successfully, to teach me to pay attention to the plain sense of things.

1

THE CITY IN A DOME

Living in an Age of
Normal Nihilism

The practice of religion has long been an incitement to philosophy, and most of that philosophy, whether apologetic or skeptical, has concerned itself with the truth of religious claims: claims about divine existence; claims about divine nature; claims about divine intention and demand. This book, by contrast, is more interested in the power of religion than in its truth, interested in what happens to that power when the claims to truth slacken their grip. In that respect, if in no other, the volume firmly belongs to the philosophical progress this first chapter will soon describe. My subject is not the credibility of any particular religion, traditional or otherwise. I intend, rather, to examine a particular inflection of our common sensibility to things, an inflection—for the moment call it religious—that has traditionally expressed itself in theological and philosophical constructions of great force and ingenuity, and also in powerful moral formations and in various styles of ethical life. I hope to understand what we can yet expect from this dimension of our imaginative life, now that its traditional expressions have begun to fade. In the book I shall try to answer three large questions:

1. What does it now mean for us to be religious?
2. What might it now mean for us to be religious?
3. What should it now mean for us to be religious?

One immediate (and, if I am correct in the story I will soon tell, quite predictable) response to these questions will be to dismiss them as dated and uninteresting, as holdovers from an earlier and more gullible stage of our philosophical culture. Are we philosophers not thankfully past the point of having to take religion and religiousness seriously? We must grant (of course) that lots of people, even some philosophers, still are religious in both vocabulary and practice; we must even grant that much of the world's (and our nation's) recent history has turned on overtly religious affiliations and conflicts. Is it not nevertheless the case that the philosophical interest of religion— as distinguished from its sociological interest, or its economic inter- est, or its political interest, or its psychopathological interest—has been largely exhausted? Can we not, and should we not, move on?

Of course we can, but only at a high price: high because it entails a form of self-denial, or at least self-forgetfulness. To think we philoso- phers have properly finished with questions about what it might mean or should mean for us to be religious is to think we have prop- erly finished with ourselves, for we—and we philosophers espe- cially—are selves that have been constituted by just such questions (and by their various answers). For us, being religious is not (or not only) a matter of explicit theological belief or sacramental practice, nor is it a matter of finding particular images and rituals powerfully affecting; it is a matter of our history, our *Bildung,* cultural if not individual, and that means of our present too. It is a matter of how we got to be the people we now are.

For good or for ill, all of us have been marked by distinctively reli- gious affections in their various intellectual, social, and political ex- pressions. We are, as Heidegger would put it, *immer schon* religious, "always already" religious, religious even in our present-day disdain for the supernatural and its outworn trappings. Our contemporary philosophical impatience with religion, an impatience real enough of course, has itself a religious root. So we need to find out what being religious means for us, and to find out whether our present way of being religious—that is, our way of being our sort of self—is the only (or the best) option available. To have finished with questions about what it means for us to be religious would be to have finished with self-knowledge.

But shouldn't a courageous philosophy intend radical and beneficial change, not merely a more adequate understanding of who we are?[1] (The dusty unwrapping of thought-mummies, Nietzsche calls it.) Why not try boldly to refuse our religious inheritance in the hope of self-

---

1. In that vein, here are the famous words of Foucault: "What is philosophy today— philosophical activity, I mean—if it is not . . . the endeavor to know how and to what extent it is possible to think differently, instead of legitimating what is already known?"

reliance? The point is well taken, and no doubt the Nietzschean ideal of self-overcoming is compelling, at least in certain of our moods. But it is worth remembering that even for Nietzsche himself a certain kind of self-knowledge is a condition of self-transformation: genealogy underwrites and empowers transvaluation. No one is asserting here that we must remain religious, world without end, amen; only that, given our history, we now *are* such, in some way or other, whether fully or privatively. And further, that it is important to us to begin to understand what that means, even (perhaps especially) if we think we do not wish to remain so. So let us turn immediately to the first of our founding questions.

The Descriptive Question

Because "What does it now mean for us to be religious?" directly puts *us* into question, and since we always are the people we have over time become, a narrative is the only proper response. But before that narrative is presented, two features of the question itself need attention.

First, we need to notice its specificity. The question quite deliberately asks, What does it now mean for *us* to be religious? The question does not ask about religiousness or religion per se, as if either had an eternal essence that could be presented once and for all by careful conceptual articulation. Nor does it presuppose an audience of bodiless spirits who can calmly survey human life in all its variety, analyzing and then synthesizing until a general account of religiousness is produced. On the contrary, the question directs itself to a particular audience, embedded in a particular history, who are thus presumed to have a particular answer to it. We ourselves, in all our specificity, are both the subjects and the objects of our inquiry here. What does it now mean for *us* to be religious? What has *our* experience of religion been?

But who are *we,* who are thus invited to question ourselves? We are end-of-century, Western intellectuals. We are not asking here what it means for a traditional Native American, or for an eighteenth-century Vietnamese Buddhist monk, or for a contemporary Hindu living in an Indian agricultural village, or for a fifteenth-century Japanese Shinto priest, to be religious. We couldn't, most of us, sensibly respond to those questions, important as they certainly are. We are not those people, nor does our history—our history as end-of-century,

Western intellectuals—directly flow from theirs. None of those ways of being religious is what it is, or what it has been, for *us* to be religious.

In saying that, I don't intend to condescend to those other forms of religious life. They are—we outsiders have every good reason to believe—at least as spiritually rich, at least as intellectually deep, at least as morally formative, and thus at least as worthy of philosophical attention, as are the major religious expressions of the West; and, for all I know, they have undergone transformations and crises comparable to the ones I will address in our tradition. Nor do I wish to imply that "the West" which figures in my question's limitation is some clear and well-defined entity, or that it should try to constitute itself as such, free of contamination by other traditions. There is certainly no assumption here that we Westerners are, or should seek to be, the center of human history, the stalwart bearers of the good and the true. Quite the contrary: we can look forward to the day when such phrases as "the West" will have only a geographical or a historical significance, when they won't be used as sticks to beat ourselves and others. But in the meantime it is still true that those who grew up by avidly reading Homer, the Bible, Plato, Cervantes, Shakespeare, Descartes, Kant, George Eliot, Nietzsche, Whitman, and Freud, and whose political consciousness was shaped by the European wars of religion and by the French, American, Russian, and Eastern European revolutions, and whose present circumstance is one of relative peace, plenty, and leisure in some one of the North Atlantic democracies, share something of a common consciousness (and something of a common fate). We are, for the most part, those women and men.

My reasons for limiting this essay to the religious sensibility of end-of-century, intellectual Westerners are two. First, I simply don't know enough about what it is like to be a Navajo, or a Hindu, or a Buddhist, to presume to speak for them about what it means for them to be religious; nor do I expect that many of my readers will be much better favored in this regard. (Some will be, of course, and all honor to them.) To try to speak for someone else on a matter of importance— especially to speak without permission, or at least without the excuse of dire emergency—is always (and at best) presumptuous; that we academics do it all the time, playing our role as expositors and interpreters of our intellectual heroes, diminishes the presumption not a whit. A certain kind of theoretician, the sort who believes in the possibility of speaking about religion *überhaupt,* the sort who tries to characterize or synthesize the phenomenon across all ages and cultures, seems to me to extend past all warrant our necessary intellectual overreaching. Wouldn't it be better for thinkers to stay closer to home where, even if distortion is still quite likely, at least the chance of giving offense is less?[2] I think so; thus I try to limit my presumption by acknowledging at the outset the particularity of the question I am asking. (To escape all presumption, of course, one would have to stick solely to the first-person singular and stop speaking about *us* at all. But philosophy, even of a fairly local sort, should try to be more than memoir.)

Past the matter of avoiding such presumption as one can, there is also the fact that we end-of-century, intellectual Westerners are yet a potent force in the world, for good and for evil. If I am right in thinking that we are always already in some way religious, and if understanding what that means can have a large measure of influence on our present attempts at self-knowledge and self-transformation, then it seems useful for us to pursue our descriptive question, limited though it is. Given who we are, and given who we might yet become, our way of being religious—of being ourselves—is still a topic of considerable interest, and not just for ourselves. That the present inquiry is ethnocentric doesn't necessarily mean that it is trivial or corrupt.[3]

2. This is not an attack on the idea of comparative philosophy or comparative religion, just a suggestion that such endeavors will turn out to be much more difficult—ethically and intellectually—than they might at first seem.

3. Having said all this, there is still the possibility that what I intend as limitation will be taken as exclusion. I fear that, in spite of my disavowals of any claim of superiority, some will always hear my talk about "us" end-of-century, Western intellectuals as an attempt to read out of our civilization, or even out of existence altogether, those voices, texts, and individuals that won't accommodate such a description. Some may see my rhetorical gesture, not as my rejection of a typically philosophical transcendental standpoint for reflection, but as comparable to the insensitivity shown (and violence done) when a teacher addresses a class as if everyone present there were white, middle-class, male, straight, Christian-Americans. In most classrooms in America today that is not—thank goodness—just who we are, and it is an affront to many of our fellow citizens for democratic education to proceed in ignorance—feigned or otherwise—of that fact. (I don't deny, of course, that such affront is still frequently given in far too many American schools and colleges.) But a single book is not a classroom or a curriculum; a limitation in the former has not the same significance as a limitation in the latter. It is one thing to set out to educate citizens of, say, the United States about what it means, and should mean, to be the citizens of that democratic republic, or to set out to initiate college students into a community defined by respect for the liberal arts and sciences; it is quite another to write a single philosophical book in the hope it may be of interest and use to some of the people who have read some of the same books you have and have been struck by those books in roughly similar ways. In our wider educational and civic tasks, a commitment to diversity and inclusiveness of perspective is always a sensible and worthy ideal. It is not clear (to me) that the same ideal should

A second key feature of the descriptive question is of course the term "religious" itself. How is it being used? A complete answer can be given only by this chapter's forthcoming narrative of what it has meant for us to be religious here in the West, but in the interim, and as a means of beginning to construct that narrative, I set out three structural features of the various forms of Western religiousness I will go on to describe. These structural features underlie, and give a certain kind of intelligibility to, the various practices of creedal affirmation, prayer, confession, repentance, virtuous action, and so on, that have been characteristic of the great Western religions: Judaism, Christianity, and Islam. These features are also centrally present in much early Greek religion and in some cultural phenomena not usually thought of as distinctively religious at all, phenomena I nevertheless shall include in my narrative.

Again I make it clear that I am not presupposing that these structural features articulate some eternal essence of religiousness, or even of Western religiousness. Rather, I take myself to be proceeding purely descriptively (if also very generally). These are features that, in various ways and to various degrees, we happen to find in the major (and uncontroversial) forms of religiousness present in our culture and its history. No claim is being made that they had to be found there, or that they must be (or must not be) found in the religious life of another culture, or even that they must be (or must not be) found in those ways of being religious (if any) that our heirs will find compelling. These three structural features are crucial parts of a purely contingent but nevertheless very important religious tradition, namely, our own.[4] To be sure, the features I shall discuss are both very general

---

always govern when one's educational aims are more modest. If one does not find oneself in the audience addressed by a book like this one, one can easily close it and walk away, perhaps in anger, perhaps in pity. That is not true when one is confronted with a textbook or with a curriculum defined by such textbooks.

4. In typical philosophical style, the account I give here seems to assume that theory must always underlie and explain practice: the structural features of Western religiousness are presented as if they are philosophical theses explicitly maintained ("believed") by the adherents of the tradition I am using them to describe. I admit that this way of presenting the material is a function of our own particular ways of construing our lives ("the age of the world picture," Heidegger calls it), but in this context it is largely harmless. At any rate to proceed in this way is (for me) unavoidable, as I don't know how to write this sort of philosophy outside the particular conventions of *vorstellendes Denken*. At best, one hopes to be able later to undo the damage one has done. (To quote J. L. Austin, "There's the part where you say it, and the part where you take it back.")

and very familiar: so general and so familiar that they usually pass unnoticed, or at least unremarked in works of philosophy. Perhaps pointing out such generalities will seem trivial to some. I disagree: "The aspects of things that are most important to us [philosophers] are hidden because of their simplicity and familiarity."[5] To call attention to such familiar simplicities is (unless one is actually Wittgenstein, of course) to run the risk of appearing simpleminded oneself, but in this case the game is worth the candle. These large, deeply embedded, and almost invisible convictions—one might almost call them elements of the spiritual grammar of the West—are the engines driving our most concrete expressions of religious theory and practice. It is important to set them out as clearly as one can.

The first of these features is the assumption of a fundamental and binary division of what there is, a division that ranges across the whole of things (and their relations) and sorts every one of those things (and relations) into one of the two basic types the division defines. We may call this division, most generally, the distinction between the *sacred* and the *profane*.[6] The division is not merely ethical or sacerdotal. At bottom it is (to use, somewhat anachronistically, a specifically philosophical term) *ontological:* anything that is, is of one sort or the other; and whichever sort it is, sacred or profane, it is that sort all the way down, in virtue of its very nature as what it is. We here in the West have seldom considered reality to be all of a piece. On the contrary, we have typically insisted that reality is divided into two distinct realms, into two different "worlds": "this world" of need and lack and change; and "the other world" (the "true world," Nietzsche ironically calls it) of wholeness and haleness and permanence.

Western religiousness makes this binary distinction fundamental to its affections and practices. When one examines the basic religious (and philosophical) texts of our civilization, from the Bible and the Koran to Plato, Augustine, Descartes, Luther, and Kant, one finds those books insisting on a deep division between (1) some things that are fully real and lack nothing in order to be what they are, things that are resplendent in their completeness, self-sameness, independence, and perfection, and (2) other things that are in some way imperfect and needy, needy in their very being (or Being), in comparison to the first. The omnipresence and familiarity of this distinction

5. Ludwig Wittgenstein, *Philosophical Investigations,* trans. G. E. M. Anscombe (Oxford: Basil Blackwell, 1953), sec. 129.

6. See Mircea Eliade, *The Sacred and the Profane,* trans. W. R. Trask (New York: Harper and Row, 1961).

should not blind us to its fundamental importance. Sensibility to the difference between the sacred and the profane has shaped our civilization in every way imaginable.

"Sacred" and "profane" are very general terms, of course, and in practice the distinction is (as we will see) fleshed out in a welter of quite different specific contrasts: gods/human beings, Forms/material things, ego/objects, nobles/slaves, and so on. But whatever the particular terms of the disjunction, and whether the vocabulary employed is exuberantly mythical or more chastely philosophical, Western religiousness has insisted upon some binary account of what there is. For our sort of religious sensibility, there is a twofold division of things at the core of reality itself. At the most basic level, we are dualists, not monists.

Moreover, and this is the second structural feature, the two "worlds" are ordered in a particular way. There is no détente at the fundamental level; the two realms do not coexist peacefully as equals. Rather, they are hierarchically ordered. One is primary and self-supporting and empowering; the other is secondary and dependent. To use here a vivid image from the philosophical tradition, the profane is always *grounded by* the sacred. The sacred ground for "this world" is what philosophers have learned to call the *subject,* the *subiectum,* the *hypokeimenon,* "that which stands under and supports."[7] There is no way completely to cash the metaphor and thus to specify what sacred "grounding" is *überhaupt:* different traditional forms of Western religiousness exploit the idea in different ways. In the Jewish tradition, to take a clear and familiar example, the first two stories in Genesis are mythical expressions of the priority of the sacred to the profane. First there was Yahweh, and nothing else; then at his command came all the other things there now are, things that entirely depend upon him for their existence and their identity. One realm is original and self-sufficient and self-same (creator); the other is patently derivative (created). But creation of "this" world by a god or gods is only one image for the priority of sacred to profane. Another, as we will see, is the Platonic notion of the Form as the perfect exemplar of the imperfect material thing, or the Cartesian conviction that "clear and distinct" insights underlie all our ordinary knowledge of the world, or Kant's idea that eternal Laws of Freedom show themselves in and through the concrete practical maxims of the virtuous life.

7. For an enlightening discussion of these matters, see Martin Heidegger, "The Age of the World Picture," in Heidegger, *The Question Concerning Technology and Other Essays,* trans. W. Lovitt (New York: Harper and Row, 1977), 139–53.

In whatever image the idea of sacred grounding is contained, this much is clear: the profane depends upon the sacred both for its raw existence and for its intelligible structure. There is no more possibility that the profane world can be adequately explained in its own terms than that it could exist only through its own efforts. Without the sacred, without the fullness of purely present Being Itself, there would be—would exist—nothing at all. And without reference to the sacred, the profane would be utterly unintelligible, a chaos lacking any stable identity or sense. Thus the philosophical metaphor of the sacred as ground has two distinguishable (if not separable) components: the ground is that which brings forth and supports, that which produces and nourishes; and the ground is that which clarifies and makes intelligible, that which justifies and rationally explains. For Western religiousness both the order of being and the order of knowledge are binary and hierarchical, and in both the basic structure is the same: the sacred (the whole, the full, the perfect, the immediately self-present, the permanent) grounds the profane (the partial, the piecemeal, the imperfect, the absent, the alterable).

But Western religiousness is more than a particular ontological perspective; it is also a form of life, a *doing*. Thus the third characteristic feature of that religiousness: a sense that the proper and harmonious relationship of sacred to profane—a relationship in which the profane world somehow recognizes and assents to its ground in the sacred order of things—has been (or at least might be) in some way breached; and, if so, that the proper order of things must continually be reacknowledged and restored in practice. The Jewish stories of the Fall vividly illustrate this loss of harmony and of the terrible consequences of that loss. So too does Euthyphro's concern that the "pollution" released by his father's role in a servant's death be cleansed by an appropriate act of piety, however personally painful. Thus the central role among us still of religious practices like ritual sacrifice, confession of error, penance, the giving of alms, and the dispensing and receiving of the sacraments. All these are ways of acknowledging in actual event both the proper relationship of the sacred to the profane ("What doth the Lord require of thee . . . ?") and the fact that this relationship has been unjustifiably put awry by us. Moreover, these practices intend to do what they can to rectify the improper relationship that now exists. If properly performed, the ritual sacrifice or the act of penance or the giving of alms to the needy does not leave the situation exactly where it was beforehand; rather, a proper connection of profane to sacred has been restored, at least temporarily. In the ritual action or in the deed of charity the part is brought closer to the whole, and the grounding Presence of all Being becomes less absent from those beings participating in the rite.

In the paradigmatic forms of early Greek religion there is less emphasis on restoring a lost harmony between sacred and profane than there is on maintaining a harmony between the two, a harmony that is fragile and complex, and thus always in danger of being lost. In other words, early Greek religion lacks the idea of shameful and personal and original *sin* so familiar to us from the Jewish traditions, including Christianity and Islam. Human beings frequently run afoul of the Greek divinities, of course, but this derives less from some innate perversity of human will than from accidents of fate, of ignorance, or of overpowering bursts of emotion. The Greek religious task is not redemption of something always already flawed ("sinful") and worthy of punishment; rather, it is to carefully avoid those pitfalls, personal and social, that would upset the proper order of things and thus bring on nemesis. Either way, Greek or Jewish, the ritual practices undertaken by human beings have as their point the overt recognition of the authoritative sway of the sacred over the profane, a recognition that either restores (Jewish) or maintains (Greek) a proper harmony between the two.

In summary, then, when one looks at those practices that most uncontroversially belong in the category of "Western religiousness"—Judaism, the Greek pantheon, Christianity, Islam—one sees at their centers the three structural features just adumbrated: a binary account of what there is; the sacred grounding of the profane; the need for proper harmony between the two and its attempted restoration or maintenance. In this way one has made a first pass at identifying what we mean by "religious" in asking, What does it now mean for us to be religious? For us to be religious is for us to have a life in which these three features show themselves in some basic way.

The Epochs of Western Religiousness

Having identified three characteristic structural features of Western religious sensibility, I now turn to a brief narrative account of their major theoretical and practical expressions. There are, I argue, four such expressions; I call them here the four epochs of Western religiousness: (1) the age of the gods, (2) the age of the Forms (Idealism), (3) the age of Cartesian ego-subjectivity, and (4) the age of transvalued values.[8] In each of these epochs one finds a particular and distinctive instantiation of the three structural features we have just noted. That is, each develops its own specific vocabulary and institutions for expressing (a) the binary differentiation of reality, (b) the hierarchical relation of ground, and (c) the proper ritual practices required to restore or to maintain a proper harmony between sacred and profane.

In my narrative I shall, for clarity's sake, treat these epochs as discrete and well-defined; I shall also present them as a determinate historical sequence. In fact, of course, the epochs overlap and interpenetrate in various ways, with quite different religious expressions jostling one another at the same place and time, sometimes even in the same texts and practices. One rarely encounters these *Weltanschauungen* in the pure forms I describe. "The theorizing mind," says William James, "tends always to the oversimplification of its materials." Furthermore, despite philosophers' self-congratulatory fantasies, philosophy is not the driving-wheel of Western history. It is unlikely that the shifts from one epoch to another are always so tightly geared to specific conceptual anomalies as I shall make them out to be. These epochs and their sequence in this narrative are *idealizations,* therefore. Nevertheless, in these idealizations we can recognize the roots and flowers of our civilization.

To call the materials of my narrative idealizations is to bring out an important feature of their production, a feature that, if not carefully noted, can confuse and anger the astute reader. In constructing this narrative account of our present situation, I shall be referring to some philosophers and their texts, just as I shall also be referring to some of the Greek myths and to the Jewish and Christian Scriptures. I shall, in fact, be trying to conjure my narrative directly out of those texts; in doing so I shall employ such phrases as "According to the Yahwist . . . ," or "Plato believes . . . ," or "Descartes asserts . . . ," or "Nietzsche claims . . ." Such phrases are most easily read as direct assertions about the views of those particular thinkers, read as elements within a respectable scholarly exposition of those views.

---

8. My potted history here obviously owes a great deal to Nietzsche and to Heidegger, but I have not burdened the reader with acknowledgments of all my specific debts and disagreements. The Heidegger essays "The Word of Nietzsche: 'God is Dead'" and "The Age of the World Picture," both in *The Question Concerning Technology and Other Essays,* are especially important for the story I tell. My narrative is also deeply indebted to my discussions over many years with Thomas Boyd Turner, and especially to his series of lectures, "What Am I Doing when I Pray?" delivered to classes in philosophy of religion at Furman in 1983 and 1984. It is a pleasure to express my gratitude to Tom for all that I have learned from him.

Though entirely natural, such a reading is in this instance mistaken. I adopt such phrases only as a *façon de parler.* My intention here is not to offer full and fully scholarly accounts of these thinkers and their convictions and arguments. Rather, I am trying to tell the story of how we came to be who we are, of how we came to exhibit the particular religious sensibility (as I understand it) of the typical contemporary Western intellectual. That sensibility can usefully be represented, and will be represented here, as a developmental narrative incorporating particular readings of some very great religious visionaries and philosophers (the Yahwist, Plato, Descartes, Nietzsche). Many of those readings, though now thoroughly traditional, are arguably oversimple, perhaps even tendentious. But it is just those readings, stark and one-dimensional as they sometimes are, that have formed us as end-of-century, Western intellectuals. No doubt it will seem crude to specialist scholars to present Plato primarily as an Idealist seeking to gaze on some transcendent ontological realm, or to make Descartes out to be a representationalist in all things epistemological. No doubt there are important facets of their thinking that cannot be captured in these standard caricatures, however brilliant, incisive, and useful they are. I willingly admit it; insist upon it, in fact. Nevertheless, these caricatures are now the standard for our intellectual culture, taken as a whole; they have shaped our typical sense of who we are and where our possibilities and limits lie.

My intention in this narrative is self-recognition. I want to describe *us*—not the Yahwist, not Plato, not Descartes—in ways that bring illumination and assent, and I want to do so in terms of our culture's gross philosophical continuities and vicissitudes. I want, in sum, to characterize what one might call the religious and philosophical mood of contemporary Western intellectuals—or, if there be more than one such mood, to characterize what I take to be the dominant one.[9] In calling the object of my inquiry a *mood,* I am trying to avoid finally reducing it to some well-defined set of philosophical theses or doctrines, self-consciously articulated and affirmed. My appeal to the word "mood" is deliberately intended to recall the German *Stimmung,* especially as that word figures in Heidegger's usage.[10] The root of *Stimmung* is the verb *stimmen,* which means (in the primary instance) "to tune," as one might tune a piano or a cello. A *Stimmung* is

9. Richard J. Bernstein also appeals to the notion of mood in his philosophical account of our situation. See his *The New Constellation: The Ethical-Political Horizons of Modernity/Postmodernity* (Cambridge: MIT Press, 1992), 11.

10. Martin Heidegger, *Being and Time,* trans. John Macquarrie and Edward Robinson (New York: Harper and Row, 1962), sec. 29.

first of all a tuning. A mood, therefore, is *an attunement to things,* a way of vibrating in relation to being struck by them, a way of sounding them out in oneself.

So understood, a mood is not a set of beliefs, philosophical or otherwise, though specific beliefs may of course be (represented as) involved in its construction or its maintenance. A mood, once established, is the way one receives whatever particular beliefs, philosophical or otherwise, then come to one. A mood shows itself in the way those beliefs are framed into one's life; it is a way of phrasing them in one's continuous self-narrative, a way of tasting them on the tongue, so to speak. Think of the difference in registering the insight "she loves me" when one's mood is confident hope rather than bleak depression. The difference may not be perspicuously expressible just in terms of what one differently believes in the two cases; it has to do with the way one's beliefs, whatever they are, strike and resound in one. A mood gives beliefs a particular *Gestalt,* a particular tone. But that is not to say that a mood is merely some sort of inner weather of the mind. Properly understood, a mood is not fundamentally "mental" at all. A mood is a way one comports oneself to what one finds; it is a way in which one *takes*—in which one "sounds out" in one's actions and reactions—what there is.

A mood, then, is a way of acting, a style of response, a specific sense of inhabiting one's life. In this chapter I describe a particular mood of ours, a mood that attunes us in a particular way to our situation as end-of-century Western intellectuals, and a mood that can (at a first pass, anyway) be represented as our identification with a particular historical sequence of religious and philosophical standpoints. If that mood has typically been conjured from caricatures of the work of some great thinkers (as I argue elsewhere that it has), then it is all the more crucial to identify, and even to trade on, those compelling caricatures. The point here, as I say, is self-recognition, not the advance of philosophical scholarship.[11] The point is that we come to ac-

---

11. My sense of having indulged the injuries of caricature is perhaps strongest in the case of Nietzsche, who has suffered terribly in this respect. The account I give of him in this chapter is flatly ahistorical, in spite of my agreement with Maudemarie Clark that ignorance of the development of Nietzsche's thought is the first step down the primrose path to misunderstanding; see her excellent *Nietzsche on Truth and Philosophy* (New York: Cambridge University Press, 1990). Again I say, my intention here is not an accurate account of Nietzsche (however that might be accomplished); I aim only at an accurate account of what Nietzsche has come to mean to us, the role he plays in constructing and maintaining our current religious and philosophical mood. As a way of acknowledging this difference, I have taken all my Nietzsche quotations from *The Will to Power,* the book that he did not live to publish. Perhaps that will make it easier for

cept my narrative, and the particular philosophical mood it creates and explains, as *our own:* as a convincing account of what it does mean for us end-of-century, Western intellectuals to be subject to religious affection.

But couldn't a more adequate account of these thinkers lead to a different sensibility? Couldn't the correction of historical caricature alter the contemporary mood I am making it my business to investigate?[12] Perhaps, but I doubt it. Sensibilities—especially deeply entrenched ones—are replaced with others, not corrected piecemeal. In this book I imagine an alternative to our present, not reconstruct on sounder scholarly principles our sense of the past.

The Age of the Gods

The first form of Western religiousness is the age of the gods. In this epoch, the sacred ground of all beings is conceived as *divine presence.* The fully present, logically prior realm that underlies and supports all that is—the sacred—is the holy and complete reality of the gods (or *a* God, if one were to be a monotheist), while everything else, and especially the human world, is partial, dependent, and lacking any secure and intrinsic order; that is, profane. The gods thus identified as the sacred ground are imagined as transcendent, willful, mysterious, commanding presences, usually personified, sometimes actually symbolized as particular human beings or animals. We all know stories from this age; clear and familiar examples can be found in the Hebrew Bible, or in Homer or Hesiod, or in the epic of Gilgamish.

Crucial to our understanding of this epoch is its portrayal of the gods as centers of transcendent and terrible will. The gods are compelling superhuman presences, instances of uncontrollable and (sometimes) incomprehensible force; the profane world makes its way under the incontestable sway of the sacred. And that sacred force is uncanny. The irresistible power of the divine, like the wind, blows wherever and with whatever force it wishes: sometimes soothing, sometimes demolishing. And human beings, though not mere debris, are finally subject to its draft. The humbling encounter with divine power, the human being's compulsion by supernatural (and fre-

---

readers to remember that the "Nietzsche" who figures in this account is no more the "real" Nietzsche than *The Will to Power* is "really" the great book of its author's maturity. The volume is a fragment, a torso; so is the philosopher found there (and here).

12. For an example of such hope, see Stanley Rosen, *The Question of Being: A Reversal of Heidegger* (New Haven: Yale University Press, 1994).

quently baffling) will, is the definitive religious experience of this epoch.

Since the sacred ground of all things is compelling divine power, in a number of stories characteristic of this epoch the physical world itself springs into being only at some god's command, compelled to exist as a world by the divine word. (The two creation narratives in Genesis, already mentioned, are familiar examples of this idea.) Likewise, human beings are frequently represented as divine products (at least on one side of their lineage), and they too find themselves always and everywhere subject to divine compulsion. In the most extreme cases, there may be literally no escape from some god's will. In Eden, for example, Yahweh commands Adam and Eve not to eat the fruit of a certain tree; the malicious serpent-god tells them to disregard the previous instruction. The human beings in the Garden thus find themselves obeying one divine power or another, whatever they do. They have no genuinely independent lives.

The gods, therefore, ground the profane with their will. The god's compelling power creates (or fashions) the profane world in the first place, and whatever intelligibility that reality may have to human beings is grasped only by referring it to the prior will of the divine. (Eden's only explanation, whether by efficient cause or by teleological one, is that Yahweh willed it. And any account of Adam's actions must refer to his obedience or disobedience of some divine power or other.)

It is equally important to see that this compelling, personal, creative willfulness of the gods may make no moral sense. As we understand the term, the gods are not moral beings at all, since for us the notion of the moral largely derives from the epoch of Idealism (to be discussed in the next part of this chapter) and is intrinsically connected to the notions of human happiness and of formal rationality.[13] Morality is not just power and the will to use it. (Think of Socrates' distance from Thrasymachus in Book 1 of the *Republic*.) That which

13. It may be that his insistence on inquiring into the morality of the gods and their directives is what got Socrates in trouble with some of his Athenian persecutors. Think in this connection of the *Euthyphro*, in which Socrates tries to move his interlocutor from the claim that piety is "what is pleasing to the gods" (a conception that emphasizes both the willfulness of the divine beings and the human necessity blindly to comply with it in ritual and sacrifice, to simply "please" the gods) to the claim that "piety is a part of justice." The latter claim seems to move in the direction of asserting the existence of some prior structure to which piety must conform. Power/will, even divine power/will, are not the final authority for things. (I am indebted to William Marion for emphasizing the connection to the *Euthyphro*.) For a stimulating and reliable discussion of these matters, see Gregory Vlastos, *Socrates: Ironist and Moral Philosopher* (Ithaca: Cornell University Press, 1991), chap. 6.

is morally good must, we believe, make sense; in the moral life willful power must answer to some standard other than itself. There must be some consistent structure of impersonal moral reasons (reasons deeply connected somehow to human flourishing in general) that specify the correct course of action in a given situation, even if we do not, in our various limitations, have full access to those reasons. Moreover, the (ideally) good action is—we footnotes to Plato believe— the one undertaken in full recognition of and submission to that structure of rational support. For us, moral beings that we are, virtue is knowledge; knowledge is virtue.

But in the age of the gods there is no necessity for divine power to be virtuous or reasonable in this sense. The gods do not have to submit their conduct to the authority of some impersonal and rational standard, and certainly divine conduct doesn't have to make human flourishing more likely. Yahweh spends a good bit of his time making things terrible for the Hittites, the Hivites, the Amelekites, and the other assorted ethnic groups who have the misfortune to occupy the land he has blithely promised to Abraham and his kin. In this regard one may think also of the classical Greek pantheon, where the only authority is the stronger or the craftier deity. Is it a matter of justice that Cronus should be able to eat his children or that Zeus should be able to turn himself into a swan to have his way with the beautiful Leda? Not at all; only power (or sometimes pity, which is a kind of condescension grounded in power) finally matters in the determination of divine conduct.

To illustrate the point, consider some events set on a mountain spiritually somewhat closer to us than Olympus: Yahweh's notorious dealings with Abraham and young Isaac as recounted in the first book of the Torah (Gen. 22). Again and again in *Fear and Trembling* Kierkegaard demonstrates the radical absence of ethical sense in the divine demand that the innocent and trusting Isaac be sacrificed in Yahweh's contrived loyalty test; nor is there any rational way to justify Abraham's willingness to submit to the god's wicked command. From the moral point of view, *our* point of view, Yahweh shows up as a capricious and bloodthirsty tyrant (one who finally, and inexplicably, decides to pity the man and boy he has tortured) and Abraham is a toadying murderer.

In this first form of Western religiousness, then, the gods want what they want just because they want it; they do what they do subject only to their own desires and to whatever external limitations on their power there may be. (In the case of strict monotheism, of course, there are no such limitations, so the god's will is boundless and unchallengeable. Recall, in this connection, God's tirade to Job from the whirlwind [Job 38:1–42:6.]) In the age of the gods, divine presence is essentially power and the will to use it; and the mundane must, sooner or later, gladly or sorrowfully, answer to that compelling force.

Just as one would expect, this age's construal of reality's sacred ground as compelling divine power specified a particular understanding of the third structural element of Western religiousness: the practical maintenance or restoration of harmony between grounded and ground. Since in this epoch the ground of all is the god's personal will (i.e., the individual exercise of his or her irresistible power), the ritual practices that bring human beings into harmony with this ground are practices that one way or another enact the limitation of human personality, the sacrifice of human will to the will and dominion of the divine Other. In the paradigmatic ritual act, one personally identifies oneself with the will of that Other; one acknowledges the compelling Other as one's god. To acknowledge another as (one's) god does not, of course, just mean to believe in the existence of a mysterious transcendent power, as I might believe in Santa Claus or in quarks. Belief—in our sense of the term—doesn't come into this sort of religion at all. In this epoch the gods are directly and immediately encountered as compelling forces, not as objects of belief. Think of Jacob wrestling with the angel at the ford of the Jabbok, and coming away with both a broken hip and a new name (Gen. 32:22–32). Here the encounter was not with something he believed in (but might not have); no, it was a struggle with a superior power, a power whose existence *as* willful power is never in question. To acknowledge something as (one's) god is to surrender to that power: to let its immediately experienced willfulness have sway over one, to serve that power. A proper relationship of profane to sacred is maintained or restored when the compelling power at the heart of things is acknowledged and then allowed to rule.

The Greek gods of the Olympian pantheon were touchy, unpredictable, and sometimes vindictive. Occasionally capable of generosity and forbearance, they more often firmly insisted on their prerogatives; and human beings were well advised to step carefully and lightly, and always to defer to the compelling dominion of the divine. Ritual slaughter of oxen, pigs, sheep, and goats was the most visible religious symbol of that dominion; it was the best way of acknowledging those limitations on human will, purpose, and power established by divine presence. "Sacrifice was the central feature of Greek religious life. . . . Gifts were constantly being offered to the gods; solidarity of the community was thereby secured and *the proper relation-*

ship between gods and humans was established."[14] A proper harmony is maintained or restored only when the unequal status of the parties is clear to all, and the willing sacrifice of one's hard-won goods makes that inequality crystal clear.

The same subservience of the human to the divine is found in the Jewish and Christian traditions. The god speaks his will; the human is supposed to obey. One need only think again of the story of Abraham, who was willing to submit to Yahweh's quirky commands long past the point of either logic or decency. He becomes the father of nations because, and *only* because, he finally obeys: first the demand that he kill the helpless Isaac; then that he substitute an equally defenseless ram. (In the helplessness of his victims, and in the arbitrariness of his bloody deeds, Abraham in his obedience tropes the God he is serving.) Indeed, the whole idea of *covenant,* upon which the Abraham story—all Israel's story—turns, is an example of the absolute priority of divine power and will. The god, for no reasons except his own pleasure, offers a human being a certain opportunity for advancement, provided only that the human being submit absolutely to the god's condition. Divine will is at the center of all, and human will must conform or perish.

The same theme of divine dominion and human obedience is found in the Christian tradition, and is best seen there, perhaps, in the centrality of the vocabulary of lordship. "No one can serve two masters," says Jesus in Matthew's Gospel (6:24), proclaiming thereby the mastery of his divine father Yahweh. Jesus' death by crucifixion, a central element in Christian theology, is the ultimate symbol of submission to the lordship of divine will. There was no reason for this exemplary, innocent man to die, except that God had willed it as the condition of human salvation. That Jesus was willing to die nevertheless, even to die the despised death of the invader's cross, is—according to Christian teaching—the decisive event in the reconciliation of the profane to the sacred. The metaphysical balance, tipped by original disobedience in the Garden, is righted only by a full acknowledgment of the power of the divine to compel obedience, even to compel (as with Isaac too) the obedient death of an innocent and trusting son. (On Calvary, Yahweh himself finally carries through the bloody filicide he remitted from Abraham on Moriah.) Divine might makes divine right; salva-

14. Michael L. Morgan, "Plato and Greek Religion," in *The Cambridge Companion to Plato* ed. Richard Kraut (New York: Cambridge University Press, 1992), 228f. The emphasis is mine. Morgan cites two classic works by Walter Burkert, *Early Greek Religion* (Cambridge: Harvard University Press, 1985) and *Homo Necans* (Berkeley and Los Angeles: University of California Press, 1983).

tion comes only through sacrificial submission of human autonomy to the god's will.[15]

The Age of the Forms

If that last sentence sounds too stark, a bit too crude and brutal, that's because we ourselves no longer live in the age of the gods. We no longer feel the pressure of divine will as more real than the pressure of our own moral scruples; we no longer wake to wrestle with angels, or worry that a god may try to rape or to murder us, as Zeus raped Leda or as Yahweh tried to murder his spokesman Moses (Exod. 4:24–26). Even our imaginative access to the texts that date from that epoch is constrained by later forms of religious sensibility, so that we instinctively try to read into those harsh (though vibrant) stories a consoling moral and rational order. The age of the gods was supplanted by the age of the Forms.

There are some texts that seem right on the cusp of the age's turn, texts in which one fancies one sees the shift of epochs taking place right before one's eyes. The *Euthyphro,* already mentioned in passing, is one such: Socrates moves his interlocutor from a thoughtless reliance on traditional religious stories (Cronos the child-eater castrating his father, Zeus binding his father Cronos in his turn), through an account of piety as whatever pleases the willful gods, to the recognition that genuine piety is a part of justice. In these few score Platonic sentences one can trace the movement from a cosmos governed by various and conflicting divine powers into the idea that the gods too must answer to something "higher," something impersonal, eternal, and perfect: justice itself. This shift from pure power to perfection is even clearer, because more compressed, in the first verse of John's Gospel, where the first words ("In the beginning") self-consciously echo the creation stories in Genesis and then are followed by the definitively Greek notion of *ho logos* (the Word), thus linking in a single

15. I don't mean to suggest there are no themes in the Jewish and Christian Scriptures that go beyond the sort of violent compulsion and obedient submission I have concentrated on here. Clearly there are. We owe a great deal of our contemporary conscience to such Jewish and Christian convictions about love and forgiveness and generosity as one finds in prophets such as Amos, Hosea, and Jesus; these visionaries have, to follow Rorty's way of putting it, allowed us to see more and more of our fellow human beings as our fellow sufferers, and thus as worthy of our compassion and aid. But in the relatively original parts of those two religious traditions there is a continuing and essential emphasis on the absolute and compelling power of the sacred over the profane, and the injunctions to charity and forbearance—real as they no doubt are—have to be seen in its light.

sentence—and apparently without embarrassment—the willful cre-
ator-god of the Jews to the idea of a rational cosmological principle.

What explains our own moral and emotional distance from the age
of the gods? The major part of the explanation lies in the advent of
Idealism, with all its powerful intellectual and ethical advantages.
With Idealism—the second epoch of Western religiousness, and an
epoch sometimes not thought of as distinctively religious at all—the
sacred ground is conceived not as personified divine presence, not as
compelling and uncanny divine will, but as the realm of rational, impersonal, and perfect Forms: an a priori cosmic order that confers
intelligible substance on things. The sacred thus becomes understood
as *the ideal*. The loci classici for such Idealism are of course the philosophical writings of Plato, especially those belonging to the so-called
middle period of his authorship. The *Republic* is the most famous
of these, and the familiar Myth of the Cave in Book 7 is a handy
summary of Idealism's major elements. In that myth some prisoners
(we ourselves, of course) are released from a subterranean world of
shadows, a place the prisoners had taken for all the world there was,
released now into the full light of day. There they encounter the ideal
objects of which heretofore they had seen only the images of images;
finally they even get to look at the sun itself, which they recognize as
the perfect and self-sustaining source of all light and thus of all vision. Then they return to the cave to tell others of the reality they
have seen outside.

Here again quite clearly is the binary, ordered differentiation of
what there is—inside the cave, outside the cave—with the former
realm portrayed as containing only the shadows (or the shadows of
shadows) of what is genuinely real. Employing a trope impossible to
overpraise for its simultaneous simplicity and brilliance, Plato conceives the well-lighted, outdoor realm of full Being as the world of the
eidai, the Forms, the Ideas. The Greek *eidos* means the visual appearance (the form, the "look") of a thing, as when one says, "Seen
from above, Perenyi's garden had the form (*eidos*) of a square, and
was further subdivided into circles and rectangles of contrasting
blooms."[16] In Plato's conception, the Form—the *eidos,* the "look" of a
thing—is an ideal condition of intelligibility; it is the fully real, perfect, immutable archetype that gives intelligible substance (a determinate, enduring identity) to the things we normally encounter.

Plato argues to the existence of these Forms by reflecting on the

16. Heidegger has made much of this visual imagery at the heart of Platonic metaphysics.

character of our ordinary experience. Here in the dim, stuffy cave of everyday life we deal with what we take to be real things, indeed the most real things of all: chairs, tables, books, and the like. But—and this is a fundamental Platonic question, and maybe the fundamental question of Western philosophy itself—what makes these things the particular things they are? They are, after all, books and tables and chairs, not undifferentiated and unrecognizable lumps of flowing stuff. The things we encounter have a quite determinate (and relatively enduring) identity; they presence before us as the specific things—books, tables, chairs—they are. Thus over time we can see them as the same as, and as different from, one another; we can identify and reidentify one as a chair rather than as a book.

But how can we do that? Are these things intelligible—recognizable and identifiable—"in themselves," as radically individual entities, each single thing having (so to speak) its own logically proper name? No, says Plato, they are primarily and originally intelligible to us as *kinds* of things, as chairs, say, or as books; and that means there must be some prior condition of their intelligibility *as* that kind of thing: there must be the archetype around which the instances cluster and which grants them their identity as instances of what they are. That prior condition of their intelligibility (and that means of their existence, since the chair *is* [i.e., appears as present] only *as* a chair) is what Plato calls the *Form,* the "look" of the thing as a chair or as a book. In the Platonic trope, therefore, the Form—the original and perfect "Look" of something—grants existence and intelligibility to specific material things (chairs, for example, or books) just as those material things grant existence and intelligibility to their images ("looks") occurring in various reflective media (e.g., mirrors, paintings, pools of water). The material objects we ordinarily (and correctly) call "chairs" are what they are only as instances of a perfect, ideal, transcendent Form: CHAIR. It is this Form that "stands under" and "supports" (that is, gives intelligible substance to) the chair in which I sit. It is the Form CHAIR that makes *this* (recognizable as, present as) a *chair,* just as it is the prior presence of Narcissus's beautiful face that gives determinate substance—specific intelligible identity *as Narcissus*—to the image appearing in the mirroring pool.

For Platonic Idealism the sacred, grounding realm of fully present Being (i.e., the world of the Forms) is radically impersonal. It is not a realm of gods, not a pantheon of willful, personified, divine presences. In the Myth of the Cave, for instance, the "true world" is imagined as a realm sustained and ordered by the regularly moving sun, not by an unpredictable deity. The realm of the Forms is thus *rational* in our typical sense of the term: it exhibits (as do the earthly seasons) an impersonal, abstract, eternal, immutable, consistent pattern. And it is a hierarchically ordered pattern as well; the Forms are ruled by the Form of the Good, the sun that ultimately allows the "looks" of things to be seen. Furthermore, the realm of the Forms is not itself a realm of action. The Forms, unlike the Olympian gods, do not war among themselves. Nor is the grounding relation of Forms to material objects one of willful, creative activity, as it was in the age of the gods, when divine beings causally produced and altered the human world as they wished: Plato's metaphors for the grounding relationship of thing to Form move from the passive trope of "participation" to the even more passive trope of "imitation." Like the hidden conceptual structure of mathematics, by which Plato was famously influenced, the Idealist's realm of pure Being is essentially static and complete. It contains no imperfection that could lead to movement and change; the Forms are immutable and eternal. From Idealism's perspective, will itself, whether human or divine, is a mark of imperfection. Being Itself lacks nothing; hence it could not want/desire/will anything.

According to Idealism, therefore, the sacred *rationally* grounds the profane. Just as the necessarily true theorems of geometry stand behind, both in the sense of empowering and in the sense of justifying, the practical work of the land surveyor or the navigator, so too do the eternal and immutable Forms stand behind our active lives in the world of appearance and change. They make possible, and give firm regulation to, our practices of identifying and reidentifying the material things on which our ordinary lives of theory and practice depend. Thus the Forms are the atemporal infrastructure of necessity upon which the various contingencies of our lives depend. The relationship of Forms to material things is not one of compelling causal power. The Forms do not, as gods do, directly create or command the material world; rather, this world is only the incomplete imitation of pure Being, only its dim reflection, distorted by the recalcitrant materiality of the medium within which the reflection occurs. The guiding image here is one of mirroring, the granting of an intelligible identity, rather than creation or control.

In Plato's account the metaphor of vision is central: one stumbles from the shadowy cave, peers about, and sees the Forms, themselves the true "looks" of things, and then finally even sees the sun that produces, orders, and enlightens all. One is saved by what one's eyes take in. By making the image of sight fundamental in this way, Plato is providing a trope for the role the abstract consciousness of reality plays in our salvation. According to Idealism, the improper relation of profane to sacred is essentially a failure of knowledge, a cognitive breakdown. To be sure, for Plato our human will is corrupt, but it is corrupted by our illusions, primarily by the illusion that the world of ordinary experience and ordinary standards is the true and only world. So long as we gaze at the shifting shadows of shadows and take them for reality, we cannot help living badly. Virtue is knowledge, and knowledge virtue, as Socrates taught. We must first see (understand, know) what endures always as the same; then we can (and we will) act as is proper in its light.

Because the idea of the sacred ground is understood in this rationalist way, the ritual practices intended to restore or to maintain a proper relationship between profane and sacred are intellectual activities, such as the study and discussion of mathematical and philosophical texts, or the Socratic method of *elenchus*. These activities are not undertaken just for utility, pleasure, or distraction. Rather, they have a quite clear sacramental function: through such activities a healing encounter with the Real can occur. Through Socratic investigation into the nature of courage, for example, it may be possible to discover (by means of the *elenchus*) what true courage is, seeing for the first time the thing itself—the originating Form—rather than its shadow; thus it will become possible for one to act truly courageously. One's action is made whole, pure, and good ("true") through its connection to the knowledge (not just opinion) that now motivates it. Even in the age of Idealism, therefore, the reconciliation of the sacred to the profane comes about through a kind of sacrifice, but here it is the sacrifice of one's illusions to a higher truth rather than the sacrifice of one's will to a mightier force. In the age of the gods one willingly submitted to compulsion; with Idealism one intellectually surrenders to perfection.

The Age of Cartesian Ego-Subjectivity

The age of the Forms was a long one, holding sway in Europe until the seventeenth century, mostly because, as Nietzsche bitterly put it, Christianity quickly became "Platonism for the people." It was, in fact, in its Christian/theological instantiation, and not as Platonic philosophy per se, that Idealism achieved its preeminence in our cultural history. Not, of course, that between (say) 350 and 1650 C.E. every European intellectual was a satisfied (Christian) Idealist, nor that between Clement of Alexandria, Origen, and Augustine (the brilliant repackagers of Christianity as populist Platonism) and Descartes (who began to poke large holes in the container the fathers of the church had used) there were no fundamental challenges put to Platonic Idealism from within the philosophical tradition itself. (One has only to think of Aristotelianism, of course.) But in our retrospect it does appear that among Western thinkers a fertile and relatively stable set of metaphysical convictions remained in place throughout this period, whatever minor (and fascinating) variations one might note. From Augustine on, most European theologians and philosophers accepted some form of what has come to be called "the great chain of Being": a conviction that reality—or, better put, Reality—is a hierarchical structure consisting of a ground of pure and ultimately substantial Being Itself, usually identified as "God," from which ground logically proceed various subsidiary orders of beings, one of which is human being. Sacred presence was thus being reconceived in the Christian West, not now as unpredictable and unchallengeable divine will, but as inescapable yet comprehensible divine order. The ultimate Order of Things—the City of God—lies open to rational survey, even if at a certain point our finite vision will necessarily fail to see all the way to its center. Furthermore, in supplement to the original Jewish and Christian emphasis on sin as a corruption of the will, the doctors of the church consistently affirmed that some metaphysical knowledge is essential to the will's sanctification ("The truth shall make you free" [John 8:32]); and thus that the harmony of sacred and profane can be reliably secured only through the human being's adequate insight into the final Order of Things. (Of course, some of this essential salvific knowledge may need to be divinely revealed rather than humanly discovered through purely rational inquiry. According to Saint Thomas, for example, the existence of a single God can be demonstrated to any rational intellect, but it takes more than mere ratiocination to see that Jesus is His only Son.)[17] During this long period of philosophical/theological synthesis the scriptural texts belonging to the age of the gods were systematically reinterpreted. In the books of Christian theologians, for example, Yahweh was transformed from an uncanny, immensely powerful center of will—a "jealous God," as the matter was put to Moses—into a supreme rational principle, into something like the Platonic Form of the Good (or the [Aristotelian] Necessary Being of Saint Thomas's Third Way). The grounding realm of the sacred was thereby transformed from a warring pantheon into a rational cosmos, from the clash of divine wills into the properly ordered world of the ideal.

17. Saint Thomas Aquinas, *On the Truth of the Christian Faith,* trans. A. C. Pegis (New York: Doubleday, 1955), chap. 3, sec. 2.

In the philosophical writings of René Descartes, however, this metaphysical and theological consensus is dismantled and a new form of philosophical—and ultimately religious—consciousness is fashioned as its replacement. The age of the Forms is succeeded by the age of ego-subjectivity, and the major impetus for the change originates in the fundamental role accorded *knowledge* in Idealist forms of religiousness, Christian and otherwise. For Idealism, as we have just noted, the key to reconciliation between the sacred and the profane is a comprehensive (and perhaps divinely revealed) apprehension of the deep structure of reality. In the final analysis, says the Idealist, only the truth—the truth of the recollected Forms, the truth of God's holy Torah, the truth of the Christian Incarnation—can make us free; only full knowledge of the Order of Things can save us. Vision, remember, is the central metaphor of Plato's progress, where we move from the darkness of the cave to the bright light of the all-revealing sun itself. My healing comprehension of reality is imagined by Plato as an immediate visual apprehension of it, as if I were somehow standing back and surveying the whole Great Chain of Being, looking at it (and myself in it) *sub specie aeternitatis.* Something analogous to this intellectual apprehension is found in the philosophical Christianity of the High Middle Ages, where the saving knowledge of God is likewise understood to be knowledge of reality's true but hidden nature. The post-Resurrection appearances of Jesus to his disciples function as a key scriptural trope for this esoteric knowledge. In those visual (and sometimes more than visual) encounters with the Risen Lord the final and saving Truth about things was revealed. These stories are the Christian equivalent of Plato's myth of the cave-dweller's blinding sight of the sun; and the apostles, like the cave-dwellers, are sent forth into the world—back into the cave—to spread the glad tidings of what they have seen.

Such a rationalist, intellectualist conception of our salvational encounter with the real depends upon certain conditions for its effectiveness. Bluntly put, the conception will hold water only when there is uncontroversial agreement about what counts as the paradigmatic sight of pure Being Itself; and most Idealist texts furnish accounts that try to remove all doubt about how that agreement is to be achieved. In Book 7 of the *Republic,* as was just noted, the vision of the sun—a vision presumably vouchsafed to the individual philosopher by rigorous dialectical thinking—is the dramatic climax of the narrative. The prisoners' quest for truth ends in the blinding presence of pure light assaulting them from its heavenly source. Such radiance, were it to appear, is of course the guarantee of its own transcendent authority: if in this direct and unmediated way I become aware of Being Itself, I shall certainly be instructed in the Order of Things, and therefore saved. One may helpfully compare this Platonic trope to the story of Paul's conversion on the road to Damascus (Acts 9:1–6), or the convincing appearance of the resurrected Jesus to his doubting disciple Thomas (John 20:19–29). In all of them there is the sight (and sound and touch) of something that answers all questions and settles all doubts; there is the immediate apprehension of, encounter with, Truth.

But what if no such compelling vision comes to me? In such circumstances, where nothing steps forth to stun one with its overwhelming assurance of eternal wholeness, Idealism totters. If we encounter no fully present Truth, we will remain sunk in ignorance, illusion, bondage, and vice. And at stake in such absence is more than just Platonism (and its Christian variants). Put in hazard is the entire "metaphysics of presence" underlying Western religious sensibility; without the assurance of—the unquestionable and full *presence* of—some absolute and sacred ground, some wholly realized Being Itself, everything is threatened by chaos. What, if not some variant of the Platonic "true world," gives determinate and enduring identity—genuine *substance*—to the world we inhabit? Maybe it's all just confusion and flux.

By the early decades of the seventeenth century, this worry had become acute among European intellectuals. Both the rise of a more empirical natural science, which seemed in some of its results to undermine the cosmology and metaphysics taught by the church and presupposed by her theology, and the extensive exploration of other lands, which called into question the familiar economic, political, artistic, and sexual patterns of European society, had combined to make problematic the very notion of knowledge itself. Alternatives began to look more and more like counterexamples. The reasoning of the intellectuals went like this: if, as now appears, we might have been wrong in what we have for so long claimed to know (e.g., that the sun goes round the earth, that the brain is an organ for cooling the blood, that the orderly inheritance of property must be patrilineal), then perhaps the whole idea of knowledge is itself a dead letter. Perhaps nothing is ever really known, but only believed by someone, somewhere, at some time. Perhaps all our most cherished claims of truth are mere opinion, an epistemic currency backed by nothing but habit, convention, and error. And if our access to fully present Being must be, as Idealism had convincingly argued, one of unimpeachable knowledge, of plain and compelling sight, then perhaps we have no such access at

all. Perhaps, therefore, we have no sacred ground on which to stand,
no secure foundation upon which to build our lives of theory and practice. Perhaps the world has no genuine substance, no stable and enduring identities, no fixed stars by which we can reckon. Perhaps everything merely floats on a rushing stream, sooner or later to sink
beneath it.

In the first of Descartes's six *Meditations on First Philosophy* (published in 1641) one can see precisely this worry being given its head.
Descartes presents himself to the reader as engaged in a search for
philosophical certainty, by which he means the search for some
knowledge incapable of being doubted, something that could *not* turn
out to be false. He is seeking, in other words, the seventeenth-century
equivalent of Plato's saving vision of the blinding sun, or Thomas the
Apostle's convincing encounter with the Risen Christ. In this search
he makes some significant (and, as we shall see, controversial) assumptions. First, he assumes that our knowledge is a hierarchical
structure built up out of many individual *beliefs,* discrete acts of intentionality, some of which serve as supports for the others, just as
piers built of individual stones might serve as the foundation for a
wooden house. The fundamental question for Descartes is, therefore,
whether any of our current beliefs actually possess the strength (i.e.,
the manifest certainty) to serve as adequate foundations for our practice. Second, and even more crucial to our interests in this essay, Descartes assumes that a belief is the mind's intentional representation
of a determinate state of affairs external to it. A belief for him is a
sort of mental picture that may or may not match what it aims to
portray; its adequacy depends on how exact its isomorphism with the
state of affairs it intends. An absolutely accurate representation
would be the actual and immediate identity of Thought (the belief)
and Being (the already existing, determinate, and self-identical state
of affairs); such a belief would be in the fullest sense *true.* And Cartesian metaphysical certainty, the impossibility of doubt (and error), is
the criterial mark of the mind's full encounter with Being Itself in its
identity with the true belief. Certainty is the sign that the customary
gap between Thought and Being, between us and the solid truth on
which we depend, has been closed. In that way, certainty is the guarantee that the world has a genuine and intelligible substance; it is the
warrant of an a priori Order of Things upon which we can reckon.

So the Cartesian quest for epistemological certainty is another form
of the Western religious attempt to encounter, and to reconcile to, the
ground of fully present, sacred Being Itself. The dramatic narrative of
Descartes's search is by now painfully familiar to us: sorting his be-

liefs by reference to the kinds of evidence—sensory, mathematical, theological—used to support them, he finds none of them immune to doubt. Why? His reasoning is simple and compelling. According to Descartes, each and every one of our beliefs about the "external world" is the result of our commitment to, and employment of, some particular principle of evidence (e.g., "Accept as true whatever your sensory experience leads you to believe to be true"). Because each and every one of the familiar principles of evidence available to us would, if consistently applied, lead us in some obvious cases to error (i.e., inconsistency) rather than to truth, then none of these principles, and thus none of the beliefs resulting from their use, is absolutely reliable (certain). Thus none of our beliefs—all of them, according to Descartes, based on our use of one or more of these unreliable evidential principles—can guarantee their exact isomorphism with reality. From a properly philosophical point of view, he (and therefore we) may as well consider our beliefs to be the malicious products of an Evil Genius intent upon our wholesale deception. Descartes's first meditation ends in epistemological—and thus metaphysical—despair. The world's substance is in question. Perhaps only the Evil Genius's febrile will, not an a priori Order, lies behind our experiences.

In Meditation 2, however, Descartes is rewarded with the discovery of a belief impervious to doubt's corruption, because it is a belief apparently so immediate as to rest on no evidential principle at all. It is, of course, the belief in his own existence as a center of consciousness, as a "thinking thing" (res cogitans). Even as he can (and therefore must) doubt the truth of all his sensory, mathematical, and theological representations (because of the faultiness of the evidential principles by which they were acquired), he cannot doubt the existence of the consciousness that doubts them: "The thinker of *this* thought does not exist" is not a thought that could ever be thought truly. *Cogito, ergo sum.* "So after considering everything very thoroughly, I must finally conclude that this proposition, *I am, I exist,* is necessarily true whenever it is put forward by me or conceived in my mind."[18]

The indubitable center of (self-)consciousness identified in Meditation 2 is the *ego,* and as a result of Descartes's skeptical maneuvers in relation to our ordinary sources of belief, all is now doubtful except the ego in its immediate self-presentation. Only in the ego's self-consciousness of itself as res cogitans is there certainty: the full identity

18. René Descartes, *Meditations on First Philosophy,* trans. John Cottingham (Cambridge: Cambridge University Press, 1986), 17. Notice the way Descartes puts his point in terms of the (necessary) truth of a proposition; that is, the certainty of a representation.

of Thought and Being. As *res cogitans,* as the "thinking thing," the ego is (in its thinking) immediately aware of its determinate and enduring identity—its self-identical Being—as *res cogitans.* Thinking about itself as thinking thing—even if that self-reflexive thinking is mere doubting—indubitably acquaints the ego with its *identity* as thinking thing: for Descartes, the identity of thinking is transparent to itself as both identity (*res*) and thinking (*cogitans*). In this way the ego, the "thinking thing," becomes the being, the *only* being, whose Being—whose determinate and substantial identity—is immediately self-given; there can be no question, no uncertainty, about the Being of this being, and this being alone. The ego thus becomes the subject, the *hypokeimenon,* the fixed and identity-granting ground of all other reality. It is the original source of the world's substance. Everything else takes its determinate identity, its true Being, in relation to this ego-subject, as one of its "objects." The epistemically privileged ego, not the Christian God or the Platonic Form of the Good, has become the first and founding link in Being's great chain.

Once the radical Cartesian doubts have insinuated themselves, thereby constructing the indubitable ego as the screen upon which various representations play, there is no possibility of immediate encounter with the gods or with the Ideal Order of Things. Metaphysical entities and hierarchies (gods, Forms) necessarily become objects of the ego's *belief,* and this is a fundamental loss of status for those entities. They are no longer the sacred ground, no longer the full presence of Being Itself. Rather, they are representations displayed as figures upon the ego-ground. It now becomes possible (and therefore necessary) to *believe* in the gods or to *believe* in the Ideal world; and, as we all know, some smart people do believe in such things, and some smart people don't. The very fact that the existence of the gods or of the Forms can be doubted, that these entities are (for us) at best the objects of belief (i.e., objects that in the first instance present themselves within representations to which assent may be granted or withheld by the ego-subject), shows that neither the gods nor the Ideal world is any more the ground of Being.

This loss of status is made clear, by the way, in the fact that Descartes himself later in the *Meditations* feels anxiously compelled to claim that the existence of God as nondeceiver is a truth on all fours with the certain existence of the ego in its self-presentation as *res cogitans.* He himself recognizes and fears the accession of the ego to the place of the subject; and thus he tries desperately to demonstrate by force of argument that God, while second in the Order of Knowledge, remains first in the Order of Being. But the attempt fails, at least according to the judgment of philosophical history. Neither the Yahwist nor Plato needed arguments, ontological or otherwise, to convince their readers of the fundamental status of their favored grounds: Jacob had his hip broken; Moses saw the bush burning but not consumed; the erstwhile inhabitants of the Cave felt the sun's heat on their bodies and were finally blinded by its overwhelming fire.[19] That Descartes does need arguments, that he recognizes that the intellect must be painstakingly tutored of the theological truths necessary for its salvation, shows that a deep and decisive change has taken place in Western religious sensibility.

Much of our lives, especially our overtly religious lives, remains problematically Cartesian. As it was for him, our intellectual integrity is still mostly a matter of refusing assent to any representation unless we have good reasons for believing that it really does match up one-for-one with what there is. Our typical religious quandaries are, therefore, essentially questions of personal belief: my students are always asking themselves (and me), "Do you believe in God?" (or in the Bible, or in Jesus, or in Scientology, or in reincarnation, and so on). Do you, that is, accept that particular representation of reality as the true one, and on what grounds? Given this sort of Cartesianism at their core, is it any wonder that our current institutional forms of religion have gradually lost their power for us? If one can only *believe* that X (e.g., Yahweh, Allah, the Form of the Good) is the ground of Being, then X is not the ground of Being, no matter what one believes. If the sacredness of X can sensibly be questioned, then X is no longer sacred.

After Descartes, then, only the ego is fully present in its self-certifying (because self-transparent) Being; all else can (at best) be known as a representation present to the ego's consciousness. The Cartesian ego's self-presentation as *res cogitans* is the grounding certainty (i.e., is the fundamental identity of Thought and Being); all other knowledge is grounded by reference to this insight. This Cartesian division of (1) the immediate, full Being of the ego's presence to itself from (2) the derivative reality of every other representation is, clearly, a recapitulation of the binary differentiation of reality we have already noted in the age of the gods and the age of the Forms. Here again is a refurbished form of the Western "metaphysics of presence": the fullness of Being Itself (the certainty of the ego-subject's self-knowledge

19. This is certainly not to say that Plato eschews all argument. But its point is always to bring the soul to recollection of an encounter already accomplished, not to bring the intellect to apprehension of a truth heretofore unknown as truth.

of its identity as *res cogitans*) contrasted with partiality and absence (the incomplete, and therefore philosophically doubtful, representations—including philosophical and theological representations—that occur in ordinary consciousness). And as before, harmony is achieved only when the latter are appropriately grounded in the former; that is, only when the certainty of the *cogito* can be clearly and distinctly seen as the axiomatic foundation of all our other beliefs.

Thus in the age of ego-subjectivity, as in Idealism, the fundamental religious practices are intellectual. The intensity of the *Meditations,* the source of much of its literary power and distinction, is itself religious. In seeking to establish something "firm and lasting in the sciences," Descartes is ultimately seeking that ground of pure Being—that source of the determinate identity of things—capable of underwriting his own particular theoretical and practical commitments. Just as much as Plato's prisoners or Bunyan's Pilgrim, Descartes has set out upon a religious quest. He is seeking, quite literally, a justification by knowledge, a salvation through certainty.

The Age of Transvalued Values

Most of the intellectual and spiritual life of our culture still proceeds within the broad conceptual limits constructed by Descartes, but there is one more turn of the screw to be noted in this narrative. And here we come to Friedrich Nietzsche, in whose thinking there is a radical refinement of Cartesianism that threatens to withdraw all its metaphysical assurances. Nietzsche begins by unmasking the Cartesian account of consciousness; in particular he wants to demolish the rationalist rhetoric that portrays consciousness as fundamentally receptive and representational. Like Locke and his other contemporaries, Descartes had taken mind to be *the mirror of Nature,* a medium wherein reality is spontaneously reflected. Cartesian "ideas," whether simple or complex, innate or empirical, were understood to be images of reality appearing on the mind's inner glass.[20] In a mirror, as with any reflective medium, various sorts of distortion are of course possible; so the first philosophical task of the seventeenth-century intellectual was to grind, position, and polish the mirror so that it could offer

20. Descartes himself famously (in Meditation 2) employs the metaphor of soft wax receiving an imprint as an image of the mind's receptive capacity; this metaphor only makes the alleged passivity of the medium clearer. The image of the mind as mirror is common to the entire so-called way of Ideas of the seventeenth century. See Richard Rorty, *Philosophy and the Mirror of Nature* (Princeton: Princeton University Press, 1979).

an accurate reflection of the reality confronting it. (Descartes's own *Discourse on Method* [1637] is a perfect example of such mental Wind-exing.) Cartesian truth is nothing but accurate representation, and representation is rooted in the spontaneous reflection of what confronts it. The ultimate rational goal for Descartes is representation *sub specie aeternitatis,* the pure reflection upon the ego-ground of the actual and comprehensive Order of Things.

In fact, as Nietzsche insists, this standard rationalist imagery is profoundly misleading, as it obscures the fundamental place of *will* as the center of the Cartesian ego-subject. Even in Descartes's own account, the ego cannot be merely a passive mirror of impressions and ideas: as a thinking thing it must either assent to or dissent from its spontaneous representations of the world.[21] Not all the Cartesian ego's representations are of equal value; some more than others reflect the actual structure of reality *sub specie aeternitatis.* Thus the ego, whose theoretical and practical salvation depends upon the acquisition of accurate and comprehensive knowledge, must pick and choose (on some epistemic principle) from the various representations that beset it. Adequate knowledge (as distinct from the grounding certainty of the ego's immediate self-presentation) is the individual's *achievement,* therefore. Our full-blown knowledge of the world is a representational structure painstakingly constructed upon a foundation of certainty; thus the ego whose knowledge this is, could not be pure receptivity and nothing more. On the contrary, *res cogitans,* the "thinking thing," is epistemic will, the will to truth.

But even if Descartes must admit—as he does in Meditation 2—that hidden in the kernel of *cogitans* is the will to truth, he nevertheless maintains that the truth the ego wills is truth conceived as the accurate representation of the real. But can one make such a claim about truth? Can one, as Descartes does, continue to construe the ego's belief as a mental picture of reality, a picture that in its ideal—truth, accurate representation—achieves the unity of Thought and Being? There seems an insuperable epistemological objection to such an account, an objection recognized early on by Berkeley and Hume and then decisively capitalized upon by Nietzsche. The objection is simple and clear: given the representational account of thinking assumed by Descartes and his fellow travelers along the "way of Ideas," there is absolutely no way for the ego directly to verify the accuracy of

21. This is clear from his discussion of thinking in Meditation 2. "But what then am I? A thing that thinks. What is that? A thing that doubts, understands, affirms, denies, is willing, is unwilling, and also imagines and has sensory impressions" (Descartes, *Meditations,* 19).

any of its representations. In ordinary life one can check the accuracy of a mirror-image or a wax impression against the available presence of the thing itself. Here is the signet ring, there is the imprint; are they the same? But the Cartesian ego cannot, *necessarily* cannot, perform such a homely act of verification. All the Cartesian ego has available to it is the set of those representations directly present to consciousness at a given time; and, no matter how coherent and convincing a particular set of representations may be, there is always the possibility of its (representational) falsity, as Descartes himself insists in Meditation 1. If thoughts are representations occurring in some reflective medium, then verification of their truth would require that one have some direct contact with the cause and intentional object of those representations so that a comparison between it and the representations can be made. The ego needs assurance that things-in-themselves accurately match up with things-as-they-appear-to-it.

But can that assurance be had? Apparently not. The very terms in which the epistemological issue has been constructed by Descartes and his peers—representation, cause, resemblance, mirroring, and so forth—seem to forbid just the sort of verification they themselves require. If, apart from its immediate encounter with itself, all the Cartesian ego has available to it are various representations of objects lying outside it, then the idea of checking the accuracy of a given representation reduces to the idea of comparing that representation to another one. The ego can never directly compare any representation to the objective reality it claims to represent. Thus the Cartesian ego's necessarily intrasubjective comparison of representations is, in Wittgenstein's wonderful image, like buying several copies of the same newspaper in order to verify the accuracy of its front-page headline. One doesn't thereby get the kind of reliable corroboration one was seeking. On Cartesian terms, the epistemic gap between representation and reality remains (and must remain) unbridgable. In this way the very idea of accurate representation of reality becomes problematic. The door is open to admit all forms of skepticism, including a rigorous solipsism. In sum, the notion of knowledge itself is again in danger of collapse, just as it was at the end of the epoch of Idealism.

Kant tried to meet this skeptical challenge halfway by arguing that human experience, and thus human knowledge, is partially constituted by the structures and operations of the ego-subject itself; at the same time, however, he fiercely held on to the ineffable *Ding-an-sich,* the "thing-in-itself," as the anchor of the representations thus constituted. But—again to paraphrase Wittgenstein—a wheel that when turned turns nothing else, is not part of the mechanism; and so it is with the Kantian *Ding-an-sich*. It performs no real function; one could eliminate it from the picture with no discernible epistemological loss. Objective reality—that opaque and resistant stuff assumed to stand over against the receptive ego and to be spontaneously reflected in its consciousness—has become a will-o'-the-wisp. In epistemic practice one is left only with the representations themselves. But this, as Nietzsche fully realized, breaks the back of the metaphor of representation altogether. If there are *only* representations, and representations of representations, and representations of representations of representations, then there are *no* representations: the sense of the metaphor itself depends upon the possibility of comparing the representation to what is represented. When that possibility of comparison is void, as it now so obviously seems to be, then the image of representation has ceased to function. The wheel one has been so furiously turning is now found to be unconnected to any real mechanism.[22] The Cartesian account of mind and knowledge has collapsed under its own weight.

So, says Nietzsche, a new, non-Cartesian metaphor for the mind must be found, and I have found it. The basic activity of consciousness is not spontaneous representation but *interpretation,* the willful imposition of structure and meaning on something—a text, a set of events, a sequence of sense-experiences—that demands it. The human being is not, as Descartes would have it, a center of passive reflection of reality, but is reality's forceful creator and manipulator.

> Not "to know" but to schematize—to impose upon chaos as much regularity and form as our practical needs require.
>
> In the formation of reason, logic, the categories, it was *need* that was authoritative: the need, not to "know," but to subsume, to schematize, for the purpose of intelligibility and calculation. (K 515)

> "Interpretation," the introduction of meaning—not "explanation." . . . There are no facts, everything is in flux, incomprehensible, elusive; what is relatively most enduring is—our opinions. (K 604)[23]

22. See "How the True World Became a Fable," in F. Nietzsche, *The Twilight of the Idols,* reprinted in *The Portable Nietzsche* ed. Walter Kaufmann (New York: Viking, 1968), 485f.

23. F. Nietzsche, *The Will to Power,* ed. Walter Kaufmann, trans. W. Kaufmann and R. J. Hollingdale (New York: Random House, 1967). All references to this work (e.g., K 515) will be to the sections in this edition. The Kaufmann edition has a good index, and

The sense of the whole Cartesian philosophical metaphor of thought-as-representation depends upon there being some avenue of access to the thing-in-itself, to the immutable, objective, absolutely given Order of Things to which Thought must conform itself in order to produce Truth. But now that a priori Order is gone, says Nietzsche, and good riddance.

> A "thing-in-itself" is just as perverse as a "sense-in-itself," a "meaning-in-itself." There are no "facts-in-themselves," for a sense must always be projected into them before there can be "facts."
>
> The question "what is that?" is an imposition of meaning from some other viewpoint. "Essence," the "essential nature," is something perspective and already presupposes a multiplicity. At the bottom of it always lies "what is that for me?" (for us, for all that lives, etc.). (K 556)

There is no sense left in the old notion of truth as accurate corre-spondence between the belief and the "thing-in-itself," just as there is no sense in the old notion of knowledge as a comprehensive structure of such truths: "Truth is the kind of error without which a certain species of life could not live. The value for life is ultimately decisive" (K 493).

"Truth is the kind of error": the apparent contradiction here is Nietzsche's ironic comment on the futility of trying to demonstrate *any* error, when the notion of error is construed as a belief's inaccu-rate representation of an immaculate "fact." Under the spell of the Cartesian/Lockean/Kantian metaphor of representation, everything can be (perhaps should be) treated as an "error," as in no case can the identity of Thought and Being be satisfactorily demonstrated.[24] That being so, says Nietzsche, the judgment that a given proposition is true (a kind of judgment we cannot stop making so long as we live) must be understood in a nonrepresentational way; namely, as the judgment that affirmation of the proposition in question is necessary (or at least very useful) to a particular form of life, namely, ours. "The value for life is ultimately decisive." To say that we have a compre-hensive and justified set of true beliefs about the world (i.e., that we have knowledge) is for Nietzsche only to say that we are operating

---

further references to what Nietzsche says about interpretation, truth, knowledge, and so on, can be found there.

24. *Pace* Descartes, this is true even with the self-presence of the ego, as we shall see.

with an interpretation (or a perspective, as he sometimes calls it) that suits our current needs. "Knowledge works as a tool of power," he says (K 480).

> Insofar as the word "knowledge" has any meaning, the world is knowable; but it is *interpretable* otherwise, it has no meaning behind it, but countless meanings.—Perspectives.
>
> It is our needs that interpret the world; our drives and their For and Against. Every drive is a kind of lust to rule; and each one has its perspective that it would like to compel all the other drives to accept as a norm. (K 481)

A given worldview (interpretation, perspective), however psychologically or even philosophically compelling it may be ("knowledge"), is for Nietzsche nothing more than the imposition of a certain point of view, a certain "meaning," upon the limitlessly plastic flux of experience, an imposition justified by nothing except its usefulness to the imposing organism's will to power.

The collapse of the metaphor of thought-as-representation and its replacement by the metaphor of thought-as-interpretation fatally damaged the traditional Platonic/Cartesian/Kantian account of human knowledge as a comprehensive and stable vision of a single and immutable reality. Knowledge now comes to be seen as a human construction, as an interpretation imposed by particular human wills in order to serve particular human purposes. Human beings are not primarily observers of reality—Emersonian "transparent eyeballs" who calmly survey the Order of Things and note with interest its salient and eternal features. No, we are *makers, doers,* organized collections of drives and needs. The worlds we inhabit are our interpretations, constructed and enforced by us upon the inherently ambiguous text of our experience. Theory necessarily takes a back seat to practice. In fact, theory just *is* the (unconscious) codification of practice, practice shaped by interests, needs, and desires.

But if, as Nietzsche declares, "Life is will to power" (K 254) (i.e., if life is always and avidly seeking novel ways to preserve and enhance itself), then what guides action in intelligent service of that will? What standard can we invoke to identify some courses of action (interpretations, perspectives) as fruitful ones and to reveal others as barren or self-destructive? Even more generally, how does reality become organized into recognizable and repeatable entities and patterns, so that the will to power—life—can extend its dominion over itself? Reality pure and simple—the Platonic dream of pure Being— cannot furnish such a standard of organization and measure, since we could have no access at all to such an immaculate realm. (And thus even the idea of that realm is finally senseless). Nor can one appeal to some quasi-positivist notion of "the facts." According to Nietzsche, "the facts" are always already themselves the products of the very interests and actions one needs to judge. Left to itself, therefore, the naked will to power is thus in danger of being swamped by its own, apparently infinite, possibilities for conception and action. Confronted with so many lives to be lived, how can it fully and joyfully give itself over to any one? What can, like the Platonic Form, serve the will to power in its need to articulate a world of things whose identity is (relatively) stable and enduring, thus creating a world within which intelligent action is possible?

At this point Nietzsche relies on the notion of *value*. Values are those fundamental structures of interpretation required and furnished (posited) by the will to power for its own preservation and enhancement; they function, one might say, as the basic filters through which raw experience is passed, thereby being modulated into a coherent and livable world:[25] "The standpoint of 'value' is the standpoint of conditions of preservation and enhancement for complex forms of relative life-duration within the flux of becoming" (K 715).

Since for Nietzsche the human being—itself a "complex form of relative life-duration within the flux of becoming"—is essentially a vector-sum of forces seeking their own continuance and expansion, his whole philosophy is anchored by the notion of value. Without some set of values to guide it in its construction and manipulation of a world to inhabit, human life would be a chaos, or, even worse, a spiral downward into passivity, reaction, and death. And thus value, some empowering and guiding structure of interpretation, some organized applications of force to other forces, is ultimately a condition of life itself.

Nietzsche has ripped the mask from the Cartesian *res cogitans*. The

---

25. To characterize values as "structures of interpretation" or as "filters" of experience, as I do here, may misleadingly suggest they must be construed as something like detachable and interchangeable lenses through which we view an independent reality, thus reinforcing in another way the Platonic visual metaphor of cognition. For Nietzsche, however, interpretations can best be understood as *organized applications of force;* they are particular organizations of action and response in relation to particular stimuli. Interpretations, one might say, are *social practices,* relatively determinate patterns of comportment that persist over time so as to constitute human beings and their world in a stable and predictable fashion. *Values* are those basic social practices that most fundamentally constitute and characterize a particular form of life; values are those ground-level interpretations—patterns of comportment—upon which other interpretations are erected to form the edifice of a culture. (This construal of Nietzschean values as organized social practices—which might not be entirely consistent with what Nietzsche himself had in mind—is strongly influenced by Heidegger; see Chapter 3.)

face revealed is unexpected and disquieting: instead of the placid gaze
of pure receptivity, consciousness glares back at us as will, as fertile
life grasping at more. Rather than as a medium of passive representation, as the humble wax waiting to receive Being's signet, mind is
shown to be essentially active; and its fundamental activity is interpretation: the creation and employment of values. To think is necessarily to evaluate: to impose sense or meaning; to create a "perspective;" to construct a (relatively) determinate and enduring world
within which the will to power can persevere and flourish. Thinking
is not (*pace* Plato) the discovery of a priori meaning instantiated in
the eternal Forms, any more than sense-perception is (as Descartes
and Kant would have it) the representational encounter with the already self-identical *Ding-an-sich*. There is no *Ding-an-sich,* no "essence," no single Order of Things that can be viewed *sub specie aeternitatis;* likewise there is no transcendent Platonic meaning (Form)
existing independently of the mind's activity. On the contrary, meaning (sense, Being, "value") always arises out of mind's own creative/
interpretive impetus in service to the will to power.

Moving in tandem with Nietzsche's critique of the epistemic passivity assumed by Cartesian/Kantian representationalism, there is
also his assault on Descartes's easy assumption of substantial selfhood. For all his self-proclaimed willingness to submit everything to
doubt, Descartes never really doubted himself, and one of the things
he took for granted was his own identity as a self; that is, as a personal, coherent, unified, single center of thought (as an *ego,* one may
say). In Western religiousness Presence has always grounded Absence; the Many must be grounded by the One. And for Descartes, as
we have seen, the ego—the pure and unitary self-presence of Being
transparently realized in the *cogito*—is this ultimately grounding
One. The Cartesian ego is therefore the *subject,* the stable and coherent foundation upon which the edifice of one's life of theory and
practice can be raised. The ego in its self-awareness is the evident
wholeness of Being Itself.

Nietzsche clearly recognizes, however, that the fully present, self-
identical, substantial Cartesian ego is itself an interpretation, a
value, not a *Ding-an-Sich.*

> Must all philosophy not ultimately bring to light the precon-
> ditions upon which the process of reason depends?—our belief
> in the "ego" as substance, as the sole reality from which we
> ascribe reality to things in general? The oldest "realism" at last
> comes to light: at the same time that the entire religious his-

tory of mankind is recognized as the history of the soul-super-
stition. Here we come to a limit: our thinking itself involves
this belief (with its distinction of substance, accident, deed,
doer, etc.); to let it go means: being no longer able to think.

But that a belief, however necessary it may be for the preservation of a species, has nothing to do with truth, one knows
from the fact that, e.g., we have to believe in time, space, and
motion, without feeling compelled to grant them absolute reality. (K 487)

That last sentence takes a Kantian insight—that space and time
are only our psychologically necessary "forms of intuition" rather
than true features of the "thing-in-itself"—and turns it against Kant,
turns it into a critique of the metaphysics of the self that underlies
even Kant's so-called critical philosophy. Kant is Nietzsche's paradigmatic post-Cartesian philosopher, the one who tries to put Cartesian
ego-subjectivity on a firmer philosophical footing. In that effort he
deploys, as is typical with him, a weighty transcendental argument:
Kant argues that belief in the unitary, substantial ego is the necessary condition for the possibility of any thinking whatsoever. "Here
we come to a limit: our thinking itself involves this belief [in the substantial ego]" (K 487). Kantian transcendental arguments intend to
move one from an initial recognition of doxastic *necessity* to the consequent recognition of doxastic *truth*: if belief in the unitary ego is necessary, as Kant here claims, then belief in the unitary ego is true, as
Descartes had asserted. But Nietzsche sees there is a devastating internal objection to this sophisticated Kantian ploy. In the Transcendental Analytic of the first *Critique*, Kant himself had argued that
"we have to believe in time, space, and motion without feeling compelled to grant them absolute reality" (K 487). By thus demonstrating
that the necessity of the "forms of intuition" (time, space, and motion)
is only a necessity of our particular psychology, Kant has himself sev-
ered any absolutely necessary connection between doxastic necessity
and doxastic truth: that we *must believe* the thing we experience to be
spatially and temporally located doesn't entail that it (as *Ding-an-
sich*) actually *is* spatial and temporal. But by severing this connection, he thereby has sapped the force of his own appeal to transcendental arguments, since all such arguments depend on that very link
between the necessary and the true. What then is left of Kant's transcendental attempt to defend the unitary Cartesian ego? Nothing.
The door is left wide open to the Nietzschean insinuation that the
Cartesian/Kantian ego is itself just a *value,* a structure of interpreta-

tion justified (if at all) only by its usefulness to a form of life as it tries
to preserve and enhance itself.

And how useful is the ego-interpretation anyway?

> The assumption of one single subject is perhaps unnecessary:
> perhaps it is just as permissible to assume a multiplicity of
> subjects, whose interaction and struggle is the basis of thought
> and consciousness in general? A kind of aristocracy of "cells" in
> which dominion resides? To be sure, an aristocracy of equals,
> used to ruling jointly and understanding how to command?
> *My hypothesis:* the subject as multiplicity. (K 490)

To us, nourished by Freud and Jung as well as by our own heightened consciousness of internal division, this Nietzschean "hypothesis"
is far from startling. The following might have been written by Freud
himself:

> The danger of the direct questioning of the subject *about* the
> subject and of all self-reflection of the spirit (*Geist*) lies in this,
> that it could be useful and important for one's activity to inter-
> pret oneself *falsely.* That is why we question the body and re-
> ject the evidence of the sharpened senses: we try, if you like, to
> see whether the inferior parts themselves cannot enter into
> communication with us. (K 492; written in 1885)

What is psychoanalysis but an attempt to enter into communication
with those "inferior parts" that so often thwart the ambitions of the
"ego" with which we normally identify ourselves? And which one of us
has not recognized in her or his self-image some of that useful men-
dacity of which Nietzsche writes here? For us, both the psychic multiplicity and the consequent struggle for hegemony that underlie our
tenuous self-identity as egos are not mere "hypothesis" (to use Nietzsche's word) but felt reality.

At this point a painful philosophical slippage has become all too
apparent. The scientific and epistemological revolutions of the seventeenth century, revolutions consolidated in the writings of Descartes,
took away all philosophical ground except the ego-subject. In the face
of the corrosive yet apparently irresistible Cartesian demand for epistemic certainty, both the gods and the Forms lost the immediacy required for any sacred ground, and only in the immediate self-presentation of the ego did there appear that identity of Thought and Being
that compels assent and underwrites virtuous action. But now, just as

Descartes undermined the Idealist forms of Western religiousness he had inherited, Nietzsche has in turn shattered the Cartesian world-view: first of all by ridiculing the philosophical metaphor of mind-as-representation and thus insinuating that the Cartesian ego-subject must be will, not receptivity (i.e., a force of interpretation, not a medium of mirroring); and second—a more radical attack—by under-cutting the philosophical idea of the grounding, centered ego itself, showing it too to be only a unifying interpretation of multifarious experience (i.e., a value, not a *Ding-an-Sich*). From the willful, inscrutable gods who make and break covenants as they wish, through the rational perfection of the Platonic Forms, to the Cartesian ego-subject in its full self-presentation, and finally to the posited values of the proliferated will to power: we seem to see here a gradual but inexorable loss of the sacred's power. Not only did the gods and the Forms pass away into being mere representations upon the ground of ego-consciousness; these representations are now seen to be posits, not mirror-images: values, not indubitably true beliefs.

Thus Nietzsche's destruction of the Cartesian system puts into question the Western "metaphysics of presence" itself. Descartes removed any possibility of sacred ground except the fully self-present ego, and now Nietzsche (not to mention Freud, et al.) has taken the ego away too, dissipated it into a pragmatically unified constellation of warring forces. One is left with no ground at all. Life is "will to power," a raging of centerless force against centerless force in which all stability is but a temporary alliance of oppositions. After Nietzsche there is nothing left that possesses the full and final presence of pure Being; there is nothing that compels our unremitting assent, nothing that stuns into a blessed silence our capacity for ironic redescription. Our values, those basic structures of interpretation created and posited by the will to power in its own service, values in terms of which our world is constructed and our conduct is justified, thus lose any claim to objectivity or universality; and we enter the shadow-time of nihilism, the twilight of Platonic-Cartesian religiousness, and perhaps the dawn of another sort: "What does nihilism mean? *That the highest values devaluate themselves. The aim is lacking: 'why?' finds no answer*" (K 2).

We can see what Nietzsche means here by "devaluation" by considering our allegiance to truth as a "highest value." As end-of-century, Western intellectuals, we have been reared to love and to serve truth before everything else. What matters more to us than getting it right, than knowing what we're talking about, than being in secure possession of the relevant facts? Nothing. And our commitment to religious truth, to our scrupulous examination (in the name of truth) of every claimant to the status of religious/philosophical ground, has led us to see, ironically enough, why such a ground must at last fail to appear. The final absence of this ground is the upshot of Nietzsche's trashing of Cartesian ego-subjectivity, just discussed: a trashing that proceeds at every point in the name of truth. But there is yet a further irony to come: the philosopher's traditional search for truth must now take truth itself as its primary object of investigation.[26] "What is the truth about truth?" becomes our cry; and in the pitiless philosophical light we have learned to focus so precisely, we see step forward in response to our prompting, not Plato's or Descartes's or John the Evangelist's Truth, weighted with the full presence of Being Itself, but just another Nietzschean value, posited by the will to power. What appears to our sight as truth is not Truth, but the *value* of truth; that is, various social practices for constructing and enforcing stable and public agreements about "the facts," agreements that always and only serve some particular instance of will to power. And this sort of "posited" and contingent truth, like any other "posited" value, can claim only our pragmatic allegiance, not our worship. Now, too late, we begin to suspect that some questions— "What is the truth about truth?"—are better left unasked. Our highest values have devaluated themselves.

To say, as Nietzsche does here, that "the aim is lacking" is to say that no single value (e.g., the Christian's God, or the philosopher's Truth) can any more serve as the permanent point and justification of all the rest. For us, values are proliferated, dispersed, historicized; they form no necessarily permanent hierarchy. Of course this proliferation is connected to our recognition of them *as values,* which is to recognize their subservience to what Nietzsche calls "will to power"; that is, to our continuing need to preserve and to enhance, to extend and to complicate, our lives of both theory and practice. We now recognize these values as deeply and inescapably our own. Because there is no assurance that the same values will always preserve and enhance life—particular values, like particular vocabularies, sometimes become impediments to our flourishing—the world constituted by some determinate set of them loses its metaphysical unity and its ultimate stability; it becomes plastic raw material to be ordered and reordered as seems necessary and useful to us. But this loss of ultimate "aim" does not mean out-and-out chaos; it means just to recog-

26. One thinks of the late John Wisdom's famous *mot:* "Every day in every way we are getting meta and meta."

nize that everything—every value—is subject to change, to loss of power, to the unpredictable vicissitudes of *moira*.

Thus nihilism—the self-devaluation of our highest values—seems the secret logic of Western culture: the worm was in the bud all along. The very idea of the sacred, of the ground of Being, has apparently collapsed upon itself. What could now present itself to us as holy and all-empowering, as the One True Source of the Being—the determinate and enduring self-identity—of things? Where now is the Platonic Form of the Good or the Christian Author of Nature or even the Cartesian ego-subject? Each has been dissolved—or, better, transmuted into a value—in the acid-bath of a truly critical reflection. All our forms of spiritual life have heretofore rested upon the distinction between the sacred and the profane, and upon the "metaphysics of presence" spun out of that distinction; now Nietzsche has (so it seems) rung the last changes on those great dreams, showing us how hopeless it is to expect any more the full meal we crave. Eat all of Plato or Descartes or Saint Paul you can hold; three hours later you're hungry again.

Nietzsche himself is unwilling (or perhaps unable) to leave the matter there, however. There is still something of a sacred ground in Nietzsche's thought, and that ground is the Overman, the *Übermensch*. Just as for Descartes all accurate representations of reality are finally grounded (i.e., certified) by and in the immediate self-presence of the ego, so for Nietzsche too all the highest values are grounded (i.e., created and "posited") by and in the self-conscious and joyful will to power of the *Übermensch*. And thus Nietzsche's work points us toward the latest, and perhaps last, form of Western religiousness; we may call it *the age of transvalued values*.

All of us live by values. All of us, that is, must adopt some basic structures of interpretation (Rorty would call them vocabularies) in order to fashion the rushing chaos of pure experience into a livable world. But for most of us these necessary values are "our own" only in the most trivial sense, as they are values we have taken over quite thoughtlessly from those powers—familial, educational, political, economic, religious—that created us. Most of us, in other words, are clones of already existing practices and institutions, not genuine individuals. We are members of "the herd" (K 274–87). And what is worse, as happy members of the herd our values don't in the main announce themselves *as* values. They are values that masquerade as something more: as God, as Truth, as Reality. Thus most of us are doubly gulled in our ordinary lives: we think we are living a life that is our own, when in fact we are merely acting out scripts written for us by others; we think our life is founded on something eternal, on Reality Itself, when in fact we are the unwitting prisoners of contingency and time.

Not so the *Übermensch*. He[27] is the genuine individual, the one who can see "the herd" *as* a herd, and can also relish his own distance from it. The Overman is "a stronger species, a higher type that arises and preserves itself under different conditions from those of the average man" (K 866).

What makes the Overman "stronger" and "higher" than the "average man' is his recognition of, and his pleasure in, himself as the self-conscious creator of the values that constitute his life. The Overman knows the power of time and contingency, and he rejoices in the freedom that knowledge gives him. To recognize that the "highest values" are not written into the fabric of the universe, but are the products of a particular form of life, is for the Overman not an occasion of denial or sadness or nostalgia but rather one of joyous self-affirmation. Like us, he is a nihilist, because in his presence the traditional "highest values" of his culture have "devaluated themselves." Their wonted metaphysical warrants have evaporated before his eyes. But he is, one might say, a joyful nihilist, not a despairing one; his is a nihilism of strength, not of weakness. He sees quite clearly the hole left by the flight of the gods, the abyss left by the disappearance of any permanent philosophical ground, and yet he sees that empty space as a region to be filled by himself. He will fill the abyss with his own will to power. He will joyfully and self-consciously create the values that constitute himself and the life he lives. "Welcome, O life. I go to encounter for the millionth time the reality of experience and to forge in the smithy of my soul the uncreated conscience of my race."[28] And those values will have to be new—"transvalued"—ones, ones that will not devaluate themselves as our own "highest values" have done. The Overman will become the self-producing artist of his own world.

Thus the three structural features of Western religiousness reappear in Nietzsche's postphilosophical vision of the *Übermensch*. The sacred ground is not some transcendent god or Form, nor even the self-recognizing, self-certifying transcendental ego; rather, the ground is the self-conscious, self-creating will to power: chaotic life that fashions itself into something more than chaos in order that it live a while longer and a bit better. The Overman, the one who knows himself to

27. In this case the male pronoun seems all-too-appropriate.

28. The speaker, of course, is Stephen Dedalus in Joyce's *A Portrait of the Artist as a Young Man,* reprinted in *The Portable James Joyce,* ed. Harry Levin (New York: Viking, 1966), p. 526.

be such a self-creation and who rejoices in that knowledge, is therefore will to power—life—that knows itself fully to be such. In contrast, the lives of most of us belong to the profane and "reactive" world of "the herd." Whether we are blissfully unaware of our contingency and still live as if we had reality's own seal upon our lives, or whether we are despairing nihilists who mourn the self-devaluation of our highest values, we lack the self-achieved self-possession and joyful power of the Overman. And what could close the gap between Overman and "average man," between sacred will and profane reactivity? Only "discipline and breeding" (K 854–1067). Nietzsche's religious sacraments are neither sacrifices of personality (the Yahwist) nor achievements of intellect (Plato, Descartes); they are practical techniques of self-possession, ways of constellating wayward forces into centers of smooth-flowing will. From such nurture will the Overman emerge. The *Übermensch* is a promise, of course, or a hope (to some, perhaps, a terrifying threat); certainly not yet a reality. We end-of-century intellectuals still inhabit the time of the "last man"; at best we can be a bridge to the (allegedly) glorious creature who will supplant us. The age of transvalued values is still only dimly visible over the horizon.

Nihilism as a Normal Condition

My narrative account of Western religiousness comprises four epochs: the age of the gods; the age of the Forms; the age of ego-subjectivity; and the age of transvalued values. So who are *we*, we end-of-century, Western intellectuals? We are those who live on the cusp of the (promised, or threatened) fourth epoch. We are those who used to encounter the gods in their holy places, who used to discover the immutable Forms in dialectical interchange, who used to know the ego-subject and its representations in philosophical meditation; and we are those who now find ourselves—happily or unhappily—to be producers and consumers of self-devaluating values. What does it mean for us to be religious? It means for us to be some sort of nihilist, conscious or unconscious, joyful or sorrowful, or somewhere in between. We can no longer serve gods, nor gaze on Forms, nor encounter ourselves as the fully present ego-subject; we can only monger self-devaluated values: values that still trade under the old and hallowed names "Yahweh," "Allah," "Jesus," "truth," "love," "reality," "evil," "I," and so forth; but values that are now a bit shopworn from our handling, and a bit gim-

crack when seen in bright light. The religious and philosophical vicissitudes I have sketched in my narrative have, in their crude com-
pulsions, gone to construct a dominant mood among us, a typical way
of comporting ourselves to the world and to one another. Nihilism—
characterized by Nietzsche as the self-devaluation of our highest
values—is that mood. Nihilism is now the way the world comes to us,
the way it sounds itself out in us; it is the way we comport ourselves
to what we are given. We are all now nihilists.

Such a characterization is easily and frequently misunderstood.
"Nihilism" is usually taken to name a pathological condition of individual or society: a paralyzing state compounded of pessimism, apa-
thy, weariness, loss of all conviction, "recession of the power of the
spirit" (K 22). Alternatively, the word is sometimes taken as a philosophical synonym for sociopathy: the nihilist is imagined to be altogether without a controlling conscience; a brute who coolly does
whatever he wishes. No doubt the term is sometimes used in those
dramatic ways, even by Nietzsche, but it need not be; and something
important may be lost if it is. Perhaps nihilism is not so uncanny a
phenomenon as we are at first inclined to think. Nietzsche, for example, sometimes speaks of nihilism as a normal condition, as *our* normal condition in fact (K 23). To be a nihilist is not (necessarily) either
to be hopeless and inert (like the catatonic) or to operate brutally and
without effective restraint (like Ted Bundy or the Nazi *Gauleiter*); on
the contrary, *all* of us now are nihilists, even those among us who are
most energetic and most scrupulous. *To say that we are normal nihilists is just to say that our lives are constituted by self-devaluating
values.* What makes these values *values* is that we normally recognize,
as our ancestors normally did not, their reality as pragmatically posited filters through which experience must be passed to become manageable; what makes them self-devaluating is that we also recognize—
and only with their help, of course—their contingency, their subjection
to history understood as the Mendelian evolution of life-forms. As normal nihilists we are aware of both the existence of radically alternative
structures of interpretation and the fact that we ourselves lack any
knockdown, noncircular way to demonstrate the self-sufficiency, solidity, or originality of our own. The only stories available to us to explain
the values we hold (or, better, that hold us) are causal stories: stories
told by intellectual historians or by psychoanalysts; not by theologians
or philosophers.[29] Under the compulsion of our carefully nurtured will

---

29. Here the influence of Rorty on my account is apparent. What I am calling *normal
nihilism* is very close to what he calls *irony*. See Richard Rorty, *Contingency, Irony, and
Solidarity* (New York: Cambridge University Press, 1989), 73 and passim.

to truth, our commitment to what Nietzsche calls "intellectual cleanliness," we have lost our confidence in those metanarratives that promised us escape from contingency.[30] And with that we also lost any sense of a genuine autonomy or self-possession. We are creatures of value, buying and selling, and that means bought and sold, in terms inherited not from Reality Itself but only from our own particular histories. We too are the products of an economy (not just financial, of course) whose true sources and rulers we do not at present see.

Thus the devaluation of our highest values: given our long commitment to the value of rigorous honesty in thinking, we have left ourselves no intellectually respectable way to dismiss the disconcerting thought that other, and radically different, forms of life have just the same claim on some sacred ground as does ours; namely, no such claim at all.[31] Our "highest values" compete with the "highest values" of others on what is, looked at philosophically, a perfectly level field of battle. And a battle it is. Even "truth"—our very highest value—is not, as our ancestors thought, the name of a triumphant power directing history from within or from without; it is just the nominalization of an adjective of our (inescapably *our*) approbation.[32] To be sure, devaluation of this sort is not total collapse; it is not "the radical repudiation of value, meaning, and desirability" (K 1). That is pathology, not nihilism understood as a normal condition. Normal nihilism is just the Western intellectual's rueful recognition and tolerance of her own historical and conceptual contingency. To be a normal nihilist is just to acknowledge that, however fervent and essential one's commitment to a particular set of values, that's all one ever has: a commitment to some particular set of values.

Moreover, and perhaps more disturbingly, to be a normal nihilist is to acknowledge that one oneself is just that set of values: one's very

30. Jean-François Lyotard, *The Postmodern Condition: A Report on Knowledge,* trans. Geoff Bennington and Brian Massumi (Minneapolis: University of Minnesota Press, 1984).

31. It should be noted that this recognition is in no way fated to lead to some form of "cultural relativism"; that is, to the (silly) idea that any particular viewpoint (interpretation, set of values, form of life) is no more, and no less, true than every other viewpoint. ("Really, the claim that the moon is a planet about 250,000 miles distant from the earth is no more true than the belief that it's an old calabash thrown up into the sky and stuck there at a level not far above the treetops.") Rather, the recognition leads us to see that what we mean in claiming that our viewpoint on some matter is true—a claim we will not and should not stop making—is less numinous than we had thought it to be. In our normal nihilism, truth retains its position as our "highest value;" only now it is a value that has devaluated itself.

32. Richard Rorty, "Feminism and Pragmatism," *Michigan Quarterly Review* 30, no. 2 (1991): 250.

subjectivity, one's deepest sense of who and what one is, presents itself as nothing more than a constellation of some historical and contingent structures of interpretation. Even the "I" that speaks or acts, the "I" that reads and judges this very text, is a value—a structure of interpretation, a set of social practices—created and imposed by some form of life, by some vector-sum of forces, in its attempt to preserve and enhance itself. Thus, gone is the free and equal rational being (the exalted ego-subject) of the Cartesian/Kantian philosophical and moral axis; or rather, not gone, but inescapably devalued: sapped of its power to command our uncompromised allegiance. Perhaps most of the time, in fact, one cannot help thinking of oneself as a whole and unitary center of rational thought and agency; that is, as the Enlightenment ego-subject so caressed by liberal-democratic theory. The normal nihilist, however, will recognize—following Nietzsche—that such "untruth" is merely a condition of [a] life.[33] To think of oneself that way, even to think of "oneself" at all, is nothing more than, nothing less than, a requirement for living in a particular fashion: it is both the result and the requirement of some specific and contingent rhetorical practices. The Enlightenment self of rational agency thus comes to be seen as a contingent human achievement, not a natural necessity. (Certainly Euthyphro didn't think of himself that way; perhaps our great-great-grandchildren won't either. And what then will they make of us?) Normal nihilism means having discovered what it means to be only a part of history, not its natural telos.

The very same point can be made, of course, in relation to the self of the normal nihilist. To find oneself to be such a nihilist, to find oneself (and everyone else) to be constituted by particular (and self-devaluating) values, is no more a discovery of one's true self than was the construction of the Enlightenment's free and equal rational person. Normal nihilism, looked at from its own perspective, is itself to be understood as just another contingent set of social and linguistic practices, just another way—our way—of cutting the cake. To see ourselves as normal nihilists is, as we normal nihilists all too well know, merely to have learned a new way of talking about ourselves (not, of course, the True way of talking about ourselves). But this way of talking about ourselves is (for us, and for a while) compelling. Although we recognize that it's not a spiritual destiny, it nevertheless seems the natural and ineluctable outcome of those other powerful ways of talking about ourselves that our most interesting intellectual

---

33. Friedrich Nietzsche, *Beyond Good and Evil*, sec. 4, in *Basic Writings of Nietzsche*, trans. and ed. by Walter Kaufmann (New York: Modern Library, 1968), 202.

ancestors (the Yahwist, Hesiod, Plato, Descartes, Nietzsche) invented and used. As a self-interpretation it is, as we realize, contingent but not (at will) dispensable.

And now one can also easily see that my own potted narrative of who we have become—the narrative that represents us as normal nihilists—is itself a distinctively normal nihilist narrative.[34] By representing our past as a series of replaceable sets of values (gods, Forms, egos), as alternative structures of interpretation succeeding one another as the varying conditions of life (intellectual and otherwise) demand, the narrative belongs to, as Heidegger would snidely put it, "the age of the world-picture" it is itself helping to define and to sustain. The narrative presents our past and future as intellectual patterns ("world-pictures") to be viewed, comprehended, and evaluated as such, and on reflection it presents itself as such a pattern as well: as a *narrative,* not the thing itself; and as *a* narrative, one among indefinitely many others, and one constructed to do a particular job. Thus my narrative places itself within its own frame, forcing us to see not only the past but also the present—this account itself—as interpretation in service to a form of life. My own account too is no more (and no less) a thought enforced by some—probably invisible—economy, of whatever currency. To us normal nihilists, obviously it must seem as if we *must* be normal nihilists: and that is right, only we must be careful not to turn the "must" into a metaphysical imperative rather than a rhetorical need. Thus devaluation devaluates the very account that succeeds in explaining our mood of devaluation. Even our normal nihilism is just a banal contingency, not an uncanny insight into the Order of Things. There are no uncanny insights any more, not even this one. And so the Pathos of self-knowledge, even of our own self-knowledge as normal nihilists, seeps away. All that is left is the economic exchange, the making and buying and selling, of values.

If one wanted a visible symbol of our normal nihilism, a contemporary alternative to Heidegger's famous philosophical representation of the Black Forest farmhouse, one could do no better than to think of the regional shopping mall.[35] Here one sees alternative values jostling one another in tenuous détente; more important, here one sees oneself operating as the consumer (and, indirectly, as the creator) of

34. I am indebted to Andru Matthews for making this point so clearly to me.

35. For Heidegger's portrait of the farmhouse, see "Building Dwelling Thinking" in *Poetry, Language, Thought,* by Martin Heidegger, trans. Albert Hofstadter (New York: Harper and Row, 1975), 160. The essay, and the farmhouse, will be discussed in detail in Chapter 4 below.

those values. In my community's largest mall, for example, a Christian bookstore sits right alongside a store selling reproductions of Early American knickknacks; just beside the shop for computer software there is a clothing store that traffics in outfits apparently designed to be worn in the Maine woods; down past the fountains are both a store full of expensive electronic gizmos and a shop decorated to look like a tropical jungle, the better to sell safari jackets and knock-off hiking boots. In air-conditioned comfort one can stroll from life to life, from world to world, complete with appropriate sound effects (beeping computers; roaring lions). Laid out before one are whole lives that one can, if one has the necessary credit line, freely choose to inhabit: devout Christian; Williamsburg grandee; high-tech yuppie; Down East guide; great white hunter. This striking transformation of life into lifestyle, the way in which the tools, garments, and attitudes specific to particular times and places become commodities to be marketed to anonymous and rootless consumers: these are the natural (if also banal) expressions of our normal nihilism. An outfit, an electronic toy for bored adult males, a book detailing an aerobic exercise program for Christians—these are, in Nietzsche's sense, *values*. They represent structures of interpretation, organized applications of force, in terms of which a stable and enduring world is constructed, and ourselves in it; they are necessary techniques of life-preservation and life-enhancement.

In my plaid wool coat driving to work, or doing my Christian aerobics to a carefully sanitized rock beat, I know who I am and who I want to be; more crucially (even if somewhat more subtly) I know I can be whoever I want. In just a few steps down the mall I can pass from glitz to tweed, from laptop computers to colonial brass sconces. Not only am I thus revealed (that is to say, constructed) as the consumer of values already manufactured; I am, if I reflect a moment, shown to be the (potential) creator of alternative structures of interpretation. The empty stores seductively beckon. One doesn't have to remain merely a plunderer of other people's lifestyles; one could, if one were both smart and lucky, turn one's own sensibility into a commodity too. As with Ralph Lauren, one's own fantasy life could be marketed as a profitable line of goods.

To visualize a shopping mall in this way is to recognize both the gain and the loss connected to our normal nihilism. The leveling of lives into economic commodities, the way in which the "highest values" of a form of life become functions of the continually evolving market economy rather than exemplars of the "true world," the sense of one's power to refashion one's identity more or less at will: these both liberate and diminish. In the culture of the mall, our highest values—even truth[36]—have certainly devaluated themselves; they have become the playthings of an impersonal and endless economic ordering (which is one currently popular way of talking about the will to power). They have become things to be peddled and traded as one sees fit. But that devaluation can also be experienced as an access of human freedom. On one's good days, wandering happily from store to store, flashing one's plastic, one seems a powerful self-creator, a person capable of radical transvaluation. When the black dog bites, however, one feels oneself a hapless consumer, victimized by the heartless purveyors of commodities and thereby laying waste to the earth and oneself in one's fruitless search for something that endures. We are gored on either horn. Most weeks we feel the prick of both.

In such normal nihilism, traditional forms of supernatural religiousness are of course decisively devalued. Judaism, Christianity, and Islam have come to be seen by us as competing sets of values, as alternative ways of interpreting (and thereby, one hopes, mastering) the opportunities and the obstacles thrown up by one's experience. Even if one might be moved—for reasons of sentiment, or of political advantage—to defend one of these sets of values over the others, one must at the same time realize that such a defense has now become necessary: no form of life is unquestionable by us; none is proof to our capacity and need for irony. Organized religion has certainly not disappeared in this shadow-time of values, but it has changed its character in fundamental ways. There are still devout Jews and Muslims and Christians around, of course, but to us they begin to look like the folks who need to wear nothing but Polo head to foot, or those who spend all their free time arguing the advantages of IBMs over Macs. The Christian bookstore is for us just another shop in the mall.

Nonetheless, it is important to see that our nihilism, considered as a normal condition of contemporary life, is itself a variant of Western religiousness, even if only privatively. Our normal nihilism makes itself felt as *devaluation,* as the self-devaluation of those values on which we most rely; and that sense of loss, the loss of any value's power to ground one's life in a finally convincing way, is a hangover from our religious and philosophical history. We may not be totally devastated by the recognition of our contingency as a form of life—

36. Consider, in relation to the value of truth, the multitude of books in the mall bookstore that self-consciously lie. I am thinking of such things as celebrity biographies, and of "as-told-to" autobiographies, and of straight-faced accounts of encounters with extraterrestrials, and of the endless parade of diet books. Enough of these books, and it's not clear any more what "truth" means.

mostly we aren't—but we are still made uncomfortably aware of our distance from what we once wanted and thought we could have. "Lost belief, like a lost fortune, has effects that linger."[37] Powerful dreams don't immediately disappear with the morning light, and the Western dream of the sacred ground persists even in our not untypical sense of need and loss, of restlessness and boredom. The religious impulse one sees in the Yahwist, Plato, Descartes, and Kant did not evaporate along with the traditional forms of the metaphysics of presence: we haven't given up the desire for wholeness, even if we think we recognize its impossibility.

To be sure, Nietzsche's Madman was telling the truth in the town square. God really is dead, dead as dirt; and we have killed him, you and I: killed him with the very weapons—a love of truth, a respect for honesty, a sense of history—forged for us by his strongest captains. But a dead father doesn't disappear just because dead, any more than a faithless lover leaves one's life merely by moving to the far side of the world. God is dead, but not gone. The role of the Big Fellow in the Western family romance is still there; only now it is empty of a living presence. So it will be filled with another one. Life itself—understood as activity, as novelty, as "multiplicity," as the endless proliferation of values, as the mall with infinitely many shops—can easily become the double for the sacred ground of our religious/philosophical tradition.

With that thought in place, we can now begin to articulate the threat posed by our normal nihilism: the way in which either the appropriation or the creation of values can be invested with the numinosity formerly attached to the fictions of traditional religion. Two dangers are apparent here. The first is nihilism expressed as a kind of runaway humanism. Confronted with the possibility—in some instances the quasi-religious demand—that we continually create new and better forms of human life, we can easily fall into an overwhelming restlessness. Life for the sake of life (the Nietzschean dream) becomes change for the sake of change. Nothing except fatigue and our failures of imagination limit our capacity to fashion ourselves and our world anew, in accordance with whatever purposes we uncover in ourselves. But novelty palls before the ever newer; the half-lives of our enthusiasms become shorter and shorter. And pretty soon we are feeding our habits by eating the earth (and ourselves) in bigger and bigger bites: the base of the pyramid must grow ever wider to support its endless ascent. Our humanism—our sense of limitless

37. Jack Miles, *God: A Biography* (New York: Knopf, 1995), 3.

inner and outer space to be filled with new selves, new worlds, new pleasures, new values—can thus leave us (and the planet) helpless before our well-confirmed predilections to addiction and to boredom. The imperative creation of new values, of new ways of ordering and mastering our experience for our own sake, can too easily slide into an ordering for the sake of a new ordering, a mastery for the sake of a fuller mastery. The driver can become the driven, with all and everything crowded into the single veering chariot.

One of the most horrifying elements of such runaway humanism is its power to obliterate, not just common goods like pure air, clean water, arable land, and pristine wilderness, but human history itself. For the normal nihilist, nothing must be preserved "as it really was"; nothing must be remembered "as it really happened." All is grist for the mill of reinterpretation in service of life's preservation and enhancement. At most, perhaps, some artifacts from the past are kept around, themselves to be commodified and marketed. (Think of our museum stores selling brooches made from reproduced Egyptian tomb-ornaments, or the hawking of T-shirts bearing mad Nietzsche's countenance.) Memory too easily becomes nostalgia; the past becomes kitsch. (How long will it be before our shops start offering souvenirs of the Holocaust, as some now trade in Nazi memorabilia? Is it really unimaginable that ID numbers tattooed in blue on forearms will at some point become fashionable in the trendy dance clubs?) Not even the reality of the past can serve as a limit on our power to re-vision ourselves and our future. Event is obscured by later event; the circle dance goes on.[38] And when the past disappears in such forgetting (or into kitschy and commodified memorial), the present can thin out into a jittery mania for pure difference. One becomes Emerson's traveler who says, "Anywhere but here."

A second and antithetical danger is nihilism expressed as the triumph of the normal. One can, in fearful or resentful response to one's sense of apparently limitless multiplicity, sink—or even joyfully plunge—into some well-defined social and cultural role, letting it define who one is and will be. The oppressive demand for novelty is rejected in favor of the comfortable bonds of what Heidegger calls *das Man,* the "anyone."[39] (One might, with some justice in our day, call this the triumph of fundamentalism.) One speaks as "they" speak; one acts as "anyone" would act. One becomes thereby, and enthusiasti-

---

38. It goes without saying that the novels of Milan Kundera have this sort of forgetting as one of their major themes.

39. Heidegger, *Being and Time,* sec. 27.

cally, a socially constructed cipher, wearing the right clothes, working at the right job, seeing the right movies, having the right responses to them, doing what is expected by "them" of "anyone." One is a model of good behavior; even one's vices are those that "anyone" might have. Sometimes it is not enough just that one find this sort of comfort for oneself; no, it must be enforced on others as well. One's own hold on normality is threatened by anything abnormal. Errancy must be condemned and attacked. One can allow to stand only what "they"—the good Christians, the true revolutionaries, the tenured professors of the Ivy League, those who have read Bataille—approve of.

As the first expression of normal nihilism tends to sacrifice the public to the private, allowing (at its worst) the fantasies of individuals and groups to consume both common goods and public norms, the second reverses the direction of the knife. At its worst, the triumph of normality destroys the private realm, and the realm of the utopian minority as well, in the name of public order. Fantasy is sacrificed to common sense, and novelty is kept within bounds set by the need for a predictable security. We all become *das Man*.

Neither of these dangers of our normal nihilism is a fate, of course. There is no inexorable logic of history, no Heideggerian Destiny, no iron *Geschick,* moving us toward either pole of the continuum I have just described. Perhaps we will escape right down the middle, figuring out how to mix private fantasy and public good in precisely the right proportions. Perhaps. But what if we do not?

Prospect

What does it mean for us to be religious? It means for us to be some kind of normal nihilist. We call ourselves, quite sincerely, Christians, or democrats, or feminists, or humanists, or some combination of such things; but we are, as these sorts of persons, in fact the consumers and purveyors of self-devaluating values. We are, as we somehow all know at some level of consciousness, *coping,* trying to make sense of things, trying on old or new costumes so as to feel at home at the party, trying to preserve and enhance—perhaps through complete transformation—whatever life we have inherited. We have finally lost our metaphysical faith, understood as a childlike faith in metaphysics, a faith in the reality and saving power of the "true world" metaphysics adverts to; but we haven't lost our desire for the Garden. We still have a powerful appetite for perfection, even if we have had to learn to be discreetly ironic about it. We aren't radical, but we remain utopian.[40] Even as normal nihilists we retain our fundamental Western religious affection—the fantasy of a healing perfection, our hunger for the "true world" that stabilizes and saves—with now no metaphysical vessel to contain it. Is it any wonder that the affection volatilizes into some form of numinous humanism? Is it surprising that the New Jerusalem appears as several hundred thousand square feet of air-conditioned merchandise to be bought and sold? And is it any wonder that, surrounded by the ransacked shopping bags of our latest spree and dressed in whatever new finery seemed just the thing at the time, we are already, and with a certain *triste,* thinking about our next foray?

Can we, or should we, or must we, be content to leave matters there? Certainly we *can.* Powerful and decent thinkers urge us to. Why should we weep and moan (or resentfully gloat) over our lost theological and metaphysical certainties when we might be doing something, teaching the world to sing a new song? "The meaning of human life is the creation of new vocabularies."[41] To be sure, there is no obvious way back, short of intellectual and spiritual suicide. The price to be paid for the stunning certainty of some new god stepping out from behind a billboard is far too high. At risk would be more than just our most cherished (and most hard-won) forms of intellectual life; such a revelation would leave us defenseless against our own well-documented need for ravishment. "Only a god can save us," intoned Heidegger in his notorious interview with *Der Spiegel.*[42] If that is true, one can see why one would not *want* to be saved; would fear it above all things, even. No doubt it's better for us to be normal nihilists, those who in our effective, though also restless and brittle, coping can hold at bay any need to be "saved," than to repopulate the earth with divinities and their demands for obedient submission. Looked at in this way, the mall is a decided improvement on the temple, or on the Nuremberg rally.[43]

40. Rorty, "Feminism and Pragmatism," 240.

41. I once heard Richard Rorty say that. Whether he would now accept it as an adequate statement of his views—I doubt that he would—is not to the point. What is, is that the statement can serve as the expression of a serious and humane point of view, one that has disavowed both nostalgia and apocalyptic hope.

42. The interview can be found reprinted in *The Heidegger Controversy: A Critical Reader,* ed. Richard Wolin (New York: Columbia University Press, 1991), 91–116.

43. I am afraid of a culture of normal nihilists, but it is not what I fear most, I hasten to add. Our value-mongering, devaluation and all, is certainly not the worst fate one can imagine. Our normal nihilism and its sorrows does not prove that the Enlightenment was a terrible mistake, nor that our traditions of democratic liberalism are

Nonetheless, I am unwilling—perhaps unable—happily to stop here. It's always a good idea, according to Iris Murdoch, to ask about any philosopher: What is she afraid of?[44] I am, I admit, afraid of our culture of normal nihilists. I am afraid that as such nihilists we will not be able to withstand for long our (antithetical) temptations to runaway humanism and to triumphant normality. I am afraid these powerful forces will beset us in vicious alternation, leaving us (and our fellow travelers on the planet, and finally the planet itself) spoiled and exhausted. I am afraid of the loss of any limit on our anthropocentrism, and (simultaneously and antithetically) I am afraid of the loss of any reliable source of energy to use against the crushing weight of *das Man*. Is perhaps the weakness I see in us, the weakness that underwrites these fears, merely a weakness projected from me? I admit the possibility, of course. If I were supremely self-confident, then perhaps I could trust the rest of us more than I do. Maybe, as Nietzsche would have it, one just gets tired as one gets old, and then mistakes one's weariness for insight. Maybe—but I'm still afraid.

Responding to the fears I have just described, the basic conviction of this book is that, although we don't need gods, we do still need sacraments: deliberate occasions for a peculiar sort of grace. We don't need to be saved, and we don't need to find a god to worship, but we do need *something* that—as the "true world" formerly did—simultaneously both limits and challenges our range of conceivable self-descriptions. Such sacraments, were we to discover and to develop them, would both liberate unforeseen energies for change and modulate that change so as to control our tendency to limitlessly aggrandize the human. Perhaps such sacramental practices would be what is left to us of supernatural religion in this age of self-devaluating values.

Somewhere Heidegger says that no one who doesn't feel the horror of the city built within a dome—the human habitation that has had to thoroughly insulate itself from its own vile poisons, which are now the material conditions of its very existence—can understand his later work. Although far from being Heidegger, I claim a variant of that thought for this book. The domed city—the shopping mall writ large—is for me too an image of some genuine horror, both because of

---

bankrupt; and it certainly does not call for a radical overthrow of our present moral and political sensibilities, to be replaced by a hearty enthusiasm for the traditional pieties of *das Volk*. There are things much, much worse than shopping malls, and I hope not to forget that. But there also may be things that are somewhat better.

44. Iris Murdoch, *The Sovereignty of Good* (New York: Schocken Books, 1971), 72.

what I imagine to be inside that city and what I imagine to be outside it. Outside, of course, are all the waste products, sentient and otherwise, created by the huge expenditures of energy necessary to keep the machines smoothly running; inside, in the cool and musical brightness, the shopping continues unabated, ordering itself in tighter and tighter circles of production and consumption, pouring more and more sludge through the vents and into the stinking pools outside.

"Drama," one will no doubt say, "not philosophy; and sentimental drama at that." True on both counts, but such images, crude as they doubtless are, mark attitudes and sensibilities out of which philosophy may—one hopes—come. It is this image, or others like it, that makes me want to move on to the second and third of the founding questions of this book. If what it means for us to be religious, to be *us,* is to be some sort of normal nihilist, some more or less self-conscious producer and consumer of self-devaluating values; and if that cannot be (for me) a happy stopping point, then it seems imperative (for me) to ask whether there might be other ways for us to be religious as well. Can we, without giving up on the history that has made us who we are, find new ways of being religious: ways of being who we are in relation to our hopeless desire for perfection that don't turn out to be just some more variations on our normal nihilism? Pursuing an answer, I turn now to some philosophical texts that can suggest the answer is yes. I begin with the work of Kierkegaard.

2

KIERKEGAARD AND THE TRUTH OF SUBJECTIVITY

The Present Age as Clearance Sale

Brief though it is, Johannes de Silentio's preface to *Fear and Trembling* (published in 1843) is a useful introduction to the whole of Søren Kierkegaard's pseudonymous authorship, especially as it helpfully situates that authorship in relation to the themes developed in Chapter 1 of this book.[1] *Fear and Trembling* is a text written in clear foresight of our normal nihilism. It is aimed at us patrons of the shopping mall, at us postmetaphysical consumers of values, values that have—under that self-devaluating description—necessarily lost some of their accustomed worth. To use Johannes's own striking image, the merchants now ruling our culture have been busily putting on *ein wirklicher Ausverkauf*, a real clearance sale (*FT*, 5). Prices have been cut to the bone. Crowds move through the market-hall of European intellectual history, fingering the bargains displayed there. Yet the goods—the "highest values" of European civilization—are strangely slow to move. "Everything can be had at such a bargain price that it becomes a question whether there is finally anyone who will make a bid" (*FT*, 5). Why should one live or (more sharply) die for something that is, after all, only a *value*, only a structure of interpretation posited by some passing form of life? The spirit of the pres-

---

1. Søren Kierkegaard, *Fear and Trembling*, ed. and trans. H. V. Hong and E. H. Hong (Princeton: Princeton University Press, 1983). References in the text will be indicated by *FT*, followed by the page number.

ent age—ours and Johannes's—is *devaluation,* self-conscious and systematic.

The most important (to Johannes) of the items currently selling at a discount is faith. Rather than the final good of a long and difficult quest, religious faith is now merely a stage on the way to something greater. "It was different in those ancient days. Faith was then the task for a whole lifetime, because it was assumed that proficiency in believing is not acquired in days or in weeks" (*FT,* 7). Not so for us: we think of religious devotion as an epistemic and cultural phenomenon, as one curious or compelling set of values (among many such sets) to be explained and thereby superseded.

As the preface makes clear, the primary villain in this devaluation is philosophy, in particular, as Johannes thinks, the philosophy of Hegel (what Johannes archly calls "the system"). Even the most elementary understanding of Hegel (and that is as much as can be ventured here) will show why Johannes is so troubled: Hegel inflates an ordinary and profitable intellectual ambition—the ambition to explain whatever needs explaining—into something grandiose and threatening. Most of our explanations are local and specific. We explain sultry southern days by reference to the stubborn persistence of the Bermuda High, and we explain the heated atmosphere of a corporate boardroom by reference to the stresses of the business cycle. Since illuminating descriptions of weather patterns are very different in character from illuminating descriptions of psychological states or of economic vicissitudes, we don't normally expect to account for all these phenomena by appeal to the same set of concepts. In ordinary life we are perfectly content to Balkanize explanation. Hegel, on the other hand, like his hero Napoleon ("the World Spirit on horseback," in Hegel's own, probably apocryphal, description), wants to bring everything together under a single authoritative rule. The Hegelian philosopher aims to deploy a basic conceptual array capable of accounting for absolutely everything, one in which the rational and the real are uniquely the same (or, better, the Same). Such final explanation requires, he thinks, a set of concepts capable of fine-grained representation of the deep structure of reality. "The system" formed by such concepts, "the system" spelled out by Hegel in his philosophical works, thus intends to be the Final Word; it purports to be an account of things given—for the first and the last time—in the things' own terms: the view *sub specie aeternitatis.* As such, it threatens to crowd out all other—and, from its point of view, primitive—ways of representing reality, religious faith among them. Hegel's "system" is genuinely totalitarian in its epistemic aims.

All this is, for Johannes, quite scary enough, but Hegel threatens also with the particular form his project of global philosophical understanding takes. Hegel tries to show that what look like fundamental and incompatible conceptual dualities in our traditional philosophical and/or theological accounts of things—dualities such as body/mind, world/God, subject/object, finite/infinte, time/eternity, determination/freedom, and so on—can be made to disappear in a higher conceptual synthesis. These apparent dichotomies can be, in Hegel's jargon, *aufgehoben,* taken up into a higher and more comprehensive concept—a third, synthesizing, term—in such a way that they are both canceled and preserved in that ascent. (Hegel is philosophically fortunate that in his native German *aufheben* means both "to cancel" and "to preserve.") In this Hegelian dialectic of the concept, the truth contained in the first term is synthesized with the truth contained in the second term; their dross is left behind (canceled); and a new and more adequate concept is the result. In its ideal, this dialectic can and should go on until all the conceptual antitheses that have bedeviled human culture have been *aufgehoben.* Indeed, this intellectual ascent to the Absolute Idea—when the real is finally the rational and the rational is finally the real—is the philosopher's defining task (and greatest glory). It is the way the thinker will find, to use a phrase from later in *Fear and Trembling,* "peace and rest." The rifts and tensions that inhere in human lives at present will disappear into the capacious lap of the explanatory Idea.

Because Hegelian philosophical understanding will resolve all differences into a higher identity, finally everything will be shown to be the Same. Everything will be understood as the working of *Geist* (mind, spirit) as it gradually comes to full self-consciousness of itself as *Geist.* Thus in the final philosophical account there will be nothing inexplicable; nothing incommensurable; nothing irrational; nothing that ruptures the fine fabric of our understanding; nothing that sets us against ourselves or one another. The gap inside the unhappy consciousness, the gap—created by reflection itself—that makes us restless and unsatisfied with our current understandings of our situation, will have been finally filled. Inside the harmonious precincts of "the system" everything will have been set securely in its proper place.

Religious life, and Christian faith in particular, is to be comprehended in these same terms, of course; and that is Johannes's true fear. What look to be the incommensurabilities inherent in that faith—for example, the allegedly vast differences between the ways of God and the ways of human beings—will disappear as soon as the philosopher can "transpose the whole content of faith into conceptual form" (*FT,* 7). Such transpositions will smoothly efface the conceptual and ethical disruptions—such as the horror of Abraham's murderous obedience in Moriah—that make the less-somnolent religious believers so uncomfortable during the Sunday sermon. Once a genuinely philosophical understanding has replaced the residually mythical and primitive accounts of traditional theology, religious faith (and Christianity in particular) will be revealed as a particular set of concepts and behaviors, as just another phenomenon the incongruities of which are to be *aufgehoben* in the superior identities of the Idea.

It is easy to see how this sort of philosophical explanation devalues the faith it claims to explain. By describing religious faith as a conceptual phenomenon, philosophy places it inevitably in relation to other conceptual phenomena; faith thus loses any metaphysically privileged position. In the Hegelian representation of it, religious faith is (just) another way of making sense of things, one conceptual array among many. Such a representation historicizes and relativizes any religious life; once faith comes to be seen in relation to other, and competing, conceptual possibilities, the question of the relative power of the competitors must be raised. And that question of relative power will partly be answered (for Hegel) by a historical account of the concepts of faith, an account that shows the earlier concepts from which they have sprung, and an account that at least intimates the later concepts by means of which they will be replaced. To describe Christianity as a particular set of concepts, and thus as concepts with a particular history and—by implication, at least—concepts with a particular future: to do that is to make it conceivable that Christian faith could be supplanted by something that "goes further" (*FT,* 7). Thus the characteristic historicist jibe: "Why stop with *that* way of thinking of things?"

These are the matters at issue early in the Exordium, when Johannes so forcefully insists that he is neither a thinker nor an exegetical scholar. He does "not feel any need to go beyond faith," as the Hegelian thinker must do in his ascent to the Absolute Idea; nor does he know Hebrew, as the exegetical scholar must know it in order to produce his convincing anthropological explanations of peculiar texts (*FT,* 9). In trying to understand what it means to be faithful, Johannes will eschew both Hegelian philosophy and biblical anthropology, since both disciplines set the matter of faith (the story of Abraham's terrible willingness to sacrifice Isaac, for example) in a context that makes it rational, predictable, necessary, explicable. In trying to account for the scandalous events on the mountain in Moriah, the philosopher will talk about the story as marking the replacement of one set of religious concepts with another, and the anthropologist will talk about the story as symbolizing the movement from a culture of human sacrifice to a culture content with the sacrifice of animals. But whatever their particular techniques of commensuration, both the philosopher and the biblical anthropologist are scientists; they serve knowledge, not passion. They seek to eliminate rupture and distress, replacing them with a comforting pattern of familiar progress.

Thus Hegelian philosophy plays the same role in relation to Johannes that Nietzschean genealogy plays in relation to us: both serve up historical consciousness as a technique of ironic detachment, and thus of devaluation. Nietzsche's account of his philosophical predecessors leads us end-of-century, Western intellectuals to see all forms of thought and of life (even our own) as temporary constellations of values, as particular structures of interpretation posited by human beings in order to preserve and enhance their existence. Likewise, Hegel's metaphysics of the Idea leads Johannes (were he to accept it) to see all history—even his own—as the progress of self-conscious conceptual reflection understood as *Geist*. As different as they are in details and motivation, both philosophical accounts in fact accomplish the same end, and that is because both are so thoroughly historicist. By making it necessary for one to see oneself as a historical *phenomenon*, as a product of conceptual, political, or economic forces—whether those forces are claimed to be directed by self-conscious teleological reason (Hegel) or by the blind and hungry will to power (Nietzsche)— both Hegel and Nietzsche produce a climate of devaluation. With their historicism both thinkers insinuate (willy-nilly) the thought that no form of life can claim the authority of the Absolute. Both thereby reduce European history to a market-hall of "values" or "concepts," the prices of which are (as Johannes says) steadily falling as more and more sets of such goods come on the market.

Hegel, of course, tries to hold out assurance of an account of things that cannot devaluate itself; namely, the account of *Geist*'s growing self-consciousness enacted by Hegelian philosophy itself. (It's as if he thinks he's written a story that could never be supplanted by a better one, an eternal best-seller in the mall bookstore.) Nietzsche explicitly, and more presciently, disavows any such metaphysical comfort. But both make it impossible for one to locate the Absolute, and thus one's own "eternal consciousness" of oneself, in any past form of life.[2] (So much, then, for the claims of Judaism, Christianity, or Islam.) And

2. By one's "eternal consciousness" I take it Johannes means something like that description of me that tells me what I finally and incontrovertibly *am*.

both—Hegel in spite of himself, of course; Nietzsche quite happily—
also make it difficult to believe in any self-defining encounter with
the Sacred even in the present; again putting one's "eternal consciousness" in jeopardy. Both thinkers thus threaten us with the despair
that comes when one's firm and defining Ground is irrevocably taken
away.

In the Eulogy on Abraham, Johannes gives voice to the danger
posed by the sort of historical consciousness traded upon by both
Hegel and Nietzsche: the danger of a thoroughly pessimistic response
to normal nihilism.

> If a human being did not have an eternal consciousness, if un-
> derlying everything there were only a wild fermenting power
> that writhing in dark passions produced everything, be it sig-
> nificant or insignificant, if a vast, never appeased emptiness
> hid beneath everything, what would life be then but despair? If
> such were the situation, if there were no sacred bond that knit
> humankind together, if one generation emerged after another
> like forest foliage, if one generation succeeded another like the
> singing of birds in the forest, if a generation passed through
> the world as a ship through the sea, as a wind through the
> desert, an unthinking and unproductive performance, if an
> eternal oblivion, perpetually hungry, lurked for its prey and
> there were no power strong enough to wrench that away from
> it—how empty and devoid of consolation life would be! (*FT*, 15)

Abraham as Counterweight to Nihilism

But Johannes himself does not succumb to the despair he so floridly
imagines in that passage. There are two resources left to us to banish
our fear of such devaluation: the hero and the poet. In this case the
memorializing poet is Johannes himself, and *Fear and Trembling* is
his "song and speech" designed to save us from nihilistic despair by
providing a heroic counterweight to the leveling explanations of Hegelian philosophy. That counterweight is Abraham, of course. He is
the hero whose deeds refuse all our philosophical and historicist attempts to "understand" them. Abraham is the hero of faith, where
"faith" is Johannes's name for a particular kind of life, the life that
cannot be sold cheaply in our culture's general *Ausverkauf*. This point
is crucial: in the religious vocabulary of *Fear and Trembling* "faith"

designates a specific way of living, a particular (and peculiar) form of life. "Faith" is not the name for some kind of special epistemic access to reality. In popular speech, at least among a certain sort of religious believer, one does sometimes hear it used in that latter way. People say, "There are things that one can only know by faith, not by reason," as if faith were something like a third eye, with which one can see things invisible to those not blessed with it. But in Johannes's mouth, "faith" does not match up with "reason" in that way. Faith is not an alternative way of knowing; it is an alternative way of living. Abraham is exemplary not because of what he knows (by whatever means) but because of how he acts.

In the Eulogy, Johannes reinforces this point by his insistence that the life of faith is not eschatological. Abraham's faith is not the hope, or even the certain conviction, that things will turn out fine in the end, in another world after death. The life of faith is not defined by reference to a time yet to come; it is a life here and now.

> Yet Abraham had faith, and had faith for this life. In fact, if his faith had only been for a life to come, he certainly would have more readily discarded everything in order to rush out of a world to which he did not belong. But Abraham's faith was not of this sort, if there is such a faith at all, for actually it is not faith but the most remote possibility of faith that faintly sees its object on the most distant horizon but is separated from it by a chasmal abyss in which doubt plays its tricks. But Abraham had faith specifically for this life—faith that he would grow old in this country, be honored among the people, blessed by posterity, and unforgettable in Isaac, the most precious thing in his life. (*FT,* 20)

The poet's task, then, is to portray Abraham's life so that the true character of faith can be seen there. The poet's difficulty is to present that life in "song and speech" without making it available for redescription in a way that will render it banal and "understandable." There is a quandary here. If Abraham is so foreign to us as to be simply a blank, the life of faith will be of no real interest; it will not be a possibility we can recognize as ours. In that case Abraham will do us no good. But if he is portrayed as genuinely one of us, if he is represented as a human possibility readily grasped, he thereby becomes material for our favored form of explanation, whatever that is: philosophical, psychological, anthropological. And thus he will be cut

down to size, no longer the hero who can free us from the clearance
sale of values we currently inhabit.

Johannes tries to skirt this dilemma by employing (simultaneously)
both a method of contrast and a method of extrapolation. He first
wants to contrast Abraham with some more readily available figures
(the tragic hero, for example), to deny that Abraham can be understood in terms of those familiar archetypes. Yet at the same time he
wants (so to speak) to *gesture* at Abraham by appeal to those very
same inadequate models. Abraham's distinctive way of living can be
attended to only by extrapolating it from certain crucial features of
these more standard forms of life. If he represents a negation of those
traditional patterns of life (and in some way he surely does), it is
negation by transcendence. He extends them past their ordinary
limits. Abraham is not the tragic hero, but that is because his heroism goes beyond that of the tragic hero. He is not the knight of infinite resignation, but that is because the knighthood of faith goes beyond that of infinite resignation. He nevertheless remains a hero; he
remains "the knight of faith." In this back-and-forth way Johannes
tries to give some intelligible content to the life of faith that Abraham
lives, but he intends to do so without leaving that life so plain that its
constitutive features can be redescribed in some reductive explanatory vocabulary.

Covenant, Sacrifice, and Murder

For Johannes the crux of Abraham's life is the abortive sacrifice of his
son Isaac to Yahweh on the mountain in the land of Moriah (Genesis
22:1–19). That event reveals the essence of faith; in that event, that
is, the true character of Abraham's peculiar, disturbing, and yet exemplary way of life comes starkly clear. So with the poet's help we
must learn to read that familiar Bible story, to see it for what it is;
and we must do so in spite of our strong temptation (nurtured—for
some of us—by years of conventional religious training) to read into it
a consoling and traditional moral ("It was a test from God, only a *test*,
and Abraham passed it with flying colors."). We must call out the
story from its ordinary entombment in sermons and in Sunday school
lessons and let it shine forth in all its awful magnificence.

Crucial to our new reading will be to see the story of that sacrifice
in terms of the larger contours of Abraham's life. The biblical account
of Abraham is found in the Book of Genesis, of course, starting with
his genealogy in the last few verses of chapter 11; his story really gets

under way in chapter 12 with the Covenant, the defining event in Abraham's life and the event that establishes Israel as a nation especially chosen by Yahweh.

> Now the Lord said to Abram, "Go from your father's country and your kindred and your father's house to the land that I will show you. And I will make of you a great nation, and I will bless you, and make your name great, so that you will be a blessing. I will bless those who bless you, and him who curses you I will curse; and by you all the families of the earth shall bless themselves." (Gen. 12:1–4)

Such is Yahweh's generous offer, but in order to receive these benefits Abram (whose name is later changed to "Abraham" in a renewal of the original agreement [17:5]) must promise to obey, to affirm Yahweh as the only god, as his Lord and the Lord of his children; and the circumcision of the foreskin of the penis is the visible symbol of that obedience: "And God said to Abraham, 'As for you, you shall keep my covenant, you and your descendants after you throughout their generations. This is my covenant, which you shall keep, between me and you and your descendants after you: Every male among you shall be circumcised'" (Gen. 17:9–10).

Essential to the fulfillment of his part of the bargain is Yahweh's promise to provide Abraham with a son, and this in spite of his great age, and that of his wife Sarah, who is long past the time of childbearing. Isaac is that miraculous child of promise, the heir through whom the blessing guaranteed in the covenant would come. And it is through Isaac that Abraham is put to his greatest test of obedience.

> After these things God tested Abraham, and said to him, "Abraham!" And he said, "Here am I." He said, "Take your son, your only son Isaac, whom you love, and go to the land of Moriah, and offer him there as a burnt offering upon one of the mountains of which I will tell you." (Gen. 22:1–2)

Abraham obeyed. He got up early the next morning, saddled up his mule, gathered Isaac and two servants, and went forth to Moriah. After three days he reached his destination.

> When they came to the place of which God had told him, Abraham built an altar there, and he laid the wood in order, and bound Isaac his son, and laid him on the altar, upon the

wood. Then Abraham put forth his hand, and took the knife to
slay his son. But the angel of the Lord called to him from
heaven, and said, "Abraham, Abraham!" And he said, "Here am
I." He said, "Do not lay your hand on the lad or do anything to
him; for now I know you fear God, seeing you have not withheld your son, your only son from me." And Abraham lifted up
his eyes and looked, and behold, behind him was a ram, caught
in a thicket by his horns; and Abraham went and took the ram,
and offered it up as a burnt offering instead of his son. (Gen.
22:9–13)

As a result of this ultimate obedience Yahweh reassures Abraham
that the covenant will be honored.

And the angel of the Lord called to Abraham a second time
from heaven, and said, "By myself I have sworn, says the Lord,
because you have done this, and have not withheld your son,
your only son, I will indeed bless you, and I will multiply your
descendants as the stars of heaven and as the sand which is on
the seashore. And your descendants shall possess the gate of
their enemies, and by your descendants shall all the nations of
the earth bless themselves, because you have obeyed my voice."
(Gen. 22:15–18)

So much for the biblical account. And what could be clearer, or
more inspiring? Yahweh offers Abraham the greatest of all gifts, the
blessing of immortality—descendants as numerous as the sands on
the seashore, descendants who will conquer a land flowing with milk
and honey and who will live in that land secure and prosperous forever—and the only condition of that gift is unquestioning obedience
to him as Lord. And Abraham does obey. He proves himself finally
worthy, and that means finally obedient, through his willingness to
offer even his beloved son Isaac as a blood sacrifice on demand. He
passes Yahweh's test, and he takes home the promised reward. Abraham's heroism—his "knighthood"—is the heroism of extraordinary
obedience.

But then what is it about Abraham that we supposedly don't "understand"? All of us certainly understand the virtues of courageous
obedience, of sticking with one's commitments even when the going is
tough; and we certainly understand the notion of a "trial," a "test" of
one's faithfulness. So isn't Abraham just a standard moral exemplar:
the man who was put to the test, whose courage was tried, and who
refused to back off? Don't we already know this good man? Certainly

we do, from a hundred sermons and a thousand Sunday schools. Only the man we know is not *Abraham*.

> We glorify Abraham, but how? We recite the whole story in clichés: "The great thing was that he loved God in such a way that he was willing to offer him the best." That is very true, but "the best" is a vague term. . . . If that rich young man whom Jesus met along the way had sold all his possessions and given the money to the poor, we would praise him as we praise every great deed, even if we could not understand him without working, but he still would not become an Abraham, even though he sacrificed the best. What is omitted from Abraham's story is the anxiety, because to money I have no ethical obligation, but to the son the father has the highest and the holiest [ethical obligation]. We forget it and yet want to talk about Abraham. (*FT,* 28)

We do not know Abraham because we forget, in our Sunday school distraction, the horrifying criminal he is actually portrayed as being. We forget the terrors of the story: Isaac's terror lying there bound hand and foot; Abraham's terror at his own willingness to raise the knife over the boy's throat; our terror at being unable either to turn away or to intervene. Abraham's unconditional obedience to Yahweh, an obedience designed to secure for him the blessings of the Covenant, has led him into an ethical abyss: "The ethical expression for what Abraham did is that he meant to murder Isaac; the religious expression is that he meant to sacrifice Isaac—but precisely in this contradiction [between sacrifice and murder] is the anxiety that can make a person sleepless, and yet without this anxiety Abraham is not who he is" (*FT,* 30).

Ethically speaking, Abraham is a murderer. It does not matter that in the end he didn't carry through with his intention. He climbed the mountain intending to kill his son at the demand of his Lord, and the sustained intention itself is sufficient to establish his ethical guilt.[3] There is no higher ethical obligation than that a father should love his son, and those who do truly love their sons will certainly balk at turning them into pieces of charred meat. Yet from the religious point

---

3. Here is a point at which one can easily see the essentially Kantian nature of Johannes's ethical thinking. What determines the rightness or wrongness of an action is its form, not its consequences; and the form of an action is given by the maxim (roughly, the subjective rule of action, the principle) it expresses. In this case it is clear to Johannes that the maxim of Abraham's action is such as to make it ethically equivalent to murder.

of view, Abraham's intention was not murder but sacrifice. He did not want simply to slaughter Isaac; he wanted to offer him up in proper obedience to Yahweh. Everything rides on the difference (Johannes calls it a *contradiction*) between these two descriptions. "Murder" and "sacrifice" belong to radically different vocabularies. What exactly makes the difference? What is it that can make an act of filicide in the one case an act of the utmost criminality and in the other an act of the utmost religious devotion?

The obvious answer is the *context* of the act, and that answer is true; but it is essential to Johannes that he avoid appealing to those contexts that devalue the descriptions they warrant. In particular, he must avoid trying to explain Abraham's willingness to kill Isaac by appealing to specific historical or anthropological features of the act as defined by the "local conditions" of its day, "local conditions" that can now (with the help of philosophy or anthropology) be seen as "local." Such historicizing is also necessarily relativizing; it devalues the act by making it impossible for us, who live in a different context, to consider the act as a genuine possibility for us here and now: "Or if Abraham perhaps did not do at all what the story tells, if perhaps because of the local conditions of that day it was something entirely different, then let us forget him, for what is the value of going to the trouble of remembering that past which cannot become a present" (*FT*, 30).

So the context that transforms a murder into a sacrifice is not historical or anthropological. It is not the presence of particular social or intellectual conditions given "objectively"; that is, as sets of facts occurring among other facts, facts the significance of which can be grasped by philosophically tutored reason. The only context that matters to such transformation is the particular sort of life Abraham is leading, a sort of life that can only be understood as a kind of "subjectivity." It is a life that takes its significances only from within, a life in no way dependent for its possibility upon temporary and inessential "local conditions." It is that Abrahamic life—the knighthood of faith—we must now try to present.

Lover and Princess

Johannes works up to his presentation of Abraham as knight of faith by way of a story designed to highlight, both by comparison and by contrast, crucial features of the kind of life lived by the patriarch.

Let's call it the story of the lover and the princess. Its basic plot can be told in a single sentence: "A young lad falls in love with a princess, and this love is the entire substance of his life, and yet the relation is such that it cannot possibly be realized, cannot possibly be translated from ideality into reality" (*FT*, 41). A love that leads to disappointment: the story is both simple and all too familiar; yet everything turns on the way the lover takes the impossibility of his love and thus his inevitable pain. The "objective" facts of the matter are not in dispute: in spite of love and its reciprocation, the connection to the princess must be broken off. A princess of the blood doesn't marry a "young lad." What matters, and what is in dispute, is the way these facts are registered "subjectively," in the consciousness of the lover.[4] The "frogs in the swamp of life," those who speak for sound common sense, see in this failure of youthful love an old (and perhaps to them comforting) tale: love does not triumph over all; considerations of money and station can count for more than does the hot breath of passion. *Pace* the old saw, marriages are made here on earth, in the careful calculations of parents and palace lawyers, in the drawing rooms and ballrooms of large houses, in the conversations of those who relish (and vouchsafe) the gradations of temporal power; not in heaven.

Everything turns, as I have said, on the consciousness of the lover. Does he accede inwardly ("subjectively") to the traditional "objective" accounts of the necessity of his disappointment, those accounts appealing to particular "local conditions" of power and wealth and their necessary conjunction in marriage? Does he accept the powerful and long-standing social and economic barriers that stand between him and the princess, and does he thereby give up the love for his impossible object? Not at all, and his refusal of that easy and ordinary capitulation makes him into a hero, into a kind of knight. In his particular kind of refusal the lover becomes, in the jargon of *Fear and Trembling*, "the knight of infinite resignation." Since for Johannes "infinite resignation" is the last stage before faith, a stage that must be lived through on the way to the kind of life that Abraham had (*FT*, 46), we need to go slowly and carefully through his analysis of its constituent features. For ease of presentation, I shall set out the "movement of infinite resignation" in four steps, with the fourth itself divided into three parts.

First, there is in the lover an extraordinary concentration of desire.

4. And perhaps in the consciousness of the princess as well, though Johannes largely ignores her.

"In the first place, the knight will then have the power to concentrate the whole substance of his life and the meaning of actuality into one single desire" (*FT,* 42f.). The possibility of this concentration depends upon a particular view of the self. Most human beings are, initially at least, creatures of desire.[5] We first of all define ourselves in terms of what we want. Some of our desires are for quite tangible and even somewhat grubby objects, such as wealth, social status, sexual conquest, and various kinds of conspicuous consumption. Some of what we want may seem more elevated: virtue, glory, learning, intimacy, happiness. But whatever the objects, mundane or spiritual, one may take it that the ordinary human life is defined by desire.

Conceived in the way of desire, our lives are most of the time marked by indecision, timidity, and outright failure. We don't quite know what we want; or, rather, we typically want too many things, things inconsistent with one another. To satisfy one desire usually means to frustrate another. Those qualities of mind and character necessary for the attainment of one sort of good turn out to be just the virtues that stand in the way of some others. Erudition, self-discipline, and a taste for delicious ambiguities may wonderfully fit one for the scholar's desk; they may, on the other hand, cripple one as a lover, or even in the Friday-night poker game down at the firehouse. And even when such trade-offs can be finessed, there is always the realization that most of our dreams don't come true anyway, especially if they are large ones. Very few of us get (and keep) what we really most want. Pain, and especially that peculiar kind of pain we call "boredom," is always lurking just over our shoulder, and gaining on us as we age.

Oppressed by such incongruities in the economy of desire, we employ two strategies designed to cut our losses. First, we try to rationalize our desires: we try (a) to achieve as much consistency among them as is possible, so as to minimize the conflict among the goods we seek; (b) to rank them in order of effective pursuit, so that the satisfaction of one may lead easily and efficiently to the satisfaction of another; and (c) to determine which of our desires are likely to be within our grasp, so that we may not spend our energies fruitlessly. Second, we try to diversify our desires: faced with the likelihood that

5. I offer this claim as a reflection of what I think is in play in Johannes's text, not as some sort of "metaphysical" view finally endorsed by Johannes, Kierkegaard, or me. The progress of the argument here bears a strong resemblance to what one finds in S. Kierkegaard, *Stages on Life's Way,* trans. and ed. Howard V. Hong and Edna H. Hong (Princeton: Princeton University Press, 1988), but I shall not complicate my argument by running down the connections.

many of our efforts will fail to satisfy, we endeavor to expand the range of our interests and pleasures. Like the wise investor, we never put all our eggs in a single basket; we spread our funds through a wide variety of instruments, hoping to recoup on the swings what we lose on the roundabout.

While both strategies are eminently sensible, neither is heroic. The hero is not an efficiency expert trying to maximize productivity. The lover does not listen to the frogs who croak at him to scale down his expectations, to diversify his desires across a wider range of objects ("the rich brewer's widow is just as good and solid a match"), or to guard himself against the dangers of too great an enthusiasm. Quite the contrary: the lover "feels a blissful delight in letting love palpitate in every nerve"; he "does not lack the courage to attempt and to risk everything" (*FT*, 42). He is not a coward, and it *is* cowardly always to count the cost beforehand; cowardly only to bet a few pennies, and then only on a sure thing. The heroic lover of our story lets his love for the princess define the whole meaning of his life. Through such concentration of desire he becomes fully who he is: the lover. That description is all we know about him from Johannes's text, and really all we need to know. He has no proper name, no history, no range of pleasures and interests. His economy of desire is as simple as it could be, defined as it is by but a solitary wish: that he have the princess for his very own. That finite desire for that finite object is now the meaning of the lover's life. He is the apotheosis of the life of desire, willing to let all significance ride on willing one thing. Such risk is a necessary condition of heroism: "If a person lacks this concentration, this focus, his soul is dissipated in multiplicity from the beginning, and he never manages to make the movement; he acts as shrewdly in life as the financiers who put their resources into widely diversified investments in order to gain on one if they lose on another—in short, he is not a knight" (*FT*, 43).

Second, having accomplished this heroic concentration of desire, having let his love for the princess "entwine itself intricately around every ligament of his consciousness," the lover now faces up squarely to the impossibility that his defining desire will be realized. He will not get his constitutive wish; he will not have the princess for his own. And this impossibility he recognizes as both (a) produced by some finite circumstance, such as the social and financial distance between his station and that of the princess, and (b) nevertheless insurmountable.

Third, faced with this finite impossibility, the lover refuses either to (a) surrender his defining desire for the princess or (b) substitute another defining desire for that one. He refuses, we might say, to *finitely resign* the princess. The lover might have surrendered his desire for the princess to despair (in which case he could become a melancholiac or a drunkard), or he might even have surrendered it to death itself (in which case he would become a suicide). He might, on the other hand, have tried to distract himself from his pain and ultimately to habituate himself to new desires through some course of frantic sensuality. Whatever their individual features, and whether they are instances of surrender or of substitution, all forms of finite resignation keep within the lover's original account of the self as defined by desire; thus all will see the circumstances of the finite world (distinctions of class and wealth, for example) as given their significance only in relation to that desire, as barriers or helps to its satisfaction. Finite resignation stays within the world as originally conceived; it merely resigns one part of that world in favor of another.

Fourth, and finally, we come to the movement of infinite resignation itself. This movement comprises three distinct moments, the first of which is fundamental to the ones that follow. This first we may call *the moment of metaphysical self-knowledge.* In this moment, as Johannes says, "I become conscious of my eternal validity" (*FT,* 46) and thereby enter into a radically new way of life. In the moment of metaphysical self-knowledge, the self acquires a deeper understanding of its nature; indeed, one may say that in this moment it comes to see that it *has* a "nature," that it possesses some solid core of "eternal validity." The discovery of such a core is a huge shift in one's self-understanding, since heretofore the self had conceived itself only in terms of lack, of emptiness. The "aesthetic" self—the self we all start out by being—understands itself to be defined solely by its desires, by what it happens to want. And since all wants are lacks, since all desires are holes screaming to be filled, the "aesthetic" self thus understands itself as void of any genuinely substantial being. Conceived purely as a center of desire, the self is something like a black hole, frantically pulling things into itself in an attempt to give itself substance, to fill itself up and thereby achieve for itself some "peace and rest" (*FT,* 45). Such a self is defined by what it doesn't have: defined as lack.

Co-ordinate with this "aesthetic" view of the self as a kind of famished emptiness is a correspondingly etiolated view of the world such a self inhabits. If I am defined by my desires, by some accidental constellation of wants, then my world will appear to me as valuable solely under the aspect of those wants. The things I confront will take their whole significance, their whole structure of meaning, from

whether or not they satisfy my desires. In this way the world too—
like the "aesthetic" self—will lack a fully determinate substance; it
will have no substantial and enduring center or form. The world's
meaning will not be given once and for all, by reference to some independent standard; rather, it will have meanings as various as the
desires of the selves who inhabit it. Conceived in this way, the world
is, so to speak, just the raw material for my happiness; and it will be
a happy world or an unhappy world only insofar as it does or does not
allow me to have what I want. Nothing will be good or bad, for example, except insofar as it serves or blocks my defining wishes.

In the first moment of infinite resignation this "aesthetic" self-understanding is replaced by another, and much more substantial, one.
Rather than a creature defined by some contingent array of desires, a
creature who in its "action" is pulled by the nose this way and that
along what look to be paths of satisfaction for those desires, the self
recognizes itself as a being capable of determining itself by appeal to
considerations of *reason.* The self comes to see itself as a substantial
center of practical agency, as a being capable of determining itself to
action in accordance with the laws that govern any rational agent
whatsoever; in sum, the self comes to see itself as capable of *obedience,* obedience to the laws of practical reason.[6] The self is in that
sense, and for the first time, *free:* free to obey or to disobey the law. I
am not, as I used to believe, a black hole helplessly seeking to fill my
lack of substance with the various objects of my desire; I am a potentially rational agent, a being capable of conforming my conduct to a
standard given independently of what I happen to want. I am a being
with "eternal validity."

Along with this re-visioning of the self, there is a corresponding re-
visioning of the world it inhabits. The significances of the "aesthetic"
world were given solely by reference to the desires of the self whose
world it was. What something meant was specified by the way that
thing did or did not enter into the satisfaction of those desires. There
was no eternal structure of value in that world, no structure of significance beyond the temporary and accidental one defined for some self
by some set of desires, concentrated or dispersed. But now things are
different. The world of the re-visioned self contains an order of value,
an order of significance, independent of the desires of any particular
self, an order given *as practical law* by the conditions of rational action itself; the self must accommodate itself to that a priori order by
obedience to those laws.

6. All this is deeply Kantian, of course.

So the first moment of infinite resignation is a radical re-visioning of the self and its world, a re-visioning that gives both self and world a genuine substance, an "eternal validity" granted by the self's identification with the laws of practical reason. The "aesthetic" self has become an "ethical" one. This change is, however, a transfiguration, not a complete metamorphosis. In this process of metaphysical self-discovery the self does not lose its particular identity; it does not "forget" its (formerly) constitutive desires and "become something new" (*FT*, 43).

This emphasis on transfiguration rather than transformation allows us to appreciate the second moment of infinite resignation, which is the redescription of all the self's finite relationships in terms of the "eternal validity" it has now discovered. Formerly, the world appeared only under the aspect of the self's desires; the significance of things was given solely by their relation to contingencies of the self's satisfaction or frustration. The lover wanted the princess, and the particular inequalities of wealth and social standing that prevented their marriage mattered to the lover only because they were barriers to the object of his desire. They mattered only "finitely," we may say; they mattered only because they happened to be in the way of what the lover happened to want. But now those barriers take on a new reality. They are redescribed in terms that give them a new significance, and that redescription depends on the more general redescription the lover has performed on himself. Whereas he had previously understood himself as defined only in terms of his heroically concentrated desire for the princess, he now recognizes his "eternal validity" as a (potentially) rational agent. As Johannes glosses the matter, when the lover recognizes that he is a being subject to eternal laws of practical reason, he also recognizes himself as a being subject to the Eternal Being whose laws they are.[7] As such a being, all the lover's opportunities and impossibilities take on a new meaning: "His love for that princess would become for him the expression of an eternal love, would assume a religious character, would be transfigured

7. This transition is a bit obscure in the text. Johannes makes an unmarked move from the lover's recognition of his "eternal validity," which I read as coming to see oneself as subject to full-fledged ethical demand, to his recognition of that demand as having reference to an "eternal being." Johannes is assuming, naturally enough I suppose, that the lover's redescription of himself and his situation will be a straightforward "religious" one, though not of course distinctively Christian. It is the burden of *Fear and Trembling* to try to make clear the difference between the religiousness of "infinite resignation" and the religiousness of faith.

into a love of the eternal being, which true enough denied the fulfillment but nevertheless did reconcile him once more in the eternal consciousness of its validity in an eternal form that no actuality can take away from him" (*FT,* 43f.).

The lover's desire for a particular person has now—in the moment of metaphysical self-knowledge—been transfigured into a love for the Eternal Being, much as in Plato there is the movement from loving the beautiful object to loving the Form of Beauty the object exemplifies. The lover now sees that his all-consuming wish for the princess is the finite shadow of his infinite need for the eternal perfection she (partially and unwittingly) represents, and thus he realizes that all is not lost. He can have what he wanted all along, but now under a more correct description: not the princess, but the perfection. By acting in accordance with the eternal law—by achieving his perfection as a being of practical reason—he can himself participate in the perfection he hungered after in the finite form of the princess. His transfiguration from "aesthetic" being to "ethical" agent gives him a new source of good. He now recognizes his true good is in his *willing the good,* in his willing himself to act in accordance with the eternal laws of practical reason itself; and that good is immediately present in the good willing itself, not in what may or may not finitely follow from it.[8]

Just as the lover now sees his love for the princess in a new light, so too does he see the finite barriers to that love's fulfillment. Those differences of wealth and class that stood in the way of the marriage are themselves transfigured by his new self-understanding. They too represent, in some way or other, the requirements of the practical law; they too are the finite shadows of infinite demands. Thus they can be seen, not as contingent and regrettable bad breaks, but as necessities to be obeyed as the will of the Eternal Being. By refusing to act on his love for the princess, by refusing to ignore the finite barriers of social distance, the lover is (*ex hypothesi*) acting in accordance with the demands of practical reason, demands that make his marriage to her impossible. "The knight [of infinite resignation], however, makes this impossibility possible by expressing it spiritually, but he expresses it spiritually by renouncing it" (*FT,* 44). By renouncing his earthly happiness, as he is required to do by the laws of the Eternal Being, he finds his true good—his true happiness—in his obedience to those laws.

---

8. The Kantian provenance of this account is of course obvious.

This dual transfiguration—the transfiguration of his love for the princess into a love of the Eternal Being, and the transfiguration of the barriers to that love into requirements of practical reason itself—makes possible the third moment of infinite resignation: the "peace and rest" that follow from the first two moments. Once the lover has redefined himself in the moment of metaphysical self-knowledge, and once that redefinition has led to the redescription of his defining wish and of its insurmountable barriers, he is not free of pain; but he is reconciled to it. "Infinite resignation is that shirt mentioned in an old legend. The thread is spun with tears, bleached with tears; the shirt is sewn in tears—but then it also gives protection better than iron and steel" (*FT,* 45). By resigning the finite (his earthly happiness as husband of the princess) in favor of the infinite (the demands of practical reason), the lover is "reconciled with existence" (*FT,* 43). In that third moment the movement of infinite resignation is complete; one has achieved "the last stage before faith" (*FT,* 46).

It is easy to see why Johannes describes infinite resignation as the work of a knight. Here the traditional knightly virtues are clearly apparent, set in a traditional heroic narrative: in the midst of his life-defining quest for the princess, the lover encounters what seems to be an insurmountable barrier; facing certain defeat, he undertakes a courageous course of self-purification; and, having reconstituted himself as a higher and worthier being, he achieves his true good at the last. No wonder infinite resignation is so rare. But the "true good" of infinite resignation is not yet the good grasped by Abraham: "The act of resignation does not require faith, for what I gain in resignation is my eternal consciousness" (*FT,* 48). Abraham gains more than that: "It takes a purely human courage to renounce the whole temporal realm in order to gain eternity, but this I do gain and in all eternity can never renounce—it is a self-contradiction. But it takes a humble and paradoxical courage to grasp the whole temporal realm now by virtue of the absurd, and this is the courage of faith. By faith Abraham did not renounce Isaac, but by faith Abraham received Isaac" (*FT,* 49).

The Tragic Hero

Before analyzing Johannes's account of Abraham as the knight of faith, we need to note one other figure Johannes uses to contrast with such a knight: that figure he calls *the tragic hero.* The tragic hero is an ethical figure. He[9] already understands himself to be a (potentially) rational agent bound in his conduct by the eternal and universal laws of practical reason, and he identifies the demands of those laws as defining the sphere of the ethical. Conceived in this way, the ethical represents the highest aspiration, the natural telos, of human being; no demand possesses greater authority for us than the demand that we exemplify in our action the very principles governing action itself.

> The ethical as such is the universal, and as the universal it applies to everyone, which from another angle means that it applies at all times. It rests immanent in itself, has nothing outside itself that is its *telos* but is itself the *telos* for everything outside itself, and when the ethical has absorbed this into itself, it goes not further. The single individual, sensately and psychically qualified in immediacy, is the individual who has his *telos* in the universal, and it is his ethical task continually to express himself in this, to annul his singularity in order to become the universal. (*FT,* 54)

To "annul [one's] singularity" means to set aside (but not to forget) the particular desires that constitute one's specific identity (such as the lover's desire for the princess) and to act instead as practical reason would demand; that is, as anyone would act. "The ethical as such is the universal." This is the familiar economy of conscience: one's desires pull in one way; the demands of the ethical law pull in another. I covet my neighbor's first edition of *Blood Meridian,* but it would be wrong (even if easy) to steal it. The ethical person will act according to the latter consideration, and will so act out of respect for the practical law per se.

There is, however, another situation of ethical conflict that needs to be noted. Sharp and bitter conflicts can arise not just between desire and ethical demand; they can also arise within the sphere of the ethical itself. Take the case of Agamemnon. Confronted by a calm that threatened the campaign against Troy, the Greek leaders appealed to the gods for wind to move their ships. In return for this favor, the gods demanded as a sacrifice the young daughter of Agamemnon, Iphigenia. What was the loving father to do? Certainly he wanted his daughter to live; he loved her, after all. And certainly as an ethical

9. Since all of Johannes's examples of the tragic hero in "Problema I" are male, in my discussion I shall use the male pronoun to refer to this sort of hero. There is, of course, no reason to think all such heroes would be male; think of Antigone.

man he was obligated to protect his daughter from harm, not to deliver her over to death. Yet he consented to her sacrifice. Iphigenia was offered up in order that the war could continue.

Agamemnon's situation at Aulis is tragic in two different dimensions. It is tragic first in that he must act so as to renounce some of his tenderest and most admirable desires. He must give up the daughter he loves, and in giving her up, he thereby gives up a large portion of his own happiness. It is also tragic in its necessity that Agamemnon act against some of his most cherished ethical principles. As a virtuous man, he knows it is his duty to protect his family from harm. By consenting to Iphigenia's death, the father is apparently failing in one of his most sacred obligations. Yet Agamemnon is a hero, not a case history. His reason for setting aside both his desire and his ethical duties as a father was, of course, a higher ethical duty. He was required to act, not just as "a single individual, sensately and psychically qualified in immediacy," and not just as a father responsible for a household, but as a political and military leader who finds himself confronting "an enterprise of concern to a whole nation," an enterprise in great jeopardy. His duties to the nation as such a leader outweigh his duties as a father to a daughter. If he is to act according to the principles of practical reason, he must allow the sacrifice to proceed.

As described by Johannes, the tragic hero thus remains firmly within the sphere of the ethical. Agamemnon (or Brutus, or Jephtha: the other examples cited in *Fear and Trembling*) does not fail to have "his *telos* in the universal"; rather, it is the demand of the universal that constantly drives his actions. That universal is, however, layered and hierarchical. Some ethical duties outweigh others. The duties attaching to one as the leader of a nation supersede the duties attaching to one as father. It is the heroism of the tragic hero not just to put aside the ordinary human desire for happiness, as does the lover; he also puts aside his lower duties in favor of his higher ones.

The Teleological Suspension of the Ethical

Yet Abraham is not a tragic hero. In some obvious ways his situation is similar to Agamemnon's: Abraham too has a child demanded as a sacrifice to a god; Abraham too loves his child as the whole light of his life, and Abraham too is an ethical man who knows (and honors) his duty to protect his son. Yet Abraham is not—as is Agamemnon—the "knight of infinite resignation," tragically resigning both desire and (lower) duty in accordance with some higher duty. He does not resign his identity as man and father in favor of some higher identity with correspondingly higher demands:

> Abraham's situation is different. By his act he transgressed the ethical altogether and had a higher *telos* outside it, in relation to which he suspended it. . . . It is not to save a nation, not to uphold the idea of a state that Abraham does it; it is not to appease the angry gods. If it were a matter of the deity's being angry, then he was, after all, angry only with Abraham, and Abraham's act is totally unrelated to the universal, is a purely private endeavor. (*FT,* 59)

Agamemnon was the tragic hero because acting as the leader of his people was for him the highest expression of the ethical; being the ruler of the nation was, so to speak, his highest ethical identity. Not so for Abraham: "There is no higher expression of the ethical in Abraham's life than that the father shall love the son. . . . Insofar as the universal was present, it was cryptically in Isaac, hidden, so to speak, in Isaac's loins, and must cry out with Isaac's mouth: Do not do this, you are destroying everything" (*FT,* 59).

Yet in spite of his love for the boy, and in spite of his recognition that he lacks any ethical justification for his obedience to Yahweh, Abraham moves steadily toward Moriah. Johannes calls what Abraham does *the teleological suspension of the ethical.* It is suspension, not ignorance, since Abraham (Johannes assumes) has made the movement of infinite resignation and is well aware of the ethical demands upon him as a potentially rational agent; he is equally aware that those demands require that he love his son, that he protect him against any power that threatens him. Moreover, Abraham's suspension of the ethical is teleological: it is undertaken in the service of another end, another telos; one assumed by Abraham to outweigh the demands of practical reason. We see here, according to Johannes, a fundamentally new sort of religious expression. If the ethical is teleologically suspended, if the demands of practical reason are set aside in favor of something "higher" than one's duty, then in that instance the ethical has the form of a temptation to be avoided. In Abraham's case, what he sees as "higher" is his necessity to obey Yahweh, to do the god's will through that obedience. But that leads to a paradox: "A temptation—but what does that mean? As a rule, what tempts a person is something that will hold him back from doing his duty, but here the temptation is the ethical itself, which would hold him back from doing God's will. But what is duty? Duty is simply the expression for God's will" (*FT*, 60).

In the thinking of "paganism" (and Kant's moral philosophy is for Johannes the highest development of the "pagan" ethical notions that originated with Socrates and Plato in fifth-century B.C.E. Athens), there can be no distinction between the will of God and one's duty. The Moral Law is the perfect expression of what an Absolutely Perfect Being would require of one as an agent. There is nothing "higher" for human beings than living in "the universal." Yet Abraham insists that he has a "private" relationship to Yahweh that requires him to act in a way that is clearly not "universally" acceptable. The ethical person acts only on those principles that anyone must act on, those principles that bind any rational agent whatsoever; Abraham acts *as an individual* in relation to God, and this in spite of his knowledge of what "the universal" demands of him:

> Here the necessity of a new category for the understanding of Abraham becomes apparent. Paganism does not know such a relationship to the divine. The tragic hero does not enter into any private relationship to the divine, but [for the tragic hero] the ethical is the divine, and thus the paradox therein [i.e., in the gods' command to Agamemnon to sacrifice the child] can be mediated in the universal. (*FT*, 60; my interpolations)[10]

Absolute and Universal

That "new category" is, of course, *faith,* and it is now time to say something directly about this unprecedented life Abraham exemplifies, a life that serves (according to Johannes) as a counterweight to the nihilism normal to us living down here at the bitter end of "paganism." Here is one of the clearest statements of the notion in *Fear and Trembling:*

> Faith is precisely the paradox that the single individual as the single individual is higher than the universal, is justified before it, not as inferior to it but as superior—yet in such a way,

10. In this section I have not challenged Johannes's claim that Abraham cannot be seen as a tragic hero obeying the higher Law. I take up this challenge below in the section "Subjectivity and Narcissism."

please note, that it is the single individual who, after being subordinate as the single individual to the universal, now by means of the universal becomes the single individual who as the single individual is superior, that the single individual as the single individual stands in an absolute relation to the absolute. This position cannot be mediated, for all mediation takes place by virtue of the universal; it is and remains for all eternity a paradox, impervious to thought. (56)

"That the single individual as the single individual stands in an absolute relation to the absolute": that is Abraham. In spite of his recognition of the necessity of the ethical, a necessity ("infinite resignation") that subordinates the desires of the formerly "aesthetic" individual to the dictates of universal practical reason, Abraham exempts himself from the universal in order to become the individual once again. He insists on his obedience to Yahweh, even when that obedience is "absurd"; that is, even when that obedience requires him to violate the Moral Law that demands that a father love and protect his child.

The notion of "an absolute relation to the absolute" is presumably to be contrasted to "a universal relation to the universal," and we can begin to get a handle on the difference Johannes is trading upon here by reflecting on what we may call "public" relationships in relation to "private" ones. By "public" relationships I mean those like parent/child, teacher/student, spouse/spouse, doctor/patient, lawyer/client, and so on. These relationships are relatively well-defined social practices constituted by roles that assign specific rights and duties to each participant in the practice. These roles are public, in that there are relatively fixed and widely shared expectations about what counts as fulfilling the role as it should be fulfilled. Some of the rights and duties attached to a given role may be expressible as definite rules ("A physician must not have sex with his or her patients."), while others are less explicit and must be learned as a kind of tacit expertise. In "public" relationships of this sort, the constitutive rights and duties are universal, or at least very general: the expectations defining excellent performance attach (*ceteris paribus*) no matter which particular individual is holding down the role. Notice that this requirement of universality leads to what one might call the "objectification" of the parties to the relationship. The wills of the individual role-players—what we might call their particular "subjectivities"—are constrained by the "rules" of the practice; in this respect, the participants cannot act "freely." If I am a psychiatrist, for example, the ethics of the medical profession forbid that I sleep with my patients, regardless of what I or my patients may happen to want. One must, as psychiatrist or as patient, set aside one's "individual" desires and live in the "universal."

Contrast such "public" relationships with "private" ones. Perhaps the best example of the latter is a love affair. Considered in relation to something like a marriage or a doctor/patient relationship, a love affair is not a well-defined social practice, especially when the affair is in its early stages, and particularly if the affair is a secret one. In such affairs there are no universal (or even very general) rules that define the roles of the lovers, and there is no set of public expectations to which the lovers are—consciously or unconsciously—trying to conform. Must lovers have sex with one another? Must lovers refrain from having sex with others? Must lovers live together? Must lovers give special consideration to one another's interests and needs? Must lovers want their relationship to become public or permanent? Must lovers share their financial resources? One could extend the questions indefinitely, and the point is: no particular answers are required. There are love affairs that are explicitly sexual, and there are love affairs that aren't. There are lovers who are also best friends, and there are lovers who aren't. There are lovers who want permanence, and there are lovers who don't. And so on.

In a relation like a love affair, the absence of any constitutive rules and of any well-defined public expectations makes the "subjectivity" of the lovers paramount. The charm and the importance of such relationships lie (at least in part) in the way such subjectivity is valorized. Our desires and the desires of our lover are crucial. What we want of our lover, and what our lover wants of us, is—in the first stages of the affair, at least—unpredictable. What it means for you to "be in love with X" is not well-defined, just as for X it is not well-defined what it is to be in love with you. The affair is in that way like good sex: the pleasure turns upon the subtle initiatives and responses that express the particular desires (perhaps never explicitly brought to awareness) of these particular participants. Just as there are no "rules" in good sex, there are no "rules" in a love affair (in the ideal, I mean, since of course we all know the power of routine to "objectify" our willfulness and spontaneity into all-too-predictable patterns of behavior). A love affair is a mutual exploration of sensibility, not a well-laid track leading to some clearly agreed-upon goal.

If, because of their constitution as role-defined slots to be occupied by an indefinite number of individuals, the doctor/patient or the teacher/student relationships can be described as "a universal relation to the universal," then a new and secret love affair can be described as (at least approaching) "an absolute relation to the absolute." The lovers are for one another absolutes, in the sense that they confront one another with unpredictable and supremely important occasions for response. In conversation with one's lover there are no a priori rules and no a priori limits. One's whole world may turn on what is said or not said in response to a simple question ("What did you think of her?"); but there is no way for one to program that response (or the fateful question that provokes it). One does not encounter one's lover (or oneself *as* lover) as a constellation of rule-governed behaviors aiming at a particular goal. (In contrast, the doctor and the patient know what their mutual goal is, and they generally know what sorts of behaviors are acceptable in pursuing it.) Thus with one's lover one is constantly off-guard, constantly scrambling to respond to a demand both unique and absolute. One must say or do the right thing, but there is no publicly defined right thing to say or do. To respond as one must, one must read the lover as an individual (as a "subject"), not as some sort of computer program comprising rules one presumes to know. And that means one has to act as an individual (as a "subject") too, for there are no rules for one to follow in responding to something not rule-constituted.

Insisting as he does on "an absolute relation to the absolute," Abraham's relationship to Yahweh is a "private" one. It more resembles a love affair than a parent/child or doctor/patient connection. The obedience demanded and promised in the original Covenant is not obedience to universal ethical principle or to the publicly recognized duties attaching to a role defined by some specific social practice. It is the obedience one absolute subject gives to another; it is unpredictable obedience to unpredictable demands, obedience that cannot be programmed as rules to follow. Thus the life of faith exemplified by Abraham in relation to Yahweh is a life of maximal "fear and trembling." There is no security for him in such a life: at any point, however obedient Abraham has heretofore been, Yahweh may make an unprecedented demand on him, a demand that suspends not just the desires that accidentally define Abraham as a specific individual but that also suspends the ethical duties constituting his "eternal validity" as a human being. Abraham lives in constant danger of being forced to destroy himself through his own choice: by willingly obeying Yahweh and sacrificing Isaac, he is (apparently) obliterating himself both as center of desire and as center of rational agency. His obedience is thus a sort of suicide; and it is, just as is suicide, therefore "absurd." How could it ever be in one's self-interest to destroy oneself?

The life of Abrahamic faith is a life of absurd self-assertion. It is

self-assertion because it represents an individual's refusal to assent
to the demands of the universal. "The tragic hero relinquishes himself
in order to express the universal; the knight of faith relinquishes the
universal in order to become the single individual" (*FT*, 75). The
knight of faith asserts himself by insisting upon "an absolute relation
to the absolute." But faith is absurd self-assertion, absurd because it
expresses itself as pure subjectivity. Such subjectivity is absurd because, knowing better, it throws away one's "eternal validity" achieved
in the hard-won movement of "infinite resignation." By insisting on
one's right to act in defiance of the demands of practical reason itself,
one destroys one's own autonomy; one obliterates that core of rational
agency that gives one an eternal dignity. And that is absurd: there
could be no *reason* for one to do that. Moreover, the absurdity of such
self-assertion is heightened by the particular form one's subjectivity
takes in the life of faith. In Abrahamic faith, one asserts oneself
against desire and ethical demand only to put oneself under subjection to some other subject. (Here there is a fortunate play on the English word "subject," understood both as *independently existing substance* [the standard philosophical usage] and as *one under the rule of
another* [a more ordinary employment].) As when the lover turns himself over to the will of the partner, willing to do anything in order to
respond as that partner wishes, so Abraham puts himself in the
hands of Yahweh. He becomes a pure *subject:* a willing subject willing
to become absolutely subject to another subject. He asserts himself—
absurdly—through self-abnegation; he asserts himself by giving himself over to the other's absolute commands.

Faith and History

In *Fear and Trembling* there is, oddly enough, relatively little discussion of Christianity per se. Of course there can be no doubt that
Abrahamic faith is supposed to be an exemplar of the life the true
Christian lives, but in this early book there is practically no discussion of how the elements of absurd self-assertion through obedience to
God play out in relation to a distinctively Christian existence; and
that is what we now need to concentrate on. For Kierkegaard, genuine faith is always in the final analysis *Christian* faith; thus it is to
his account of Christianity as true faith that we now turn.

Kierkegaard's most philosophically self-aware description of the
form of life he calls "becoming a Christian" is the *Concluding Un-*

scientific Postscript (1846), and late in that work Johannes Climacus (the pseudonymous author) makes a distinction between *Religiousness A* and *Religiousness B,* a distinction intended to recapitulate and clarify the book's earlier distinction between Socratic ignorance (which Climacus takes to be the highest religious expression of paganism) and Christian faith.[11] Both A and B are forms of "existential pathos," the internal transformation of an individual's existence by reference to the possibility of his eternal happiness (*CUP,* 348, 350). That is, as characteristic forms of Western religiousness they depend upon one's seeing the difference between the "here" (this vale of tears) and the "hereafter" (the place of perpetual joy)—upon, that is, the individual's recognition of his or her finitude, which recognition requires a correlative recognition of the infinite as that upon which the finite depends and for which it hungers. (Here, of course, are the three structural features discussed in Chapter 1: the infinite grounds the finite, and the latter strives for a proper harmony with the former.) This existential recognition of one's finitude necessarily produces a sharp suffering, a sense that one is nothing before God, and a dying away of the immediate: "And as one who is sick and cannot move because he feels pain everywhere, and as one who is sick and cannot keep from moving as long as he lives, although he feels pain everywhere—so the religious individual lies fettered in the finite with the absolute conception of God present to him in human frailty" (*CUP,* 432).

So much is common to A and B. Their difference lies in the locus of the criterion of perfection by means of which one undertakes to transform one's existence so as to seize one's eternal happiness. A is "the religiousness of immanence," by which Kierkegaard means that the sense of what eternity demands of a given individual is sought within that individual herself, within that part of her that is eternal (*CUP,* 508), a part she shares with everyone else. The criterion of perfection is (potentially) fully present to one (to anyone), because one is (potentially) fully present to the perfection already lodged within oneself. The eternal (the perfect, the infinite) is immanent in the temporal (the imperfect, the finite), which it grounds and judges.

Socrates, for instance, relies upon an immanent criterion of perfection when he appeals to his recollection of the perfect Forms, a recollection that depends upon the soul's preexistent encounter with them.

---

11. Søren Kierkegaard, *Concluding Unscientific Postscript,* trans. D. F. Swenson and W. Lowrie (Princeton: Princeton University Press, 1968). Further references will be designated by *CUP,* followed by the page number.

Only because of such immanent acquaintance with the Forms can the Socratic dialectic move—haltingly, to be sure, and incompletely—toward the truth, a truth that equally binds us all because it is equally present to us all. What is crucial to Religiousness A is that one's relationship to the eternal come directly from the eternal itself, so to speak. The "true world" is everywhere and in all of us, waiting to be realized. So far as is possible, but always without losing the sense of oneself as an existing individual, one tries to get in touch with the eternal (the infinite, the selfsame, the completely present) to oneself and then use it as a standard for ordering one's life: "In the religiousness of immanence therefore the individual does not base his relation to the eternal upon his existence in time, but the individual's relation to the eternal, by the dialectic of inward appropriation, determines him in transforming his existence in accordance with this relation and expresses this relation by the transformation" (*CUP*, 508f.).

There is paradox in such religiousness, but it is the familiar paradox of appropriation, the recognition of the necessary failure of the finite individual's attempt to do justice to the infinite truth from which she—"the child that is born of the infinite and the finite, the eternal and the temporal" (*CUP*, 85)—legitimately descends. The pathos of the life transformed by Religiousness A is both the embarrassment inherent in ignorance (as with Socrates) and the guilt inherent in acting with less than the knowledge one needs: "The scandal of Religiousness B is its rejection of an immanent criterion for self-transformation; instead, it asserts that the eternal has come into being in time, and therefore that the criterion for self-transformation is historical, not eternally immanent. The criterion is outside the individual, in a particular historical event, and thus can only be known, like any historical event, through a process of approximation" (*CUP*, 510).

Here Climacus is of course thinking about the Christian teaching of God's incarnation in Jesus of Nazareth, a teaching that certainly exhibits enough internal conceptual incongruity to make its affirmation in thought and life absurd. (Just as a matter of conceptual consistency, how could the eternal God become the temporal man? It makes no sense.) But it is crucial to note that for Climacus the particular scandal of the Incarnation does not lie just in its conceptual self-contradiction. The Incarnation is the claim that history—a specific historical set of events, indeed—is the final, decisive, and complete locus of divine revelation, of the *truth*. One might say, therefore, that the scandal of the Incarnation is the scandal of history itself.

The most obvious aspect of that scandal is epistemological: that one's relationship to history is always uncertain, that one's knowledge of a historical event is always partial. But this epistemological uncertainty attaching to Christian faith is not essentially different from Socratic ignorance, which rests upon an immanent criterion of divinity; so one must look deeper for the particular absurdity of the Incarnation. The true scandal of considering history the locus of revelation is the necessary particularity of history. To be a part of history is necessarily to be one thing rather than another; it is to be a particular individual. But in Western religiousness God has traditionally not been considered such an individual, says Climacus, accurately: "In immanence God is [not] a something (He being all and infinitely all)" (*CUP*, 498). Because God is not a something, he can be *ubique et nusquam*, even while concealed in the individual by the actuality of existence (*CUP*, 506). In the religiousness of immanence God is not *in* history (as one thing but not another), but his presence everywhere *underlies* history, grounds it, gives it meaning; and his immanent presence to us makes possible what grasp we have of that meaning. Notice the obvious "metaphysics of presence" in the structure of Religiousness A: the differences and absences of history are grounded in and accounted for by a hidden and universal presence, just as the noises and silences of speech are supposed to be made into language by the operation of hidden (acts or entities of) meaning. The metaphysical pattern one sees here is always the same: the "true world" (full and abiding presence) makes the "apparent world" (with its various absences) possible and intelligible.

But in Religiousness B God appears *in history itself:* "The historical assertion is that the Deity, the Eternal, came into being at a definite moment in time as an individual man" (*CUP*, 512). "As an individual man": which means, as one man but not another. And that means "existence is abandoned by the concealed immanence of the eternal" (*CUP*, 506). This abandonment is the true scandal of the Incarnation. In Religiousness A, the same knowledge of the eternal is possible for all of us, since all of us are equally gifted with the eternal's immanent presence. There are no irreconcilable differences between one human being and another; the universal immanence of the eternal is the basis for an ideal of universal human community, a community that has put by (*aufgehoben*) all ethnicity: an identity that overcomes all differences. But history is defined by difference, not identity: "Religiousness B is discriminative, selective, and polemical: only upon a definite condition do I become blessed, and as I absolutely bind myself to this condition, so do I exclude every other man who does not bind himself. This is the incentive of particularism in universal pathos" (*CUP,* 516).

If there is to be community in Religiousness B, it will be determined historically—in time—by the decisions of particular human beings, and it will be determined by reference to history, by reference to a particular event in time. A universal moral community based on a common, ahistorical human nature is not an ideal of Climacus's version of Christian faith. Athens is not Jerusalem. God is *in* history. This emphasis on history, by the way, lets us see Abraham as a paradigm of Religiousness B. Certainly his religious consciousness, his criterion of self-transformation, was specifically rooted in a particular historical event: his Covenant with Yahweh (one neighborhood god among many, presumably) and in the obedience it required. Abraham's absurdity consists in treating that historical revelation as final, in letting it extinguish in practice all the immanent and universal demands of the ethical. Just as all the heroic lover's other relationships are defined in terms of the particular historical relationship to the loved one, all Abraham's relationships, even those to wife and son, are determined by obedience to the promises and demands of the Covenant with Yahweh. And notice that it is a Covenant that stresses difference, not identity: it establishes a particular relationship between Yahweh and Abraham, a particular god and a particular man; a relationship that excludes every other family, and that (among other things) underwrites the conquest of Canaan by Abraham's descendants, now become the Chosen People of Yahweh. For Abraham, Yahweh *is* the God of the Covenant; that is, a god revealed in that particular history, not in immanence.

But a historical god cannot be the ground of history. And yet for Johannes Climacus that is precisely the absurdity of the Incarnation: that God was in Christ, reconciling the world unto himself. Just here is the crux of Kierkegaard's thinking, and—not unexpectedly—here one finds him at war with himself, trying to straddle a geological fault-line. It would be tempting to interpret the form of life shaped by Religiousness B as a self-conscious attack on the entire Western metaphysical tradition of "full presence." Does Climacus succeed, as Johannes de Silentio tried to do with Abraham, in describing a way of life that can't be understood by means of the traditional philosophical categories of "paganism"? Surely it is clear that to insert eternity into time is just to displace the idea of eternity itself; to incarnate the "true world" in a particular Jewish rabbi—who could be more pervaded by difference than a Chosen One of the Chosen Ones?—is to bring the whole Platonic paper-chase of truth and universality to an end, isn't it? Isn't Religiousness B the *reductio* of all onto-theology, and thus an escape from the nihilism that tradition contains?

Subjectivity and Self-Awareness

In *Fear and Trembling* Johannes defines faith as (1) the individual's grasp of the finite (2) in virtue of the absurd.[12] The *Postscript* discussion of Religiousness B puts us in position to see how these two characteristics are one for the Christian: faith's grasp of the finite is the absurd affirmation that a particular part of that finitude, namely, a particular set of historical events, *is* the infinite, *is* the eternal, *is* "the truth," and therefore *is* the criterion of worth to be employed in one's pursuit of one's final good. All one's relationships to self and others—all the *Pathos* of one's religious self-transformation—are to make reference to that bit of history as the standard. Thus Christian faith (Religiousness B) clearly goes beyond the highest faith of paganism. The most scrupulous form of paganism, Socrates' philosophy, also takes a particular historical expression—namely, the best current result of the Socratic dialectic—as a guide to one's self-transformation; but this is a guide one always knows to be finally inadequate, and one knows this through one's immanent (if tacit) acquaintance with the eternal truth at which the dialectic is aiming. The Christian goes much further. She absurdly affirms that the full presence of eternity, and thus the final standard for self-transformation, is to be found in a particular set of temporal events. So the heroism of the Christian is not (as with Socrates) to act as if one's own tradition were finally true, when one very well knows it might not be; Christian heroism is, absurdly enough, to act so as to affirm the ultimate, final, and eternal truth of a finite, historical tradition, a tradition that itself incorporates and depends upon the sharp distinction between the finite and the infinite, between the ways of God and the ways of human beings. Johannes Climacus's "Christian faith" is the most vivid example of an

---

12. See, for example, the crucial paragraph on 49: "Temporality, finitude—that is what it is all about. . . . By my own strength I cannot get the least little thing that belongs to finitude, for I continually use my strength in resigning everything. By my own strength I can give up the princess, and I will not sulk about it but find joy and peace and rest in my pain, but by my own strength I cannot get her back again, for I use all my strength in resigning. On the other hand, by faith, says that marvelous knight, by faith you will get her back by virtue of the absurd."

ethnocentric form of life that recognizes its own ethnocentrism for what it is and (yet somehow) persists in treating it as absolute.

Thus one can appreciate the tremendous tension the life of Christian faith demands. Abraham's "fear and trembling" in Moriah is present in every moment of the Christian's life. The Christian must always be conscious of the adamant distinction between the eternal and the temporal, and of the metaphysical dependence of the latter upon the former, while at the same time the Christian must override that distinction with the doctrine of the Incarnation. And this can be done: while it is not possible for anyone to *think* the Incarnation, it is certainly possible for someone to *live* it. One can transform oneself and one's relationships in accordance with the norms of the Christian tradition, taking thereby (as Kierkegaard himself did) the bitter with the sweet, while at the same time being inwardly aware of the ultimately unjustifiable ethnocentrism of such transformation. The fact that a form of life continues self-consciously to violate its own most fundamental scruples—whether intellectual or moral—does not mean that it cannot nevertheless be lived, provided one can persist in laying out the necessary emotional capital, which is of course astronomically large.

But why would one want to? Why would Climacus believe that Religiousness B is a form of life that in any way commends itself to human beings? What could possibly be the good of such self-consciously paradoxical ethnocentrism? The answer is clear: it is the extraordinary level of psychological tension produced by Christian faith, a tension intrinsic to that form of life, that for Climacus is its specific virtue. Let us see how.

In his contrast in *Fear and Trembling* of faith to "infinite resignation" Johannes constantly connects faith to *passion;* and in the *Postscript* the same connections are made by contrasting (what he calls) "the subjective reflection" (a reflection that "makes its way inwardly in inwardness") to "the objective reflection." The latter sort of reflection is characteristic of Religiousness A, while the former sort is central to Religiousness B. It is clear enough that a certain amount of passion, a certain amount of emotional tension, a certain amount of *suffering,* is produced in an individual living the life of Religiousness A. After all, such a person is betting her life on objective uncertainties; and, since that life may be the only life she will get, there is bound to be some anxiety once *les jeux sont fait.* The objective uncertainty of her choices "repels in the inwardness of the existing individual"; and because of that repulsion—much as the resistance in a wire causes electrical glow—the individual's inwardness, her sense of herself *as herself,* is thereby intensified. Out of the suffering occasioned by doubt, self-awareness is born, maintained, and enhanced. In her willing subjection to the uncertainties of the objective, she comes to know herself more fully as the willing subject she is.

With Religiousness B, however, that sense of subjectivity is terrifically increased: "But since [with Religiousness A] the paradox is not in the first instance itself paradoxical (but only in its relationship to an existing individual), it does not repel with a sufficient intensive inwardness. For without risk there is no faith, and the greater the risk the greater the faith; the more objective security the less inwardness (for inwardness is precisely subjectivity), and the less objective security the more profound the possible inwardness. When the paradox is paradoxical in itself, it repels the individual by virtue of its absurdity, and the corresponding passion of inwardness is faith" (*CUP,* 188).

Here all the key terms are identified with one another: faith, passion, inwardness, subjectivity, risk. If one is anxious—as Socrates is— at gambling one's life against long odds (or even against short ones), then how much more anxiety, how much more bravado, how much more "fear and trembling," in putting down one's chips when one knows the game to be fixed for the house. If in the first case one is inwardly alive, acutely self-conscious, full of spirit, then how much more in the second. It produces, to be sure, a certain amount of passion to gamble one's life savings on the turn of a wheel; but it produces infinitely more passion—more suffering—to pitch one's whole fortune into a bog, and especially to do it daily, one diamond at a time, while the world stands by and jeers. The life of Christian faith is an absurd grasp of the finite as the final locus of divine revelation; it is ethnocentrism that knows itself to be such but answers to its own absolutistic demands nonetheless. Living such a life produces for the individual an unprecedented level of suffering (passion), and that suffering produces in its turn a uniquely intense self-awareness ("inwardness"): "Faith is the objective uncertainty due to the repulsion of the absurd held fast by the passion of inwardness, which in this instance [i.e., Christianity] is intensified to the utmost degree" (*CUP,* 540).

"Intensified to the utmost degree": it is this quality of supreme self-awareness that is the final good of Christian faith, according to Climacus. In the passion of my inwardness I am aware of myself as an existing individual, as a thinking/willing subject, as a synthesis of finite and infinite, and so on. So now we have a much clearer picture

of the form of life supposed to be an alternative to our normal nihilism. Both Father Abraham and the contemporary Christian—the
true Christian, of course, not just the ordinary citizen of Christendom—live a life of absurdly heroic self-assertion through absurdly
heroic self-abnegation. By asserting oneself as subject, that is, both as
a self-grounding center of will and as one willingly ruled by the will of
another, the person of faith turns up the volume of self-awareness as
high as it will go. As the absurdly obedient Abraham, obeying a God
who contradicts simultaneously both himself and the demands of the
Moral Law, my suffering is a constant spur to self-consciousness.
Every step up the mountain in Moriah drives the sharp stick of practical and ethical absurdity deeper into my flesh, thus keeping me
awake and terrified, keeping me aware of myself as willingly obedient
to this mad tyrant with whom I have covenanted.[13] And as the absurdly obedient Christian, asserting that the eternal and transcendent meaning of human life and history is incarnated once and for all
in an obscure Near Eastern teacher and political criminal put to
death by the Roman governor of Judea two millennia ago, my suffering is equally intense; and thus my self-awareness equally strong and
undeniable. As I live the witness of the Christian cross, committing
thereby the *practical* absurdity of giving up my life in sacrifice for the
poor and downtrodden on the basis of the *rational* absurdity of the
Incarnation, I am most fully aware of being myself. Through my suffering ("passion"), modeled on the passion of my Lord, I become fully
aware of myself as willing what I hereby will; namely, that the will of
another (Yahweh, Lord Jesus) absolutely determine my own. My subjectivity is enhanced through my suffering, through my will's willing
subjection; the bright pain of my "fear and trembling" before the
Cross, or before the altar in Moriah, is the best goad to full and lasting self-awareness.

13. In *Fear and Trembling* too little attention is paid to the practical absurdity of
Abraham's obedience. Setting aside the gross immorality of what Yahweh commands,
how could it possibly be in one's rational self-interest to trust a god who seems now to
be taking back just what he promised? The Covenant was supposed to guarantee
Abraham immortality through Isaac. How can that immortality come to be if Isaac is
slaughtered? Isn't Yahweh obviously going back on his word? And even if it occurs to
Abraham that maybe Yahweh will change his mind before the bloody deed is actually
done (as he in fact does), or perhaps perform some miraculous act of resurrection ("Sur-
prise!"), how could any rational agent trust a god who would be so capricious? How can
Abraham be sure that Yahweh won't change his mind again? Wouldn't the rational
calculator of self-interest think it best to stop dealing with this whimsical (and cruel:
how will either Abraham or Isaac forget this trip?) divinity?

Truth as Subjectivity

But, again, what is supposed to be so wonderful about such self-awareness? Granted that Religiousness B fosters a sense of oneself that is extraordinarily (perhaps uniquely) intense, why should such "passion of inwardness" be sought? What makes this form of life attractive enough to be a counterweight to nihilism? Certainly Climacus cannot justify the Christian's pursuit of self-knowledge as Socrates justifies his. For Socrates, knowledge of the eternal was immanent within the individual, and the peeling of the self's onion could—potentially, at least—bring one into contact with the objective ground of one's being. But the "accentuation of existence" in Religiousness B has (so it is claimed) given up every vestige of immanence (*CUP*, 510). If, as the Incarnation teaches, the eternal is located only in a particular historical individual, not immanently in us all, then my knowledge of myself as a subject that makes its way inwardly in inwardness (knowledge which is of course maximally intensified by my absurd affirmation of the Incarnation) can seem pointless.

It is not pointless, however, since that self-awareness is also—*mirabile dictu*—an encounter with the eternal. That is why supremely passionate self-awareness is for Kierkegaard the final good of faith. Here, unfortunately, one encounters a contradiction—not merely an edifying paradox—in Climacus's thinking. Immanence is denied there only in the service of another immanence; Religiousness B returns by a devious route to become a disguised form of Religiousness A. After all, immanence just means the possibility of encountering the eternal within oneself, and that is precisely what happens in the passion of affirming the Paradox: "It is only momentarily that the particular individual is able to realize existentially a unity of the infinite and the finite which transcends existence. The unity is realized in the moment of passion. . . . In passion the existing subject is rendered infinite in the eternity of the imaginative representation, and yet he is at the same time most definitely himself" (*CUP*, 176).

The same point is expressed in the different idiom of *The Sickness Unto Death*: "This then is the formula which describes the condition of the self when despair is completely eradicated: by relating itself to its own self and by willing to be itself the self is grounded transparently in the Power which posited it."[14]

14. Søren Kierkegaard, *The Sickness Unto Death*, trans. W. Lowrie (Princeton:

Passion—the suffering of subjectivity/subjection—is, of course, the utmost possibility for the self; indeed, the self *is* passion, as the affirmation of the Paradox in thought and in life so intensely demonstrates to it. Thus, in the self, in the moment of its passion, is always the possibility of "a unity of the infinite and the finite which transcends existence." "In passion the existing subject is rendered infinite . . . and yet he is at the same time most definitely himself." What could this possibly be but the description of an immanent encounter with the eternal? For the self to be "grounded *transparently* [my emphasis] in the Power which posited it" is also surely the description of an immanent encounter. Such transparency is, so to speak, to be able, by means of willing to be oneself, to *see through* oneself to the constituting Power within. By looking without, to history, one can come to see what is truly within.

Now certainly the encounters described here are quite different from the enlightenment produced by the Socratic dialectic. In the latter case the immanently eternal is approached by means of critical rationality, by the avoidance of self-contradiction; and in that activity of ratiocination, passion and its peculiar access of self-awareness can only be a hindrance. It is only at the limits of reason (i.e., of reason as appropriated by an existing individual) that Socratic faith must throw up its bridges. The eternal is grasped by Socrates *with* passion but not *by means of it*. In Christian faith, however, passion—suffering and the extraordinarily acute self-awareness it produces and maintains—is the fundamental *means* of appropriating the eternal; indeed, it is the only way one fully encounters it. But this difference from the Socratic dialectic, important as it is, does not alter the immanence of the eternal in the moment of the self's passion. The eternal encountered there is not truly *in* the historical, even though that is the (absurd) affirmation one makes; the eternal is encountered in the flash of passionate inwardness that occurs as one makes (over and over in word and in deed) that (absurd) affirmation. That is to say, the eternal is encountered directly in the self by means of the self's (absurd) denial of the immanence of the eternal. But that remains at bottom the religiousness of (disguised) immanence.

This inconsistency is far from being a minor slip; indeed, it undermines Kierkegaard's claim (essayed in both *Fear and Trembling* and the *Postscript*) to have described a form of life that goes beyond the highest reach of paganism. To be sure, Kierkegaard mercilessly ridi-

---

Princeton University Press, 1953), 147. Further references to this work will be designated by *SUD*, followed by the page number.

cules the metaphysician's claim to have closed the gap between subject and object. Our existence, he says, constantly conspires to keep
that gap open. The identity of Thought and Being, while the proper
ideal for philosophical thought, must remain only an ideal for the
thinking, willing subjects we all are. In sum, philosophical truth
founders on the fact of human ego-subjectivity. For that reason as
well, as Kierkegaard sees, human history (considered objectively)
must remain for the alert philosophical thinker—as it was for Socrates—only a process of approximation. From the point of view of pure
reason, all traditions, institutions, scientific generalizations, and particular empirical judgments must, to a greater or a lesser extent, fall
short of the full presence (truth) at which they aim. Human life is
always and inevitably riddled with difference and absence, with "approximation" and "falsity."

Given these insights, it can seem that Kierkegaard is on the thresh-
old of a critique of the pagan ideal of "full presence" itself. By recognizing the ground of thought (the ego-subject) to be passionate, suffering will, he seems just a step away from displacing the entire Platonic
("pagan") problematic of transcendence of the temporal through
thinking. And at first glance he seems actually to be taking that step
with Religiousness B, where the eternal is (absurdly) *identified* with
the temporal, as it is done paradigmatically in the Christian teaching
of the Incarnation. By such an affirmation of the individual's necessary historicity, by insisting upon the inescapability of ethnocentrism
in any life lived intensely, he seems to be breaking with the whole
Greek ideal of a universal moral and intellectual community based on
an immanent awareness of the "fully present" truth. (He announces,
after all, that true Christian faith must be more than "paganism"; it
must go beyond both "infinite resignation" and "Socratic ignorance.")
All that is now lacking is a genuinely radical critique of truth itself, a
critique that would mark Kierkegaard as a proto-deconstructionist (or
proto-pragmatist: they are much of a muchness in this respect).

That critique never comes, of course. What one gets instead is just
the claim that truth is subjectivity, which is finally only a shift in the
locus of truth, not a break from the metaphysical ideal of truth itself.
Climacus's assertion that truth is subjectivity, which is of course central to the argument of the *Postscript,* is not just the claim that objective truth is impossible in either metaphysics or history; it is also the
claim that the ideal of subjectivity is an adequate replacement for the
ideal of objectivity. (The "true world" has not disappeared; it has, so to
speak, been discovered wholly *inside* one.) The objective ideal of truth
was the identity of Thought and Being, the closure of the gap between

subject and object: in other words, the full presence of Being in identity with Itself. Climacus is now claiming that this ideal is only possible to accomplish in ego-subjectivity itself. That is, only by heightening the self-awareness of the ego-subject to its highest possible pitch
can ego-subjectivity be (momentarily) overcome: "It is only momentarily that the particular individual is able to realize existentially a
unity of the infinite and the finite which *transcends existence*. This
unity is realized in the moment of passion" (*CUP*, 176; my emphasis).

Only in this most intense moment of self-awareness, when the ego-
subject is most acutely aware of its own concrete subjectivity, is the
self "grounded transparently in the Power which posited it" (*SUD*,
147). In the fullest presence of the self to itself, there is momentarily
a respite from the ordinary gaps and absences of existence. This
acutely enhanced self-presence is in no way a break from the "metaphysics of presence" that defined the highest expression of paganism.
The goal of the life of Christian faith is still the Platonic goal of the
healing encounter with the fully present: the harmonious unity of
Thought and Being, of subject and object, of soul and Form, of self
and God. In Platonic philosophy, as we noted in Chapter 1, such
encounter is pursued by means of strengthening the individual's capacity for abstraction, understood as a means of self-transcendence
through thinking. Such abstraction seems to offer a way of ascending
to the reality that authorizes the particular practices that constitute
a life or a culture. (For example, once the abstract and selfsame
truths of geometry have been comprehended, then the various
methods of land survey and measurement can be codified and legiti-
mated by reference to such truths.) Abstract thinking apparently offers one both a way to escape from the particularity and difference of
one's history (from one's "existence") and a way to harmonize one's life
with what is always whole and self-same. Abstraction thus confers
authority.

In Christian faith, however, existence is transcended not by ascent
from one's subjectivity by means of abstract thought, but by deeper
penetration into that subjectivity itself. Existence is transcended "existentially," as Climacus puts it (*CUP*, 176). Full presence is vouchsafed (though only momentarily, to be sure) through the utmost increase of self-presence. And this self-presence is enhanced by means
of concreteness, not abstraction. Abstract thinking on the "pagan"
model takes me away from myself; it raises me above my particular
history, resolves my quandaries and self-doubts, and sets me down in
an utterly impersonal and universal community, in which I might as
well be anyone. Under the guidance of such abstraction, I think and

act as if I were no-one in particular; I become a ghost, the spirit of Reason itself. But Christian faith turns this familiar philosophical progress on its ear, seeking presence on the other side of the will's felt absences. Faith uses my historicity, my partiality, my internal and external differences from other human beings, as a spur to my sense of self. By locating the eternal in the temporal, that is, by absurdly identifying some recognizably particular and partial historical tradition as the final basis for all one's praxis, faith turns up the volume of one's willfulness to an almost unbearable level; in that fear and trembling, in the suffering produced by one's recognition of one's practical and conceptual absurdity, the self is made fully present to itself. By forcing the self to recognize itself as will and thus to will its own concrete destiny, which destiny is the willful and passionate surrender to the will of another, the terrifying affirmation of the Incarnation is the way by which the self—the will—wills itself; so that in *that* willing, subject and object are indeed one. The snake takes its own tail in its mouth, closing the circle of the self and composing a mandala of wholeness. In the adrenaline rush of the will that wills its own willfulness, a willfulness that shows itself in the willful surrender to the will of one's Lord (whoever and whatever that may be), there is given, according to Kierkegaard, "a unity of the infinite and the finite which transcends existence" (*CUP*, 176).

Subjectivity and Narcissism

We now are in possession of the central elements in Kierkegaard's representation of a form of life he thinks capable of standing as an alternative to our normal nihilism, and we have seen that his paradigmatic account of that life (in the *Concluding Unscientific Postscript*) fails to cut it free from the philosophical assumptions of the "paganism" he explicitly hopes to supersede. The heroic self-assertion of one's subjectivity through one's willful and absurd subjection to the will of another is still for Climacus grounded in a standard philosophical ploy: the claim that "truth is subjectivity." In one's absurd subjection one's "truth" as a "subject" is revealed to one, and revealed in a fullness of self-presence that closes the gaps of one's ordinary existence. One now knows who and what one "really" is. This philosophical chestnut of a fixed and eternal "human nature," of what is called in *Fear and Trembling* one's "eternal validity," thus compromises Kierkegaard's claim to have broken with the Platonic tradition that leads inexorably to our normal nihilism. Assertions about what I "naturally" am—a willing subject that makes its way inwardly in inwardness, for example—are just as eviscerated by Nietzsche's knife as are any other metaphysical claims. Thus Religiousness B is no more supported by claims of "truth" than is any other form of life. It's just another shop in the mall, hawking values, not "eternal validity."

Perhaps it would be premature, however, to take that as the end of the matter. Could we not detach Kierkegaard's account of this form of life from its philosophical underpinnings? Could we not consider it purely as "phenomenology," as describing and commending a kind of life that is (as he thinks) a counterweight to normal nihilism; describing it and commending it without in any way attempting to justify it philosophically?

No doubt we can, though we must still ask whether it succeeds even in that more limited aim. Here we need to go slowly. Certainly there are religious folk who claim—some quite loudly—that the rationally and practically absurd ethnocentrism of Kierkegaardian Christianity provides an existence immeasurably rich and satisfying, an existence free of any hint of self-devaluation. Moreover, it is unseemly in a philosopher flatly to contradict such enthusiasm. Philosophy possesses no privileged point of view from which forms of life can be pronounced to be either real or illusory, satisfying or ultimately disappointing: in the final analysis, the proof of the pudding is in the eating. That does not mean, of course, that philosophy can do nothing in the way of criticizing a Kierkegaardian life detached from its philosophical buttresses. Not all criticism is transcendental criticism; not all criticism, that is, pronounces something impossible according to conditions discovered by pure thought to be necessary for that sort of thing to be. Perhaps it is possible to live as a distinctively Kierkegaardian Christian, and perhaps that form of life does offer something as proof against the threat of nihilism. Nevertheless, some questions remain for philosophers properly to ask. First, how likely is it to do these things? And second, at what cost?

About a positive answer to the first of these questions I am frankly skeptical. I think it quite unlikely that the form of life Kierkegaard describes will, for most of us and for the long run, be stable and effective in the face of the philosophical progress sketched in Chapter 1, a progress now an inescapable part of our history and our present mood. The problem with Kierkegaardian faith is that, even when cut loose from "pagan" attempts to ground it, it remains firmly tethered to a representational epistemology and philosophy of mind, and to the Cartesian subject/object schema and to the notion of "objective truth" that go hand-in-hand with them.[15] Dozens of passages from a variety of Kierkegaardian texts could be offered in illustration of my claims, but perhaps the clearest is the well-known discussion of objective and subjective reflection in chapter 2 of the *Concluding Unscientific Postscript*. Climacus begins the chapter by sketching two accounts of truth: the empirical, which he characterizes as "the conformity of thought to being"; and the ideal, characterized as "the conformity of being to thought" (*CUP*, 169). In both cases the familiar epistemological template of thought-as-representation is readily apparent. "Thought" is one sort of thing; "being" is another; and the task of epistemic reflection is to bring them into "conformity" (*CUP*, 169). What could be more representational than that? What is "conformity" but a post-Kantian synonym for Cartesian "mirroring"? This representational template is essential to formulating the *Postscript*'s famous distinction between subjective and objective reflection. Consider the following famous paragraph, italicized in the original.

> When the question of truth is raised in an objective manner, reflection is directed objectively to the truth, as an object to which the knower is related. Reflection is not focused upon the relationship, however, but upon the question of whether it is the truth to which the knower is related. If only the object to which he is related is the truth, the subject is accounted to be in the truth. When the question of truth is raised subjectively, reflection is directed subjectively to the nature of the individual's relationship; if only the mode of this relationship is in the truth, the individual is in the truth even if he should happen to be thus related to what is not true. (*CUP*, 178).

An objective reflection achieves truth by getting the subject into a proper relationship with an object, namely, a relationship of justified belief about an object that actually is what the subject justifiably believes it to be. A successful objective reflection produces objective truth, that is, a clear "conformity" of "thought" (the subject's belief) and "being" (the actual object). The representational structure here is unmistakable. Even the subjective reflection, in which attention is focused primarily on the relation of the subject to her belief rather

15. By a representational epistemology I mean only the claim that thoughts are made true, and thus knowable as true, by standing in some sort of more-than-causal relationship to things. A representational philosophy of mind is the claim that human intelligence is suited to construct and/or recognize that sort of more-than-causal relationship between thoughts and things.

than on the relationship of that belief to the object it intends, depends essentially upon the notion of "conformity." In the subjective reflection the point is to increase subjectivity at the expense of objectivity, and that can only be done if some notion of thought/being "conformity" is presupposed as the basis of objectivity in the first place. Remember: for Climacus it is the *failure* of thought's objectivity, the breakdown of any assured "conformity" between thought and being, that begins to ratchet up the quotient of subjectivity in a religious life, whether Socratic or Christian.

Even in his commitment to a life of objective reflection Socrates was a great subject because he affirmed (and therefore lived) propositions that he knew to be objectively uncertain: he lived a life he knew might not "conform" to the way the world really is. Thus he lived with a certain amount of "fear and trembling." The subjective reflection of the Christian, however, proceeds by the affirmation of propositions that she knows to be objectively absurd, not just objectively uncertain. To absurdly affirm the man Jesus to be the one true God, and thus, equally absurdly, to take up his shameful cross for oneself, is to ratchet up one's "fear and trembling" to its highest possible level. One has turned up the volume on one's subjectivity as high as it will go. So both Socrates and the Christian depend on the familiar philosophical notion of "conformity" in order to achieve their heightened sense of self. In each case the anxiety that provokes the enhanced self-awareness, the full self-presence that "transcends existence" (*CUP*, 176), depends upon the recognition that one's affirmations lack that proper relation to reality that produces objective truth. Socrates is uncertain (of his truth), the Christian is certain (of her absurdity); but both depend upon the philosophical idea that there is such a thing as objectively "getting it right." Both operate on the assumption there is some favored relationship of "conformity" between one's affirmations (whether practical or linguistic) and the reality those affirmations are "about," such that when that relationship is in place one is objectively "in the truth."

But once one has, following Nietzsche, come to see that a representational epistemology and philosophy of mind make no sense, that it is useless to postulate some more-than-causal relationship to reality that our affirmations must have in order to count as true, will one's worries about being "in the truth" be as intense as they formerly were? Will one *suffer*, as Socrates or the Christian suffers? I think not. Likely there will be a slackening of one's epistemic superego; likely a more tolerant and experimental spirit of inquiry will replace the sharply moralized demand that one at every point "get it right." And with that new spirit will also come a diminishment in the "fear and trembling" associated with error. An "experimental" (i.e., nonrepresentational) Socrates will still be conscious of the possibility of error, of course, and presumably will want to replace his erroneous beliefs with more adequate ones; but I doubt he will feel so strongly (or for so long) the horror of being wrong, of being "out of touch with reality." He will recognize that all his beliefs are, and never can be more than, attempts to get what he has learned (and is learning) to want. Error is not therefore an affront to a godlike reality that demands our proper worship in the form of true ("objective") reflection; it is merely a less-than-adequate set of interpretive tools brought to bear on some problem one is facing. Error does, so to speak, no injury to the reality it purports to represent; at most it injures the one who cuts his hand when the dull chisel slips. So too for the "experimental" Christian. To affirm the "absurdity" of the Incarnation is now only to adopt for oneself a rule of action that is communally and perhaps personally disconcerting or disadvantageous. "Becoming a Christian" is only to act so as to get things most people don't want, or it is to act so as *not* to get things most people (perhaps including oneself, under some descriptions) do want. No doubt such deviance from the norm will (especially in the second case) cause a certain amount of distress for one, but surely less than before, when one saw oneself as foolishly and willfully affirming a representation of things known with certainty by everyone to be false. (Gone is the alternately heady and terrifying sense of blasphemy one had as one willfully thumbed one's nose at reality.) If now one suffers at all, one suffers the pangs of fallibility, or at most of eccentricity, not of full-fledged absurdity; and the sting of fallibility, and even of eccentricity, is intermittent and fading. One (gratefully) gets accustomed to lacking philosophically solid ground for one's parade and to being out of step with the other marchers.

Thus the post-Nietzschean collapse of the representational epistemology and philosophy of mind in terms of which Kierkegaard's account of faith is couched will correspondingly weaken the *Pathos* of the form of life he describes. To recognize that one's beliefs no more and no less "conform" to reality than anyone else's, and that one's form of life is to be judged in terms of its power to provide what one wants, is (I think) to diminish the capacity of that form of life to provide a constant spur to one's self-awareness through suffering. To begin to see one's beliefs as tools is a step toward having those tools disappear in the efficient functioning they are designed to facilitate.[16]

16. It might go another way, of course. Seeing one's beliefs as tools of interpretation

Moreover, the subject/object schema in terms of which the life of Kierkegaardian faith is described cannot survive the Nietzschean assaults on it. Rather than a discrete, willful subject—"that individual"—confronting a range of fixed and determinate objects, we now begin to see ourselves as constellations of forces engaged with other forces in a struggle for hegemony. No doubt an important asset in that struggle is (or at least has been) my sense of myself as an individual, as a single "subject" directing myself through a field of "objects"; but after Nietzsche I now come to see such individualism as a self-interpretation designed to enhance and preserve a particular form of life. The life of maximal subjectivity valorized by Kierkegaard is *one* form of life, not life itself. Even the terms in which it is described lack any final validity.

But could not that recognition—the recognition of the contingency even of the terms in which one's self-interpretation is carried on—be a further spur to the sort of "fear and trembling" that is wanted by Johannes and Climacus? For a while, perhaps; but the *frisson* that feeds one's self-awareness is unlikely to last. Why? Because the shudder that contingency provokes in us depends upon its contrast to some intelligible alternative. Error is frightful for Socrates or for the Christian because it so neatly contrasts with truth, understood as the conformity of thought with being. The contingency of one's own self-interpretation is frightening, an occasion of suffering, for one only if one postulates a self-interpretation that *wouldn't be* contingent; contingency is scary—rather than mildly interesting for a while—only to the extent one fears one might not be "getting it right." In Nietzsche's reflections, however, the whole representational construal of "getting it right" is exploded, or at least unburdened of its numinosity. Once one realizes that self-interpretations are not the sort of thing that anyone ever "gets right," and that because there's no objective "right" to "get," then the power of that recognition to cause anxiety or resentment—and thus through suffering to increase one's self-awareness as a subject—is inevitably diminished (even if not entirely extinguished). In our normal nihilism, fear of contingency is soon replaced with a dull sense of loss and with a fitful restlessness, neither of which can do the job of Kierkegaardian "fear and trembling." One

---

designed to facilitate the preservation and enhancement of a form of life might cause one to abandon those tools, either because they aren't working very well or because one can now see that this is not the form of life that one on reflection wants to preserve and enhance. But that abandonment will (*ceteris paribus*) be preparatory for taking up some new set.

gets used to one's ethnocentrism, which is—among us normal nihilists—just another name for one's finitude.

Thus I do not believe the life of faith described and recommended by Kierkegaard as a counterweight to our normal nihilism will do the work he claims for it, even if that life is disengaged from any attempt (such as is found in the *Postscript*) to justify it philosophically. Without (as we post-Nietzscheans are) the spur of capital-T Truth against which to gore ourselves, and without (equally gone for us) the sense of splendid isolation fostered by the subject/object schema, the life of faith will likely soon seem, even for those who are living it, just another sort of life, a life that after a while grows—like any life—routine and comfortable.

But one may feel (I sometimes do myself) that my criticisms so far are largely beside the point. The true force of Kierkegaard's thinking is ethical, not philosophical; he appeals to us finally as representative of a rare and costly way of living, as the finder of a pearl of great price, worth—he believes—whatever it takes to buy it. It is that form of life—maximally enhanced subjectivity—that must ultimately be judged in our balance, not its particular philosophical trappings. What finally matters is not Kierkegaard's (admittedly outdated) recipe for cooking up the life of subjectivity ("objective uncertainty," "absurdity," and so forth); what matters is that life itself. I now turn to that question: Is the life of Kierkegaardian faith a good one? At what cost is it to be lived? Let us imagine—against all the likelihoods just canvassed—that the life of faith could sustain itself long-term: that one could discover some sufficiently sharp stick with which to poke oneself so that through one's suffering one remains constantly aware of oneself as subject (in both senses of the term). What would such a life be like?

It is sometimes said in criticism of Abraham that he is both externally and internally indistinguishable from the madman; and that may be true, since the voice in terms of which he absurdly defines himself as obedient subject is a voice that contravenes both personal desire and impersonal ethical demand. In his willingness to sacrifice the beloved and innocent Isaac, Abraham does seem, perhaps even to himself, a psycho killer. Both for him and for us the voice of Yahweh urging him toward the mountain altar seems the sort of communication that should best be squelched with large and steady doses of Thorazine. Thus the psychological and social costs of living this sort of life are enormous, for him and for everyone else (especially Isaac); far too high, I would say, to make it an attractive way of being religious for most of us. If the only alternative to our normal nihilism is

indeed Abraham, then most of us will happily stick with our devaluated values. Better the mall than Moriah.

Nevertheless, could it not be a mistake to think that all knights of
faith must assume the shape of an Abraham? Could not the kind of
absurdly enhanced self-awareness he exemplifies be produced by
something other than the contravention of fundamental ethical norms
and heartfelt desires? Johannes himself seems to think so, since he
spends almost three pages of *Fear and Trembling* describing a knight
of faith who "bears a striking resemblance to bourgeois philistinism,
which infinite resignation, like faith, deeply disdains" (*FT,* 38). This
Copenhagen burgher, who "looks just like a tax collector" (*FT,* 39),
lives an apparently ordinary life: "He attends to his job. To see him
makes one think of a pen-pusher who has lost his soul to Italian book-
keeping, so punctilious is he. Sunday is for him a holiday. He goes to
church. No heavenly gaze or any sign of the incommensurable betrays
him; if one did not know him, it would be impossible to distinguish
him from the rest of the crowd, for at most his hearty and powerful
singing of the hymns proves that he has good lungs. In the afternoon,
he takes a walk to the woods. He enjoys everything he sees, the
swarms of people, the new omnibuses, the Sound. Encountering him
on Strandveien, one would take him for a mercantile soul enjoying
himself" (*FT,* 39).

Presuming that Johannes is not being ironic here in describing
such a man as a knight of faith, we must believe the burgher has
discovered some way of heroically heightening his self-awareness as a
subject, but a way that does not require him to step outside the ordinary constraints of social and ethical life. His absurdity is neither the
absurdity of ethical villainy nor the absurdity of religious fanaticism;
presumably, however, there is some other way in which he is constantly and painfully reminded of the absurd idiosyncrasy—the utter
lack of any "universal" justification—of the life he is living.

I find it difficult to imagine what such a reminder could be. To the
extent that the outer forms of one's life smoothly mesh with the conventional expectations of one's community, surely it would be hard to
keep reminding oneself of one's complete and absurd willfulness in
living as one does. Johannes and Climacus insist that the suffering
induced by the life of faith is the key provocation to one's awareness
of oneself as subject. Does the Copenhagen burgher suffer? Not from
being out of step with the rest of the world, certainly. And how else
could internal suffering be fostered and sustained for the long term?
Let us assume, however, that these questions can somehow be satisfactorily answered and that there is some way of treading the earth

as steady as a postman while at the same time constantly being aware of the black abyss into which one is always willfully stepping. What would one say of such a life? Does it possess advantages sufficient to make it an attractive way for us to be religious?

I should think its implicit narcissism would give one pause. Granted, it can be quite a bad thing to find that one's life has lost some of its accustomed savor, and has lost it through one's hard-won recognition of that life's lack of any final claims, whether on oneself or on reality. We all know the experience of sitting back in the dark anonymity of the *Philosophisches Kino,* of seeing one's own life screened up there as one set of events among many, and thereby feeling its peculiar *Pathos* begin to seep away. It was no doubt more satisfying to have been able to live with the illusory consolations of Truth and Right. For a long time it has been one of the ambitions of religion in the West to prevent that sense of one's diminishment at the hands of the objective thinker, or at worst to restore one's (battered) convictions of specialness; and certainly Kierkegaard should be understood in just these terms. Any attentive reader will hear Kierkegaard's dismay at the way things can turn out to be so ordinary in their most intellectually compelling representations. The forces of banality ("the frogs in life's swamp" [*FT,* 41], constantly croaking their single note) are powerful and ubiquitous; their vanguard is the philosopher who insists on "an objective point of view." Looked at "objectively," of course, everything *is* less than it heretofore seemed: love for a princess is just a young man's self-seeking; the philosopher's doubt is just a rhetorical ploy; and religious faith is just the need of a person or a people for a stable and life-enhancing worldview. No wonder the great cultural clearance sale is now going on, and no wonder the customers turn out to be such hard-sells. The world revealed in objective reflection is, for Kierkegaard at any rate, flat and without piquancy. "In the world everything is as it is, and everything happens as it does happen: *in* it no value exists—and if it did exist [there], it would have no value."[17]

As I have said, no one of us can doubt the reality, and the intermittent distress, of such an experience of the world's banality. But one can nevertheless wonder whether it's best to respond to the nihilism of total objectivity with the narcissism of total subjectivity. For that's

17. Ludwig Wittgenstein, *Tractatus Logico-Philosophicus,* trans. D. F. Pears and B. McGuiness (New York: Humanities Press, 1974), sec. 6.41. The *Tractatus* is in many ways a quite Kierkegaardian book. For an attempt to draw some useful connections between Wittgenstein and Kierkegaard, see my *Ethics Without Philosophy: Wittgenstein and the Moral Life* (Gainesville: University Presses of Florida, 1982).

what Kierkegaard's work seems in the final instance to represent: the retreat into the self as the final locus of what is valuable, of what gives strength and flavor to life. Shorn of its various metaphysical trappings, the claim that truth is subjectivity is the claim that a life of constant self-awareness gained through constant (and preferably humiliating) self-stimulation is the life one should most want for oneself. There is something uncanny (and therefore profoundly attractive) about the Copenhagen burgher under this description, living his real life behind permanently closed doors, so to speak; but there is something horrifying as well. And in both cases—the attraction and the horror—it is the same thing we attend to: the man's necessary inability to express publicly what he is; his glorious imprisonment in a self that, in order to stay alive and interesting as a self, must hie itself away from the world, away from the common life and its entanglements. He buys vitality as the price of the most profound isolation. For him the closet is a palace of delight. Presumably not even his wife and children—or whoever is nearest to him—know of the constant seething behind this man's petit-bourgeois countenance. And yet it is just that seething—and nothing else—that counts for him: "Subjectivity is the truth." Can any of us deny the *Pathos,* in every sense, such a picture evokes?

The danger of Johannes's use of Abraham as a paradigm of faith is that we might only be appalled by him: the ethical transgression of child-murder may loom so large in our thinking that we miss the exquisite appeal of his closeted and boiling subjectivity. That appeal should be easier to see in the burgher, and likewise our repulsion from it should be all the more acute. The appeal is a godlike freedom and invulnerability—or at least the illusion of these. The burgher is not *in* the world, neither defined by its ordinary significances nor subject to its ordinary dangers. He escapes both banality and injury. Whatever happens to him will merely be fodder for his own appropriation of it, an appropriation that makes it a spur to a more intense and interesting subjectivity.

What, we wonder, is the blade that cut the burgher free? For Abraham it is easy to see: after the knife raised in Moriah, he will never again be at home in the world. No-one will ever look at him with an ordinary glance; he will always be the man who almost killed his son for God. So too for the genuine Christian: she with her voluntary poverty, and with kissing the sores of lepers, and with leaving the dead to bury their dead, she too will easily avoid the clutches of the everyday that threaten to swamp subjectivity. The world will constantly offer to these two, Abraham and the Christian, reminders of their failure to be a part of it, and of its ordinary significances; thus it will force on them the willful assignment of meaning through—and to—the self. But what of the burgher? What is the nail he twists into his palm in order to stay self-aware? Johannes does not say.

For the Kierkegaardian "subject," the meaning of the world is not out there, in the everyday concordances with others in supermarket, bed, boardroom, or playground; it is *in here,* in the self whose private theater those ordinarily public spaces have become. But for such a self the other is never quite real—or is real only in relation to the self-awareness he or she can provoke in one. And that sort of hungry self-enclosure, though ugly enough, is not the worst. One's *own* self, the self one has fed with greater and greater doses of various stimulants, threatens to disappear the first moment those stimulants cease. Cut loose from being defined by the relatively stable (though of course inevitably banalizing) significances of the public world, the narcissistic self is always on the verge of vaporizing. Once CPR ceases, will the heart continue to beat on its own? Only if its connections to the larger organism have been reestablished. Once one stops slapping oneself into full self-awareness, will one remain awake? The threat to the narcissist, the terror that drives him, is that oblivion will quickly return and conquer.

A self defined purely privately—"Subjectivity is the truth"—is not a stable self at all. Neither Abraham nor the Copenhagen burgher lives in steady harmony with his world. Each must constantly turn aside from things, turn *inside* the self, in order to remain real to himself. In his terrible need to avoid the lee shore of everyday society, the narcissist, like the *Pequod's* Bulkington, must trade the comforts of ordinary intercourse for a life of (internal) distance and hidden significance. "The land"—the life of honest connection to the world, the life of real others and public tasks—"seemed scorching to his feet." Bulkington requires the lonely deck in the freezing rain of sea gales; for him, signing on for voyage after voyage, "in landlessness alone resides the highest truth, shoreless, indefinite as God."[18] Yes, but only at the cost of endless wandering and the loss of any intimate human engagement. For me, such a self is too precarious and brittle to be a worthwhile ideal.

Thus my objections, both philosophical and ethical, to Kierkegaard's conception of truth as subjectivity. But must one conceive this notion quite so individualistically? Could not one interpret the life of

---

18. Herman Melville, *Moby-Dick; or, The Whale* (Berkeley and Los Angeles: University of California Press, 1981), 111.

subjectivity as leading to a more *communal* narcissism, as playing into a sort of political autochthony? Conceived this way, truth as subjectivity means the achievement of full self-presence through affirmation of one's ethnic, racial, ideological, or national difference from "the others": here subjectivity means one's formation as a subject by one's subjection to *this* community, a community itself formed by its recognition of its difference from all other communities. If the analogy to the individualistic case is to be complete, the most intense (most truthful) communal subjectivity derives from a sense of oneself defined by a community itself defined by its subjection to a single and absurd will; here the community-defining will of *der Führer* functions as does the will of Yahweh in the covenant with Abraham.[19] Perhaps this way of reading the notion of truth as subjectivity removes some of the philosophical objections to it, but a great deal of its ethical menace remains. (Indeed, it increases.) If the danger of the more individualistic account is that the self will finally evaporate, the danger of the other account is that the self will finally coalesce into an obdurate part of a mass, willing, probably eager, to find its animating thrill in its instantiation of the will of the Leader.

So either way, the Kierkegaardian ideal of truth as subjectivity fails to offer a wholesome response to the threat of normal nihilism. If this is what it should mean for us to be religious, better that we try not to be religious at all.

19. For an example of such thinking, consider Martin Heidegger's sentence from 1933, "The Führer alone *is* the present and future German reality and its law." The statement is found in a political text of 1933, translated by William S. Lewis and published in *The Heidegger Controversy: A Critical Reader,* ed. Richard Wolin (New York: Columbia University Press, 1991), 47.

3

HEIDEGGER AND THE OVERCOMING OF SUBJECTIVITY

Kierkegaard's religious response to the devaluation of his highest values—that is to say, his resistance to the world's steady transmutation of New Testament Christianity into a banal and morbid Christendom—is inflected with a particular philosophical understanding of what it means to be a human being, and thus of what it means to be an authentically religious human being. That philosophical understanding, which may of course be a misunderstanding, we may properly (if also somewhat pompously) call *transcendental ego-subjectivity*. For Kierkegaard the human being is first and foremost the ego-subject: a freestanding, self-identical, and self-aware center of will and passion. Only subjects who are fully conscious of their own subjectivity can, he thinks, carry out their authentic relations to the world and to God.

In this commitment to transcendental ego-subjectivity (and to its correlative ideal of objectivity), Kierkegaard remains fully within the flood of Western philosophy running from Plato to Descartes, thence to Kant, and thence to Husserl. *Fear and Trembling*'s remarkable account of Abraham as the knight of faith—as the heroic subject of an absurdly enhanced subjectivity—must be seen as just another variation on Plato's quest to find the eternal and perfect ground[1] of all

1. For "ground" read also: *hypokeimenon, subiectum,* "subject," "that which stands under and supports." Details of this philosophical and linguistic history can be found in Martin Heidegger, "The Age of the World Picture," in Heidegger, *The Question Concerning Technology and Other Essays,* trans. W. Levitt (New York: Harper and Row, 1977), 139–53.

Being, a quest that took a fateful turn with Descartes's demonstration that only the fully self-present ego can be the foundation upon which the various figures of life are displayed. As "that individual," as the one who insists upon "an absolute relation to the absolute," Abraham is (in Kierkegaard's representation of him) a nineteenth-century avatar of the Cartesian "I," but one who has substituted willing, desiring (and thus suffering: "passion") for thinking as the distinctive mark and content of selfhood. For such a subject, its "objects" are first of all the objects of passionate desire; they are not the objects of a cool and disinterested cognition, but they are the ego-subject's objects all the same.

This continuity with the Western philosophical tradition damns Kierkegaard's pseudonymous books—beautiful as they are—to impotence in face of their strongest ambition. Offered as an alternative to our normal nihilism, his account of Christian faith fails to meet the bill. Indeed, Kierkegaardian faith seems nothing more than a peculiarly intense instance of such nihilism: normal nihilism with the volume turned all the way up, so to speak. Kierkegaard's suffering subject of desire—the desire for wholeness, for perfection, for salvation, for eternal life—who chooses maximally to increase that suffering by seeking its balm in the absurdly ethnocentric affirmations of Christianity, and who thus in the heightened sense of self produced by that terrifying passion discovers the wholeness all along being sought: that subject is only an extreme example of *us*. We too know, know all too well, the desire for a rounded and satisfying completion, and we too scour the shops—Kierkegaard's *wirklicher Ausverkauf* of European intellectual and spiritual history—for some trinkets to still our fears of nullity and emptiness. But we are, most of us, luckier than Abraham (or Kierkegaard), since the values we buy to fill in our cracks don't cost us quite so much as his cost him. Most of us don't need, thank goodness, a life of theoretical and practical absurdity to produce a reliable (reliable enough) sense of self. We are content, rather, with meager comforts sufficient unto the day. The shop patronized by the Kierkegaardian Christian sells its goods, however well or ill they may wear, at far too high a price.

But even in that shop—ruinously expensive, and disguised not to look like a shop at all—one is still a consumer, still a normal nihilist trying to preserve and enhance oneself through the appropriate choice of values. Even the Kierkegaardian Christian herself, making her absurd and costly choices of faith, must know that she is finally choosing her form of life for the personal advantages she gets from it.

Since she makes choices that are both theoretically and practically absurd, she can't be making them on grounds of ordinary truth or rationality. She knows that in no way, practically or theoretically, is she compelled to choose the form of life she does. Desire, then, must be the root of her decisions. She must be freely shopping for what she wants, and thus she too is one sort of normal nihilist: one who has purchased a particular set of values for the incredible rush of selfhood it offers. But it is a rush unlikely to last, and a rush unwholesome to contemplate in its narcissism. The Kierkegaardian Christian seems not only—to herself and to us—a normal nihilist, a consumer of self-devaluating values (truth itself is devalued by its truthful Kierkegaardian identification with subjectivity); she also has succumbed to purchasing a particularly dangerous set of those values. In spite of his religious vocabulary of radical transcendence, Kierkegaard turns out to be a runaway humanist.

If we are to escape that fate (presuming, as I do here, it is something rightly to be feared), perhaps we must break the hold of our philosophical tradition itself; and particularly the hold of the picture of the human being—the value-consuming, value-creating ego-subject—that now seems to be the tradition's inevitable result. The philosophical work of Martin Heidegger can be seen as just such an iconoclasm. Indeed, in my view his is the most fully developed criticism we have of that tradition of ego-subjectivity. If we are to find a way for us to be religious—to be *us*—that escapes our normal nihilism, then it will be useful for us to examine Heidegger's radically non-Cartesian account of human beings. That is what we shall be doing in this chapter. Is there another and (to use Heidegger's own mythical idiom) "more primordial" account of who we human beings are? Can we get back behind, or anyway off to the side of, the original Cartesian creation of the ego-subject, and can we thus avoid the normal nihilism that seems to be the fate of such a subject, even in its Nietzschean deconstruction? And can we do that without falling back into some sort of Idealism or supernatural religion? Heidegger is grappling with just these large and daunting questions.[2]

2. In no way am I claiming that the use to which I put Heidegger here—as showing a way in which we may escape transcendental subjectivity so as to imagine a new way of being religious—reveals the "real meaning" of his enormous and rich philosophical production. Part of what makes his work so powerful is that it resists such reduction to a single and master significance; or, to put it positively, that it lends itself to so many diverse philosophical projects. Mine is only one of many.

Transcendental Subjectivity

It has now become something of a commonplace to divide Heidegger's philosophical work into two parts: there is the "early" Heidegger, whose great work is *Being and Time,* published in 1927; and then there is "later" Heidegger, the author of those essays and lectures done after "the turning" (*die Kehre*), an event conventionally dated in the mid-1930s. No doubt such a simple story won't do as definitive philosophical history, but for the purposes of this book such a neat division is actually useful; in Chapter 4, I shall focus on some Heidegger essays from the 1950s as presenting an account of what it might mean for us to be religious, and I shall claim that those essays can be read as responding to what Heidegger came to see as inadequacies in his account of human being developed in *Being and Time.* There are, of course, great and fundamental continuities in Heidegger's thinking, "early" and "late"; but there is equally no doubt that the philosophical emphases of 1930 and 1950 are quite different. Both the continuities and the differences will be crucial for us. This chapter will focus on *Being and Time.*

Because one constant in Heidegger's philosophical thinking was his attempt to overcome transcendental ego-subjectivity as an account of what it means to be a human being, we must begin with an understanding of that account. For Heidegger transcendental ego-subjectivity is not a freestanding part of our philosophical history; rather, it proceeds from an unnoticed answer to an unasked but essential question, what he calls *die Seinsfrage,* the question of the meaning of Being.[3] *Being and Time* famously opens by adverting to that question, and by deploring its loss as a topic for philosophy.

It is not surprising, though, that the question has fallen on hard times. Posed in Heidegger's unapologetically traditional vocabulary—"What is the meaning of Being?"—the *Seinsfrage* seems a paradigm case of just the sort of question philosophy should stop asking, a question so vague as to be meaningless, the kind of windy question that gives philosophy a bad name.[4] But underneath the obscurity of Heidegger's formulation, there is a genuine and fundamental philosophical question struggling to be asked. Think about it this way: here in my room right now are various kinds of things. There are books,

3. Martin Heidegger, *Being and Time,* trans. John Macquarrie and Edward Robinson (New York: Harper and Row, 1962), 19ff. References henceforth to *Being and Time* will be noted in the text by *BT,* followed by the page number.
4. Heidegger recognizes this, of course. See *BT,* 21ff.

chairs, a sleeping cat, a videotape of an Errol Morris film. That's what those things truly are, or Truly Are: books; a cat; a videotape. They aren't just indeterminate, "meaningless," nonspecific blobs of being-stuff; they are determinate (kinds of) things, things self-identical over (some period of) time as the (kinds of) things they truly are: books, a cat, a videotape. But what "makes" a cat a cat? What "gives" the video its specific reality as a video? What makes them just those particular and determinate and relatively continuous (kinds of) things, things with just those particular and determinate and relatively continuous "identities," identities recognizable as such in our sight, speech, and practice?

It's not just that I call the cat a cat and thus "make" it one.[5] No, it *is*, really *is*, a cat before I (in particular) speak to call it so: not a dog, not a pillow, not a piece of pie. It's a cat, and that's why I (in particular) call it what I do. Again, the philosophical question is, What "makes it possible" for this (kind of) thing *to be* just the determinate and self-identical (kind of) thing it so definitely is, and that I can recognize it as being? (One has to work hard at first not to hear that question as begging a straightforwardly causal answer. If one can *only* hear the question of what makes a cat a cat as a question about some sequence of events linked causally, and thus a question to be eventually answered by one of the natural or social sciences, then one will always have a tin ear for philosophy, Heidegger would say. One will not be able to hear the question as distinctively "transcendental.")

The "transcendental" question of Being is, What is the "source" or "origin" of a thing's determinate "identity," of its self-identical "Being," as precisely the thing it is?[6] What "makes" it just the particular (kind of) thing it is (a book, a cat, a videotape), and not some other (kind of) thing (a fountain pen, an otter, a compact disc)? At a first pass, then, the "question of the meaning of Being" is the question of how the definite "identity" of some particular kind of thing arises, of what "grants" to something its determinate significance as the something it actually is. And then of course there is the even more funda-mental question behind that one: the question of how *anything* is the

---

5. In one trivial sense, of course, it *is* "just that I call it" a cat. I am, that is, a speaker of English; if I were speaking German I would say "eine Katze." But the point is clear: what makes "eine Katze" a translation of "a cat" (and vice versa) is that they are both used to refer to cats. Whether in Greenville or in Garmisch, cats are really there—Really There—to be spoken of, spoken of *as cats*, as a particular kind of thing.

6. I use "Being" (with a capital B) as a translation of Heidegger's *das Sein*. I use "being" (interchangeably with "entity") as a translation of *ein Seiendes*.

determinate (kind of) thing it is. How (why) is What-There-Is always already articulated? How (why) do things—beings, entities—originally and inevitably get their "Being" as the (kinds of) things they always already are? Why (how) is there Something—some stable structure of temporally enduring (kinds of) things—at all, rather than the Nothing of constant Heraclitean flux? That question is *die Seinsfrage* in full flower.[7]

Heidegger conceives the history of Western philosophy as a series of attempts to answer that Platonic question, with the first and paradigmatic answer being Plato's own, of course: what "makes" a cat a cat, or a book a book, or a videotape a videotape, is its relation to some preexistent Form of the Cat, or the Book, or the Videotape. The eternal and perfect existence of the Forms originally and inevitably articulates sublunar reality into its structure as determinate kinds of things. For Heidegger, Plato's answer about "Being" is paradigmatic because it accounts for the Being—the "identity," the significance—of a particular (sort of) being (e.g., a cat) by asserting the prior and necessary existence of another sort of being—a "perfect," "fully present" being; a being the Being of which is immediately self-given—the Form. The Being of the ordinary entity is thus "accounted for" in terms of its relation to the extraordinary entity. The extraordinary being "grants" Being—a particular identity, a particular significance, a particular "sense," one might say—to the ordinary one.

For Plato, then, a thing is the thing it is, a cat for example, because it "participates" in the Form of Cat. Its "participation" in that particular Form, rather than some other Form, is what "makes" it the particular (kind of) being it is: a cat rather than a dog or an otter. Thus the Being of "this" world, the world of changing and mortal cats, books, and videotapes, is "grounded" in another world, in the world of the

---

7. This decidedly Platonic way of explicating *die Seinsfrage*—and that means this way of glossing "Being" as the determinate "identity" of the entities that are—will in the long run turn out to be objectionable to Heidegger himself, as it buys into classical Greek's conflation of the "is" of pure presence with the "is" of predication. That is, it asks: "How (why) is Noddy Boffin a *cat?*" rather than "How (why) *is* Noddy Boffin there at all?" In this way, the question obscures the "ontological difference" by assuming that Being (which Heidegger ultimately wants to gloss as pure presence itself) is always the Being of some (determinate kind of) being. For a convenient and elegant summary of the philosophical and linguistic details, see Barry Allen, *Truth in Philosophy* (Cambridge: Harvard University Press, 1993), chap. 5. But the point of my explication here is not a full account of Heidegger's views about Being; I want merely to show how the Western philosophical tradition of transcendental subjectivity arises from Plato's question about the Being of entities—however much that question is, from Heidegger's perspective, badly formed.

eternal and immutable Forms. The "identity" of any ordinary entity is "given" to it by the entity's relation to some other, and superior, entity. And thus we have the classic pattern of Western metaphysics and religion: the Being of "this" world of entities is rooted in "another" world of (super)entities, a "true world" that "stands under and supports" the Being of beings like cats, books, and videotapes.

One can, as Heidegger famously and brilliantly does, tell the story of Western philosophy after Plato as putting forth, one after another, a line of candidates for the "perfect" entities that grant determinate identity and sense ("Being") to the ordinary and "imperfect" ones. The clearest example of such perfection is perhaps the Christian God, understood as the sole Creator of all beings and (in light of Platonic philosophy) thus as the ground of all Being. If all beings are created ex nihilo at the conscious desire and will of an omnipotent and omniscient creator, if (so to speak) all of Nature is a book written by a single and fully self-aware author, then it's no wonder that things have the specific "meaning" they do. Their "Being" as what they are is the result of their having been "made" (i.e., created, willed) to be what they are. God is thus the absolutely necessary "subject" that "stands under and supports" the system of significances that is the world.

As we've already noted, in the seventeenth century, and particularly in the work of René Descartes, an extraordinarily powerful new understanding of the "subject" replaced the creator God of Platonist/Christian Idealism.[8] When all things were bathed in the corrosive philosophical doubt decanted in Descartes's Meditation 1, only the ego—the thinking, speaking "I"—retained its certain warrant as what it is. Only the ego had Being (as *res cogitans*) that was unmediated by anything else: a Being (an "identity," one might say) that was immediately self-given and self-certain. Standing unharmed and alone in the wreckage of the world, only the "I think/I am" was capable of being the ground upon which the Being of beings was to be re-erected. Everything (else) thus became an "object" for this self-given, self-identical "ego-subject." After Descartes, an entity "is"—is something in particular—only as the "object" for the epistemologically invincible "ego-subject."

Soon Descartes's relatively crude *res cogitans* had been refined into Kant's "transcendental subject"; but it was Heidegger's own teacher, the phenomenologist Edmund Husserl, who gave the account of transcendental subjectivity that marked the true culmination of the Cartesian epoch. The transcendental subject constructed by Western phi-

8. See Chapter 1, "The Age of Cartesian Ego-Subjectivity."

losophy from Descartes to Husserl has three central features. First, transcendental subjectivity is *a pure and immediately self-given self-awareness of itself as the awareness of "objects."* The Cartesian/Husserlian transcendental subject is potentially self-transparent: it can know itself purely and directly *as* the self-identical subject it is; it can commune with itself privately and thoroughly, simply by turning its attention upon itself through the *ascesis* of philosophical self-reflection. And by so doing, in the course of what Husserl calls his sequence of philosophical "reductions," the "I" finally comes to encounter itself as *self-identical awareness of awareness of the intentional (i.e., subject/object) structure of awareness.* This, then, is the full and final presence of the self to itself: intentionality becomes the intentional object of intentionality itself; the subject isolates itself as pure (self-) consciousness of itself as the self-identical subject of all objects.[9] Second, although the transcendental ego—understood as this just-described full presence of the subject to itself—is not to be identified with any concrete human body or specific historical identity (it can't be identified with JCE, for example), it remains an *individual:* it remains something that can legitimately address itself as "I." Third, this ego-subject is properly *transcendental* in that all forms of consciousness, and in particular all acts of cognition, are grounded in it. The existence of such a self is the necessary condition for the specific consciousness of anything else as the particular thing it is. In this way, the transcendental ego is the necessary ground of all "objects" and their characterizations. It is the ultimate and original source of their "identity," of their "significance," of their "Being," as what they are.

Thus, given all three features taken together, the Cartesian/Kantian/Husserlian transcendental ego-subject is the avatar of the Platonic Form: it is the "perfect" (i.e., fully present, self-identical, self-knowing, self-warranting) being in relation to which the Being of all other beings is determined. The ego-subject's perfection inheres in its perfect self-transparency: it knows itself immediately as what it is, as pure point of intentionality with intentionality itself as its object. In its ultimate self-reflection (Husserl's "transcendental reduction"), therefore, the subject has become fully aware of itself as a self-aware whole. The circle has been closed and no gaps remain.

As we have seen, Plato's answer to the question of the meaning of Being was paradigmatic in its postulation of some sort of "perfect"

---

9. This, I take it, is the outcome of the "transcendental reduction" in Husserl's thought.

being as that which "grants" the Being of beings. For Heidegger it is that paradigmatic (what he calls the *metaphysical*) structure of Plato's answer that makes it so dangerous, since that structure—the "true world" of the Forms (or their avatars) grounding "our world" of particular beings—makes it so tempting to *identify* the Being of beings with that set of "perfect" beings that allegedly grounds them. If one succumbs to that temptation, Being becomes "reified;" the Being of beings becomes confused with a special kind of being (i.e., an entity, a *super*entity). Plato's metaphysical account of Being thus encourages us to forget what Heidegger later comes to call "the ontological difference": the difference between Being and beings. "The Being of entities 'is' not itself an entity," he says (*BT*, 26). And it is just this *Seinsvergessenheit*, this "forgetfulness of Being," that has so sadly marked the philosophical history of the West, thinks Heidegger. We have forgotten what it means for something to "Be" (i.e., to be what it specifically is); in particular we have forgotten what it means for *us* to be specifically what we are. In our Platonic assurance that the Being of beings must itself be "given" by some "true" and "perfect" being, we have come to think of *ourselves* as that superbeing. By failing to see that we have always already asked and answered (and badly answered) the *Seinsfrage*, we have come to accept (and even to insist on) an erroneous account of what it means to be us. We have come to think of ourselves as transcendental ego-subjects.

Dasein and the Question of Being

Heidegger is convinced that the fundamental philosophical question of the meaning of Being is best approached by interrogating that being—we ourselves—that is most essentially characterized by its self-interrogation on just this matter of Being. We are that being; we are Dasein (Being-there).[10] Dasein, as Heidegger says, "is an entity which does not just occur among other entities. Rather it is ontically [i.e., factually] distinguished [from other entities] by the fact that, in its very Being, that Being is an *issue* for it" (*BT*, 32). That is what it means to say that Dasein "exists": it is a being that always, in one way or another, is asking itself what it means to Be the being it is.

10. As Hubert Dreyfus points out in *Being-In-The-World* (Cambridge: MIT Press, 1991), in everyday colloquial German, *Dasein* means something like "ordinary human existence" (13). This is perhaps the place to acknowledge my deep debt to Dreyfus for his reading of *BT*. In this chapter I have largely followed his excellent lead.

Dasein is therefore a self-interpreting being; existence is self-interpretation.[11] Most of *Being and Time* is trying to describe what it means to be Dasein, and to do that work of description in such a way that Dasein doesn't turn out to be the Cartesian/Kantian/Husserlian transcendental subject described above. That will not be easy, since the idea of ourselves as a freestanding center of intentional self-awareness has now become a part of our (philosophical) common sense. When we begin self-consciously to reflect on ourselves, it is overwhelmingly tempting to think of the "I" as a kind of discrete *thing,* as (so to speak) the transparent eyeball that sees and assigns significance to whatever there is to be seen. Heidegger intends to offer another interpretation of the Being of Dasein, one that avoids such reification.

First and foremost, Dasein is the being that says "I." Dasein, as we might put it, is the being that can *speak for itself.* Correlative to this "I," to this sense of "mineness,"[12] is the sense of what is *one's own.* I am *I* just insofar as there is something that is *my own:* my own point of view; my own life; my own world. "The world is *my* world," says Wittgenstein in the *Tractatus,* and in *Being and Time* too it is just that sense of the world's "mineness" that delineates the self as such. Heidegger's goal (like Wittgenstein's, in fact) is to avoid reifying the self thus revealed: a difficult task, because Dasein tends to import into its own self-interpretation an ontology that has been useful to it for the interpretation of beings other than Dasein. Specifically, Dasein has tended to interpret itself in the same terms in which it has traditionally interpreted its world. In trying to understand itself as a Cartesian subject, Dasein has quarried its self-interpretation from the ontology of the Cartesian object. Thus, in order that an inadequate ontology of world not be taken over into our self-interpretation, we must first offer a more adequate interpretation of the Being of Dasein's world itself. Self and world must be interpreted (i.e., reinterpreted) together.

In that work of interpretation, we shall encounter three distinct ways in which Dasein "owns" its world, three ways in which Dasein

11. Dasein's interrogation of itself is not necessarily carried out under the patronage of philosophy, of course. Most of our self-interpretation is done quite unreflectively, and shows itself in the way in which we take on for ourselves those interpretations of what it means to be Dasein that are already available in our culture. An accountant choosing for herself a newly designed business card is an example of Dasein's self-interpretation, as is the way she answers the phone or treats her secretary.

12. The word Heidegger uses is *Jemeinigkeit.*

does or does not "own up to" its life.[13] There is first of all what Heidegger calls "the undifferentiated mode" of Dasein's existence, the kind of life in which Dasein is caught up in current and ordinary ways of interpreting itself and in which no explicit reflection on those interpretations is occurring. Most Dasein lives this sort of life most of the time, the life of "average everydayness." We play out the scripts we are handed, normally without calling to mind that they are scripts. Most days I get up, go to school, carry on with my professorial tasks, and so forth; and I do these things thoughtlessly and smoothly, untroubled by any sticky questions about their "meaning." Living in this ordinary way, I am not "owning up to" my life at all; indeed, it would make good sense to say that my life is living me, not the other way round.

Sometimes, however, we are pricked into a disconcerting awareness of our submersion in these well-defined social roles. Perhaps one day I arrive at school only to find the adjoining office empty and dark, because my colleague—hurrying to meet an early class—has been killed in an automobile accident. I might then well ask, "Why was it so important for her to be on time?" and from that question I might be led into questioning the larger life my friend and I shared: a life in which promptness for class is just a symbol for a more general sense of punctilious responsibility to others and to institutions. Where does that powerful sense of responsibility come from? What gives it its authority over me? Does it, in fact, have any such authority at all?

If in response to such reflection I were to assert (perhaps on the basis of philosophical or religious conviction) that my acceptance of my identity as defined by these roles—the prompt professor, the responsible citizen—is *necessary,* that it is somehow grounded in a metaphysical reality that establishes permanently fixed meanings and assigns specific and eternal significances to things, then I am living as *inauthentic* Dasein. ("God in His providence made me what I am and put me here at this station, and I must never flag in carrying out its duties. May God's will be done!") In such a case I am, in a way, "owning up to" myself and my life, but I am doing so in a way that sloughs responsibility off onto some "higher power," some "true world" to which I must answer in my Being who I am. Thus I find "peace and rest" (to quote Kierkegaard) by establishing my metaphysical identity and its concomitant obligations. Such consolation is the defining mark of inauthenticity. If, on the other hand, I were to meet such

---

13. I owe this splendid way of putting the matter to Dreyfus.

reflection in such a way as both to forgo such "metaphysical comfort" and yet to find a way of Being what I am, a way that is (at the margins) genuinely "my own," then I am *authentic* Dasein. This is one's fullest way of "owning up to" oneself. (We shall discuss authenticity in detail later in this chapter.)

It is tempting, Heidegger admits, to focus on authenticity (and thereby on its opposite, inauthenticity) in our attempt to give an account of the Being of Dasein; but it would be a mistake to do so. Most of Dasein's existence is neither authentic nor inauthentic. Most of our life is the life of "average everydayness," and authenticity and inauthenticity are just occasional and transient modifications of that mode. If we are to understand what it means to be us, and in that way to get a leg up on the *Seinsfrage,* we need to account for ourselves as we are "proximally and for the most part" (*zunächst und zumeist,* as Heidegger says), and that means in the "undifferentiated mode" of our average everydayness. Most of Division 1 of *Being and Time* is devoted to that account.

Being-in-the-World

Heidegger believes that we tend to reify the "I" because we import into ourselves an ontology originally at home in relation to (a particular conception of) the world: the transcendental "subject" conceives *itself* as a peculiar sort of "object." The Being of self and world, he thinks, are always given together. Thus a more adequate interpretation of the "I" will depend upon a more adequate interpretation of the world in which that "I" lives. Dasein is, as Heidegger puts it, *In-der-Welt-Sein:* Being-in-the-world. The temptation of our philosophical common sense is to think of that world we are "in" as a collection of discrete and inherently meaningless "objects," "objects" that must as such be present before a meaning-granting "subject" that holds ("constitutes") them in its vision. (As an example of such philosophy, think of the old "sense-datum" picture of perception so beloved of empiricists: what meets the eye are just patches of color and shape until the ego-subject mentally forms them, perhaps incorrectly, into various physical objects.) Heidegger is offering another, and—as he thinks—more revealing, interpretation: the world (*die Welt*) of (some particular) Dasein is always the environment (*die Umwelt:* the "around-world") of (some particular) Dasein. "World" is not the mere occurrence before a subject of a number of discrete and meaning-hungry "objects;" rather, it is the *gathering of things* into a holistic system, just as the physical environment of some creature is an already operating ecosystem within which that creature has its particular "role" to play, as do all the other parts of this environment.

The specific character of Dasein's environment thus is a world of things, not "objects." In *Being and Time* Heidegger is attempting to recover (what he thinks of as) a more primordial sense of "thing," one that goes behind the (Cartesian) understanding of "things" as *res* to the Greek understanding of "things" as *pragmata*: "that is to say, that with which one has to do in one's concernful dealings (*praxis*)" (*BT,* 96f.). Things aren't mere "objects," mutely standing there apart from one another and oneself, waiting upon some "subject" to assign them their significance. No, things show up for Dasein in terms of its "concernful dealings"; the things that appear to Dasein always already appear as what they are in relation to those dealings. Things therefore always already present themselves *holistically,* as part of a "referential totality" of things. A thing is not an anonymous "object"; it is (for example) a pen, or a desk, or a lectern, or a notebook, or a teacher.

As the thing it is, a pen has its Being—its meaning or significance—in terms of two sorts of "assignments" or "references": first, it is what it is in terms of the project(s) within which it appears (a pen is an instrument for *writing,* within the various project[s] of Dasein that depend upon writing); second, it is what it is in relation to the other things (like paper, ink, desks) also involved in such projects. The pen is thus "defined," given its determinate Being as the thing it is, by these two sorts of "references." The pen exists, one might say, at the intersection of these two axes of "reference." There is (so to speak) the "forward" reference in terms of (some of) Dasein's project(s) yet to be accomplished (the pen is for *writing,* for *writing a book of philosophy,* a book for *getting tenure,* for *proving one's father wrong,* and for *vindicating Platonic metaphysics*), and there is the "sideways" reference to other things also involved in those project(s) (the pen writes in a *notebook,* placed on a *desk,* taking down the words of a *teacher,* who stands at a *lectern*).

In this way, according to Heidegger, a thing is the thing it is as *Zeug,* as equipment or gear for the accomplishment of some project(s) or other (*BT,* 97). A pen is a part of the referential totality of Dasein's writing gear; a lectern is a part of Dasein's educational gear; and so on. As *Zeug* a thing has a particular kind of Being, what Heidegger calls "readiness-to-hand" (*Zuhandenheit*); and this kind of transparent availability for Dasein's projects is very different in character from the vivid but static "presence" that an object would have for a Cartesian subject. The pen when being used as a pen "disappears" in that use into the work it is doing. While there is of course a kind of circumspect awareness one has of the pen in one's hand (Heidegger's word for such awareness is *Umsicht*), the focus of one's attention is not on the pen, not on the writing gear, but rather on the writing actually being done, or even, one might say, on the "significance" or "point" of that writing. "The peculiarity of what is proximally ready-to-hand is that, in its readiness-to-hand, it must, as it were, withdraw in order to be ready-to-hand quite authentically. That with which our everyday dealings proximally dwell is not the tools themselves. On the contrary that with which we concern ourselves primarily is the work—that which is to be produced at the time; and this is accordingly ready-to-hand too. The work bears with it that referential totality within which the equipment is encountered" (*BT,* 99).

In Heidegger's account, then, the Being of a thing is given to it (as that particular [kind of] thing) by the holistic context of back-and-forth references created both by some project of Dasein and by the other things likewise involved in that project. Things are not Cartesian "objects," standing there (as Heidegger puts it) "present-to-hand" (*Vorhanden*), waiting to be assigned their Being—their meaning, their significance—by some self-aware subject. On the contrary, things always already are what they are as a result of their place within a referential totality of other things given alongside them. Thus the world of Dasein is always already a world of significance granted by things in their relation to one another in the context of some project(s) of historical Dasein; it is not a world of freestanding *res* that stand silently and discretely in front of the detached, ahistorical, meaning-giving "I." The "worldhood of the world" is found in the holistic Being of the things that appear as *Zeug* to Dasein in its various projects.

Notice that in this Heideggerian "ontology" of the thing, the thing is never reified as a "pure individual." It never is what it is independent of the other things that appear alongside it; it is what it is as gear in some project(s) of (some) historical Dasein. Thus it is given its Being, its significance, not by some other and single and superior being the Being of which is fully present in itself: by some avatar of the "true world" such as a Platonic Form or a creator God or a Cartesian ego. Rather, it is "made" what it Is by its role within an economy of beings formed as such by some projected action of Dasein. In the final analysis, therefore, it is apparently Dasein that grounds the Being of things.

> The primary 'towards-which' is a "for-the-sake-of-which." But the 'for-the-sake-of' always pertains to the Being of Dasein, for which, in its Being, that very Being is essentially an *issue*. We have thus indicated the interconnection by which the structure of an involvement leads to Dasein's very Being as the sole authentic "for-the-sake-of-which" . . . (*BT,* 116f.)

Dasein in its inevitable projection of its own Being is thus the necessary condition for the possibility of the Being of things. But doesn't this seem still to be a kind of transcendental subjectivity? Isn't Dasein still the maker of meaning, the granter of significance, the ground of Being?

Dasein as the "They-self"

Dasein would be this maker of meaning only if Dasein were itself the "pure individual"—the fully self-present, unitary entity—that could serve as the significance-granting subject, and it is not. And yet, as Heidegger himself recognizes, it is extraordinarily difficult for us to avoid the reification of the "I" into the transcendental ego.

> Even if one rejects the "soul substance" and the Thinghood of consciousness, or denies that a person is an object, ontologically one is still positing something whose Being retains the meaning of present-at-hand, whether it does so explicitly or not. Substantiality is the ontological clue for determining which entity is to provide the answer for the question of the "who." Dasein is tacitly conceived in advance as something present-at-hand. (*BT,* 150)

The almost irresistible temptation to reify the "I" springs from two ways in which that "I" seems to designate a "pure individual." One might call these the two aspects of Dasein's individuality, and both seem immediately to spring into view the moment one begins to take stock of oneself as the "I". The first is individuality understood as a kind of *existential discreteness.* Dasein seems to find itself as having a kind of fundamental separateness from everything else. To be Dasein seems to be a freestanding entity, essentially apart from all other selves and things. I am "here"; everything else is "over there." My reality as the "I" seems independent—potentially, at least—of the reality of every other entity; it seems to me that I could exist even if, *horribile dictu,* nothing else did. In Meditation 1, Descartes classically expresses this sense of existential discreteness by claiming to be able to imagine that everything he believes to exist (excepting himself, of course) is only a delusion produced by an all-powerful and evil spirit. From there it is but a short step to doubting the reality of the deceitful demon as well. One is left with the idea that, like the cheese in the children's singing-game, the "I" stands alone. Cartesian individuality means radical independence.

The second aspect of Dasein's individuality is individuality understood as a kind of *unique perspective* on things. Dasein seems to find itself, so to speak, standing in a particular place, and seeing what it sees in a particular way, from a particular location. This "perspective" is not (of course) only or even fundamentally spatial, though spatial imagery—such as I have just used—is almost indispensable for expressing the immediately felt reality of Dasein's perspectival relation to things. "The world is *my* world." What I see is *mine,* seen from right here, not from anywhere else. And that sense of "mineness" means that everything in the world has a particular and unique significance, a significance granted by its specific relation (or lack of such) to me: this is *my* room, and that one isn't; these are *my* books and papers, and those are someone else's; these are *my* thoughts, and those aren't. And this sense of "mineness" seems to go far beyond anything that could be publicly understood and accounted for. They aren't just *JCE's* books; they are *my* books, for *my* name is JCE.

If Heidegger is to replace our understanding of the "I" with an understanding that avoids turning it into some present-to-hand "subject," he will have to account for both our individuality understood as our existential discreteness and our individuality understood as our unique perspective. In regard to both aspects of individuality, Heidegger's tactic is the same. He does not want to deny the felt reality of either phenomenon: we do, at particular times, feel ourselves to be existentially discrete ("alone, alone, all all alone") and to be uniquely personal ("this is *my* world"); under the spell of such occasions, it is natural, even commonsensical, that we should interpret ourselves to be some sort of transcendental ego, separate and unique. Heidegger's response to such an interpretation is to try to show that it proceeds, not from what is true of us "proximally and for the most part," but from circumstances in various ways outside the normal stream of Dasein's life. Having shown the peculiar character of the circumstances from which this particular philosophical interpretation arises, Heidegger thinks he has at the same time undermined the claims of this interpretation to being "obvious common sense." It will have been revealed *as* an interpretation.

The first aspect of our individuality—our sense of our existential discreteness—is belied by our everyday experience of ourselves as Being-in-the-world. We have seen that the ordinary world of Dasein is a world of things ready-to-hand, things whose significance as things is given in terms of a holistic context of back-and-forth references to lots of other things, each of which has its significance given in the same holistic way. I am holding a *pen,* and am writing on *paper,* for the purpose of making a *book,* and so forth. No one of these things is the thing it is (a pen, for example) without its reference to the other things (paper, ink, books) with which it is caught up in some of Dasein's projects. These "other" things (paper, ink, and so forth) are quite literally *present along with* the thing (the pen) to which for some reason my attention was originally drawn. The pen is therefore not a "pure individual" that I confront as discretely present-at-hand. It does not "stand alone."

In the same way, other Dasein is equally present along with me and the things I encounter as world. The pen was *made by* some worker, and was *given to me by* my wife; the book will be *read by* some readers; the thoughts are thoughts *about* Heidegger.

> In our 'description' of that environment which is closest to us—the work-world of the craftsman, for example—the outcome was that along with the equipment to be found when one is at work, those Others for whom the 'work' is destined are 'encountered' too. . . . When, for example, we walk along the edge of a field but 'outside it', the field shows itself as belonging to such-and-such a person, and decently kept up by him; the book we have used was bought at So-and-so's shop and given by such-and-such a person, and so forth. The boat anchored at the shore is assigned in its Being-in-itself to an acquaintance who undertakes voyages with it; but even if it is a 'boat which is strange to us', it is still indicative of Others. The Others who are thus 'encountered' in a ready-to-hand, environmental context of equipment, are not somehow added on in thought to some Thing which is proximally just present-to-hand; such 'Things' are encountered from out of the world in which they are ready-to-hand for Others—a world which is always mine in advance. (*BT,* 153f.)

Thus, "[t]he world of Dasein is a *with-world* (*Mitwelt*). Being-in is *Being-with-Others*" (*BT,* 155). Dasein does not—"proximally and for the most part"—find itself discrete from other selves and things. Rather, one finds oneself always there *with others.* "I" am not a free-standing, radically independent entity; rather, one is always already caught up with others in one's projects and with the gear necessary to those projects, gear that one always (in some ways) shares with others. Therefore the philosophical interpretation of oneself as the discrete "pure individual" is an interpretation flawed by the extraordinary partiality of the data on which it operates. Such an interpretation does not uncover the structural features of who Dasein "really" (i.e., *zunächst und zumeist*) is.

Of course Heidegger does not deny that sometimes Dasein finds itself alone (alone in *fact*), and he does not deny that by focusing its attention on those times Dasein can be led—*mis*led—to interpret itself as the kind of entity that exists separate and apart from all others. Sitting in his cozy oven, or bleakly staring down at people (or are they perhaps merely cloak-draped automatons?) in the street, Descartes *is* alone; and because he does his philosophical thinking in such circumstances, it is no great wonder that in that thinking he thinks of himself as the freestanding ego, as the lonely eye that sees what is "over there." But in so doing, he forgets all those times in the tavern or in the street when he is happily (or unhappily) one among many; more important, he forgets that even when he is in the oven or in the high window there are others there too. To characterize what he sees, or thinks he sees, as a *cloak* or a *pumpkin* or a *meat pie* is already to populate the world with others, others engaged along with him in the ordinary tasks of agriculture, cookery, and tailoring. The world he sees or thinks about, from wherever he is placed, is never (*pace* his own philosophical interpretation of it) just his world; it is a world inhabited, always and already, by innumerable (even if unknown and absent) colleagues. "Being-with is an existential characteristic of Dasein even when factically no Other is present-at-hand or perceived. Even Dasein's Being-alone is Being-with in the world" (*BT,* 156f.).

So much, Heidegger thinks, for individuality understood as existential discreteness. But what about my sense of personal uniqueness, and what about the peculiar significances of things that seem to go with that? Here too Heidegger does not deny the reality of the feeling. No doubt there are occasions when one feels oneself to be a peculiar sort of "perspective" on things, when one feels oneself to be a kind of self-conscious "center" from which everything else is viewed and in relation to which everything else gets its final significance ("The world radiates from *here*—no-one else can see things exactly as *I* see them."). Under the spell of such occasions it is tempting (even plausible) to interpret oneself as the transcendental ego of the philosophical tradition: the constituting center of the world. But is that "really" what one is? Are we forced (to use a Wittgensteinian idiom) to accept the Cartesian/Kantian/Husserlian grammar of the self that forces itself upon us on such occasions? Heidegger thinks not.

He begins by challenging our conviction that our sense of our own uniqueness is primary and grounding. Most of the time, says Heidegger, we are not aware of our personal differences from other Dasein; on the contrary, most of the time the others are precisely those from which one does *not* differ.

> By 'Others' we do not mean everyone else but me—those over against whom the "I" stands out. They are rather those from whom, for the most part, one does not distinguish oneself— those among whom one is too. (*BT,* 154)

Most of the time, as I am doing those things that I normally do, such as feeding the cats or teaching my students, I am thoughtlessly and effortlessly and *necessarily* making use of a whole range of public "understandings" in order to define and to accomplish my goals. These public "understandings" identify particular projects (e.g., teaching, feeding one's companions) as possible and needful to be done, and as possible and needful for me to do; they also identify what counts as doing them, and what counts as the gear appropriate to that doing. As I use the opener on the cat-food can, or turn on the water to rinse the fishy spoon, or rest my book upon the desk, or pick up the chalk to write "phenomenology" on the blackboard, I am trading upon a basic set of public expectations of what various things are (i.e., of what those things are "good for"). I do not and cannot (*ceteris paribus*) figure out from ground zero what wants doing and how to do it; I simply avail myself of the projects and the tools (can-opener, chalk, words) already there and ready-to-hand for me. And this is the crucial point: those things I am doing and using are there for *anyone* to do and use. This gear is not, in the first instance, specifically *my* gear for *my* unique and personal projects; it is gear that anyone can— and in fact does—use to do what is possible and needful. The world of Dasein is a *public* world, a world comprising gear to be used in standard ways in order to accomplish standard tasks with standard goals. Things are not in the first instance *mine;* they are *ours.*

So my basic and normal sense of myself—shown in my ordinary
comportment toward things—is not the sense of myself as someone
different from everyone else; rather, it is the sense of myself as one
among the anonymous many: as *one* cat-feeder in America on this
winter morning, as *one* teacher of philosophy here at Furman; not as
the cat-feeder, nor as *the* philosophy teacher. The can of Fancy Feast I
opened was not packed just for me but for anyone with the forty cents
to buy it, and the classroom I vacate at 10:50 will be occupied at 11:00
by some other teacher, who will rest her book on the same desk and
use the same chalk to write many of the same words on the same
blackboard. And as I do the things I do, I do them (more or less) as I
was taught to do them, and that means I do them (more or less) as
"they" (who taught me) do them. By availing myself of these public
and prior understandings of what is to be done and how it is to be
done, I am—proximally and for the most part—doing what "they" do.

Perhaps the most forceful illustration of Heidegger's point is language. My words, which are the indispensable gear of almost all human practices, are certainly not "my own;" they are not personal to
me. I speak English, not "Edwards." As I shop or teach, I necessarily
trade upon the public understandings of what words like "cat food"
and "phenomenology" mean. I use those words as I was taught to use
them, as "they" use them, more or less as "anyone" uses them. My
basic sense of myself, a sense vouchsafed to myself as one who speaks
and thinks (and thus as one who can shop for cat food and teach
philosophy classes), is the sense of myself as one among many, not as
the unique and personal "center" of significance.

Heidegger calls this basic sense of oneself, *"the 'they' (das Man)"*
(*BT,* 164). "The 'who' [of Dasein] is not this one, not that one, not
oneself, not some people, and not the sum of them all. The 'who' [of
Dasein] is the neuter, *the 'they'"* (*BT,* 164). In the first instance we are
not the Cartesian/Husserlian self shut up inside its own consciousness and wondering what is outside; nor are we the self that assigns
meanings to things in relation to our distinctly personal ambitions
and understandings. No, we are Dasein caught up in our publicly defined projects, and caught up with the others who participate alongside us in those projects either as our colleagues and/or as our (potential) replacements.

> In utilizing public means of transport and in making use of
> information services such as the newspaper, every Other is like
> the next. . . . In this inconspicuousness and unascertainability,

the real dictatorship of the "they" is unfolded. We take pleasure and enjoy ourselves as *they* take pleasure; we read, see and judge about literature as *they* see and judge; likewise we shrink back from the 'great mass' as *they* shrink back; we find 'shocking' what *they* find shocking. The "they," which is nothing definite, and which all are, though not as the sum, prescribes the kind of Being of everydayness. (*BT,* 164)

In that last sentence Heidegger has two distinct things in mind. The "they" prescribes the Being—the meaning, the significance—of the things there are. The can-opener or the classroom is a can-opener or a classroom because "they" use it as a can-opener or a classroom, not because it is a can-opener or a classroom "in itself," or because it stands in some relation to a Platonic Form, or because it has been granted its meaning—"consitituted"—by a Cartesian/Husserlian ego-subject. And the "they" likewise prescribes the Being of Dasein itself. Dasein is first and foremost "one of them" (or, better, "one of us"). Dasein is not *zunächst und zumeist* a unique and discrete "center" of iterated self-consciousness that assigns a peculiar significance to things from its personal "perspective"; rather, Dasein is the "they" that speaks and thinks and attaches significance in a decentralized language that "they" already speak and think, and that acts and reacts according to already established public understandings that "they" act and react to as well. Proximally and for the most part, Dasein is the "they-self."

Dasein's Philosophical Misinterpretation

But what of those times when I do seem to myself to be a unique "center" of self-consciousness? Just as there are times when—as the result of some breakdown—we become aware of our tools in a new way (as when, confronted by a broken hammer, we become aware of it as pure present-to-hand material "stuff," as [now] just some chunks of wood and iron), there are also times we can become aware of ourselves outside our involvement in the normal practices of the "they." We can become "withdrawn" from our normal practices in the same way the broken hammer "withdraws" its availability from our circumspect use of it to repair the shelf. But just as we don't think that the broken hammer—confronted by us then as useless lumps of wooden and metallic material—is the "real" hammer, so too we should not think of the self that has become aware of itself as separated from its normal involvement in public practices as the "real" self. And yet that is just the self-interpretation (i.e., self-*mis*interpretation) that lies behind the Cartesian/Kantian/Husserlian account of the transcendental ego.

Why should this misinterpretation be so powerful? Its power rests both in (1) the normal power of the "they" to blind Dasein to the actual character of its everyday Being *as* the "they" and in (2) Dasein's explosive reaction to that everyday Being when it hears what Heidegger names "the call of conscience." In the ordinary course of things Dasein is not a Socratic questioner, demanding of its life that it answer to universal and eternal standards of adequacy. On the contrary, normally Dasein is wholly and unself-consciously taken up in its constitutive projects (feeding the cats, teaching *Being and Time*), using the gear available to it ready-at-hand in order to make its way in the world as "they" require and recognize. This absorption in the ordinary fabric of one's life Heidegger calls *falling*: "Being-lost in the publicness of the 'they'" (*BT*, 220). In spite of the moralistic resonance of the word "falling," Heidegger insists that this submersion in the "they" is not a matter for criticism or regret; it is normal and proper (indeed absolutely necessary) that in its average everydayness Dasein should operate unself-consciously according to the public norms defining "our" projects and "our" gear. Falling shows itself vividly in such phenomena as idle chatter, curiosity, and ambiguity; and in ordinary circumstances Dasein's falling is a state of bland and unreflective contentment.[14] Dasein's everyday activity in accordance with public norms is calming and anodyne, and the public world of the "they" offers Dasein a whole range of manageable challenges and satisfactions.

> The supposition of the "they" that one is leading and sustaining a full and genuine 'life', brings Dasein a *tranquillity*, for which everything is 'in the best of order' and all doors are open. Falling Being-in-the-world, which tempts itself, is at the same time tranquilizing. (*BT*, 222)

14. Idle chatter is saying what "they" say: gossiping; passing the word along. Curiosity is "seeing, not in order to understand what is seen . . . but *just* in order to see." Ambiguity is the inability to decide what is disclosed in a genuine understanding, and what is not. These indicators of falling Dasein, which Heidegger insists (not altogether convincingly) are not to be understood as having a disparaging connotation, are discussed in *BT*, secs. 35–37.

But even in the tranquillity of falling, Dasein can be shocked into awareness of its actual Being; it can come to recognize its subjection to "the publicness of the 'they.'" And when that happens, Dasein hears "the call of conscience": "Conscience summons Dasein's Self from its lostness in the 'they'" (*BT,* 319). Dasein recognizes that its ordinary life is a life into which it has been "thrown" by various contingencies outside its control (e.g., who its parents were, the age and culture and language into which it was born, its genetic assets and liabilities, its particular toilet-training, the schools it went to, the books it read, and so forth); and it further recognizes—this recognition producing "anxiety" (*Angst*)—that the particular life it is living is only one among many possible and actual lives, that it lacks any sort of metaphysical grounding that would warrant it as *the* life for Dasein to live. The anxiety consequent upon the recognition of Dasein's "thrownness" and lack of "ground" produces a sense of "uncanniness," according to Heidegger. (The German word translated as "uncanny" is *unheimlich,* the root of which is *Heim,* meaning "home.") Beset by the anxiety of groundlessness, Dasein now finds itself *not at home* in the life it has been living; it now finds itself for the moment withdrawn from those public norms and expectations that had heretofore constituted its daily fare. Confronted with that sort of breakdown, but not recognizing its peculiar character *as* a breakdown, Dasein can be powerfully tempted to interpret itself as philosophically and essentially "homeless"; that is, as a freestanding center of reflexive self-consciousness capable of living outside all particular public norms. From there it is but a short step to a philosophical self-interpretation in which Dasein becomes the ultimate ("transcendental") source of the norms themselves. And part of what makes such self-interpretations so powerful to us is that they don't seem to be interpretations at all. Under the spell of a writer like Descartes, for example—as we all to some degree now are—it seems the baldest common sense that the "I" is a "pure individual" self-conscious of itself as such.

One might put it this way: Dasein's occasional, uncanny (and deeply impressive) sense of itself as withdrawn from any particular actual life is an existential phenomenon that the Western philosophical tradition has (brilliantly and powerfully) misinterpreted as a metaphysical reality. It is a normal feature of one's existence as Dasein that one periodically finds oneself in circumstances that provoke a peculiar sense of distance between oneself and one's particular constitutive norms and practices. That periodic sense of uncanniness, expressed in "the call of conscience," is both real and powerfully emotive; it is, one might say, a structural feature of the kind of Being Dasein has.[15] But everything turns on what sort of philosophical interpretation one gives of the (periodic, uncommon) experiences of such distance. Does one have to account for them by reifying the existence of the "I" into a "pure individual" like the transcendental ego of Descartes or—more clearly—of Husserl? No, says Heidegger. The existential phenomenon can and should stand on its own; it does not demand a particular metaphysical representation.

Think of déjà vu. There is no doubt that the experience is both real and powerfully impressive: occasionally we seem to be doing things that we have done just this way before, as in a forgotten dream or in an earlier life. When it happens to one it produces an uncanny sense of oneself as something stranger and deeper than one knew. It is so impressive, at least at first, that it cries out for some sort of interpretation. But do we need to account for—to interpret—the phenomenon in any one way? Do we, for example, actually have to believe that we have lived this very life before, or that we have dreamed the future—*this* future—and then forgotten it? Certainly not. We can treat déjà vu as, for example, just a strange electrical phenomenon of the brain, on the analogy of the distortions in radio reception produced by a thunderstorm. If during a thunderstorm I receive the signals from a Pittsburgh radio station more clearly than I receive the signals from downtown Greenville, does that mean that "really" Pittsburgh is closer to me than is the station downtown? Of course not; that would be a mistaken—though on its face experientially plausible—interpretation of the phenomenon at issue. In the same way it would be a mistake to interpret déjà vu as showing that one really has lived (or dreamed) this life before, or to interpret Dasein's occasional experiences of uncanniness as an indication of the reality of the transcendental ego.[16]

---

15. One could even (unlike Heidegger) think of these experiences of "uncanniness" as having a physiological root: as being the result of a chemical imbalance in the brain, say. That might make it easier for one to distinguish the experiences themselves (understood as existential phenomena, as normal [though rare] parts of Dasein's life) from the metaphysical interpretation our philosophical tradition has given them.

16. A similar point can be made, by the way, for near-death experiences. There is, so far as I can see, little reason to doubt that they sometimes happen, and little reason to doubt that similar features are present in many of them (moving toward a bright light, seeing dead relatives and friends, feeling at peace, and so forth). But a great deal turns on what sort of interpretation one gives of the experiences. As with déjà vu, there's no good reason blithely to accept the interpretation that seems (because of our history and our needs) not to be an *interpretation* at all.

Authenticity

Rather than indicating a fundamental metaphysical distinction between the self (understood as a reflexively conscious "pure individual") and the world (understood as a conglomeration of present-to-
hand "objects"), the sense of one's uncanniness vouchsafed in the call
of conscience is really the recognition of the possibility of what Heidegger calls *authenticity* (*Eigentlichkeit*). The call of conscience is an
existential reminder of one's typical "lostness in the 'they'"—the banality and contingency of one's ordinary life—and it demands to be
answered with some modification, however marginal and temporary,
of that normal existential situation. Dasein in its "average everydayness" lives a life into which it has been "thrown," a life constituted by
a range of already existing, well-developed, overlapping social practices (being a teacher, being a husband, being a son, being a male, and
so forth), each with its own set of public norms and expectations. Indeed, it is better to put it more strongly: in its average everydayness,
Dasein just *is* some set of social practices. As the "they-self" it ordinarily is, Dasein is (some set of) social practices "all the way down."[17]
First and foremost Dasein is the language—the various languages, in
fact—it has been taught to speak, and which it normally speaks as
"they" speak; and that is so for the languages of Dasein's own self-
understanding as well as for the languages it uses to describe and to
evaluate its world. Proximally and for the most part, Dasein is what
"they" have required it and recognized it to be, and nothing more. In
this average everydayness, there is nothing in one's life that is genuinely one's own (*eigen*). The life one is living—the language one is
speaking—is not a life (or language) one "owns," or even has "owned
up to."[18]

When the call of conscience comes, provoked by whatever event of
conflict or breakdown in one's ordinary identity, one must in some
way or other own up to oneself; that is, own up to those constitutive
social practices into which one has been "thrown" by one's history.[19] As

17. I believe the application of this vivid locution to Heidegger's idea is due to
Hubert Dreyfus. I first heard it used at a summer institute on Husserl and Heidegger,
directed at Berkeley in the summer of 1979 by Dreyfus and by John Haugeland. I
presume it consciously echoes the famous story about William James and "turtles all
the way down."

18. As noted above, this excellent way of putting the matter is due to Dreyfus.

19. From Heidegger's point of view, the events that produce the call of conscience
must always be collisions of social practices with one another. In my life as a teacher,
for example, the ruling public norms and expectations governing my behavior may in

was noted earlier in this chapter, there are two major ways in which that "owning" of oneself can occur. The first is what Heidegger calls *inauthenticity* (*Uneigentlichkeit*). The inauthentic response is one that claims some sort of metaphysical warrant for identifying oneself with some particular set of one's constitutive social practices. Inauthenticity metaphysically privileges one of one's self-descriptions; it claims that one's identity *as something* (as Christian, as teacher, as male, as free and equal rational being) has overriding metaphysical authority. That is who one Really Is. Confronted by some crisis with the need to clarify one's Being in relation to a particular practice into which one has been "thrown" (the practice of being a teacher, say), one may avail oneself of the comfort of insisting that one's constitution by that practice is somehow *necessary*. One may inauthentically deny one's contingency by claiming in some way that one *must* be a teacher: that it is a vocation given one by God, for example; or that it is a way of life true to one's own defining nature; or something of that sort. What is crucial to inauthenticity is that in some way or other one conceals from oneself one's own contingency as Dasein constituted by—"thrown into"—metaphysically "groundless" social practices. Inauthenticity conceals this contingency behind some claim of metaphysical necessity. This concealment allows one to throw oneself (or, better, to be thrown) even more willingly into whatever social role(s) one has been playing. Given the (inauthentic) assurance of its necessity, one enthusiastically submerges oneself (or is submerged) in one's life as a teacher; one's "identity crisis" has been happily resolved.[20]

Notice that when one's conflict about "who one is" is resolved inauthentically, one's captivity to the current "state of play" in the practice is essentially complete. If I come to believe it is somehow necessary that I be a teacher, I shall at the same time come largely to accept that *what it means* to be a teacher is something already in its essentials defined by (some part of) the practice with which I am identifying myself. By identifying myself necessarily *as* some already actual social practice, a practice that—through my own assertion of

---

various ways conflict with the norms and expectations constituting my life as a husband or as a friend. Thrown as I am into all these practices, and confronted with inconsistent directives, I may be brought to a standstill. Who am I, teacher or husband or friend? Notice that there is no necessity to interpret this conflict in such a way that "I" am somehow "metaphysically" separable from these practices. The question is, Which, if any, of these practices (and under what description of that practice) am I? Which way of talking about myself and others will I "own up to," that is, will become definitive for this historical Dasein?

20. Dreyfus, *Being-In-The-World*, 26.

its necessity for me—I am assuming to be in some way "grounded" over and above my own (or anyone's) enactment of it, I am closing myself off from identifying and instantiating certain heretofore unrealized possibilities in that practice. In my inauthenticity I shall continue to play the game as it "should" be played, and that means: as it has been played by (some of) those whom the practice recognizes to be its standard exemplars.

The alternative response to the call of conscience is what Heidegger calls *authenticity* (*Eigentlichkeit*). Here too Dasein recognizes its "lostness in the 'they'" into which it has been thrown, but in this case it does not respond to its "falling" by concealing (from itself and from others) the contingency of its thrownness. Nor is authenticity any (necessarily illusory and futile) attempt to escape from that contingency. Authentic Dasein is still and always the "they-self" (*das-Man-selbst*). Authenticity—fully "owning up to" oneself—is not an abrogation of the "they."

> [A]uthentic existence is not something which floats above falling everydayness; existentially, it is only a modified way in which such everydayness is seized upon. (*BT*, 224)

> *Authentic Being-one's-Self* does not rest upon an exceptional condition of the subject, a condition that has been detached from the "they"; *it is rather an existentiell modification of the "they"—of the "they" as an essential existentiale.* (*BT*, 168)

Authenticity is the constitution of Dasein in social practices that in their normal and normalized behaviors *acknowledge their Being as practices;* that is, as contingent ways of Dasein's Being that are always ranged alongside an indefinite number of other actual and possible ways for Dasein to Be. Within such practices (call them nonself-concealing practices), Dasein (as constituted by such practices) is constantly aware of its existence as radically contingent, as "groundless." Authentic Dasein's own languages of self-description and world-description are languages that (in some way or other) acknowledge their contingent particularity. (They would be, so to speak, languages that systematically put into question their own vocabularies and grammatical conventions.) Speaking those languages Dasein knows that it is not "necessarily" or "essentially" what it (at that point) takes itself—takes itself *truly*—to be. Nor is Dasein's world any less contingent than Dasein itself: the world too—the true world, this actual one—is just that constellation of gear necessary to "groundlessly" self-interpreting Dasein in its various projects.

Such authenticity is clearly not the norm. Most of the practices constituting Dasein are practices that in no way raise the question of their "ground"; they certainly don't raise and negatively answer such questions within the practice itself. Most practices are thus unconsciously self-concealing; instead, they carefully but surreptitiously cover over any sense one might have of their contingency. And of the few practices that do gesture in the direction of "grounding" themselves, most offer Dasein some sort of "metaphysical comfort" by insisting on their own necessity. I once heard a stockbroker lecture to the effect that free-market capitalism is peculiarly expressive of our divinely created human nature, and thus that his profession—no less than that of the physician or the priest (those were his examples)—is ordained by God. If such a lecture were to become part of the standard training of stockbrokers, then that training and its subsequent practices of buying and selling equities would form a clear example of inauthentic Dasein. Authentic Dasein, on the other hand, is constituted by practices that call specific attention to their lack of such assurance.

Within such nonself-concealing practices Dasein can be what Heidegger calls *resolute* (*entschlossen*). Resolute Dasein can find in its constitutive practices unexpected ways of Being what it truly is, ways that are "uncovered" or "unlocked" (*ent-schlossen*) by the acknowledged groundlessness of the practices. Take, for example, the social practice of teaching philosophy to undergraduates, which is one of the practices constituting what it means to be JCE. What if that practice were somehow to include within itself the explicit acknowledgment that it is only one practice among many, that it is a practice that might never have been an actual possibility for any Dasein, and thus that its centrality to the Being of JCE is a mere contingency lacking any warrant of metaphysical necessity? What if the practice of teaching philosophy to undergraduates were somehow to highlight any historical Dasein's "thrownness" into it, and what if that practice were to contain within it certain mechanisms that would prevent one from ever being able (inauthentically) to claim for that practice, and for one's own constitution by it, any sort of metaphysical standing? In such a case, Heidegger thinks, it would be possible for Dasein to be resolute. It would be possible, that is, for Dasein to uncover particular, perhaps novel, ways of being a teacher of philosophy to undergraduates, ways that would be invisible to the teacher who was—either in average everydayness or in inauthenticity—lost in the "they."

> In resoluteness the issue for Dasein is its ownmost poten-
> tiality-for-Being, which, as something thrown, can project itself
> only on definite factical possibilities. Resolution does not with-
> draw itself from 'actuality', but discovers first what is factically
> possible; and it does so by seizing upon it in whatever way is
> possible for it as its ownmost potentiality-for-Being in the
> "they."

> *The resolution is precisely the disclosive projection and deter-*
> *mination of what is factically possible at the time.* (The first
> passage is from *BT,* 346; the second is from 345.)

Thus resolute authenticity is not an escape from the "they-self"; it
certainly does not give oneself a sense of oneself (a "Being") as a
metaphysically distinct "pure individual" that exists outside any and
every particular social practice. Authenticity is rather a peculiar modification of the "they-self," a modification vouchsafed by the disclosure
of specific factual possibilities within the identity constituted by the
"they-self," possibilities that would not be disclosed were I not so
aware of the contingency of that identity itself. To return to the earlier example, once I become aware of the radical "groundlessness" of
my Being as a teacher of philosophy to undergraduates—ultimately
because I am aware that it is mere happenstance that Dasein has
constituted itself as philosophers, teachers, and undergraduates[21]—
then I am no longer bound to the current state of play in the practice.
Previously unremarked-upon possibilities (may) become apparent to
me. Perhaps, to take a banal instance, I now recognize I can fruitfully
substitute a couple of novels for Kant's *Groundwork* in my ethics
class—and still be teaching philosophy. After all, the syllabus for "a
course in philosophical ethics" is not a natural kind; it is just as much
a historical contingency (and thus just as much subject to reinterpretation) as is philosophy, or ethics, or the university where both are
taught.[22] All these social and linguistic practices, I presumably now
see, are instances of Dasein's defining concern with what it means to

21. These words do not name natural kinds established as such from the foundation
of the world. A philosopher is just as much a historical accident as is a David Letter-
man fan: both depend for their existence on twists and turns in the culture that could
easily have gone otherwise.

22. This is not to say that "anything goes" in such interpretation. Part of the force of
calling these *factical* possibilities is that *in fact* one will find it possible to get away
with them: for example, most of one's colleagues in the practice will agree that, yes,
this still counts as teaching philosophical ethics.

Be Dasein; thus all are equally "groundless." Notice, however, that this capacity for innovation is just the freedom to see new possibilities already "factically" there in the practice of teaching philosophy to undergraduates. It does not show me what such teaching "really is," nor does it reveal me to be something really "other" than a teacher of philosophy (a transcendental ego, say). It just lets me see better something of what it means for me to be that sort of teacher I am: I become aware of "my ownmost potentiality-for-Being in the 'they'" (BT, 346).[23]

Authenticity and Normal Nihilism

We have been looking at Heidegger's account of what it means to be Dasein, considering (as I do) that account to be contemporary Western philosophy's most fully developed attempt to avoid transcendental subjectivity as a description of human being. Dasein is not a freestanding, individual center of reflexive self-consciousness (Descartes, Husserl); nor is it a self-possessed center of restless, passionate desire, able to shift itself at will from one coveted object or form of life to another (Kierkegaard). Dasein is, proximally and for the most part, the "they-self." It is, "all the way down," some fairly stable and enduring set of overlapping social (i.e., linguistic, behavioral) practices: nor-

---

23. It is important, though difficult, to keep in mind that authenticity and inauthenticity are themselves just particular (and marginal) modifications of the social practices constituting the Being of some historical Dasein. They are not, as they can so easily seem, "attitudes" or "states of mind" that the reified "I" can freely assume in a moment of decision (*der Augenblick*). (That's the typical "existentialist"—one might almost say Protestant Christian—reading of Heidegger, and one that Heidegger himself sometimes does not make it easy to avoid.) Remember, for Heidegger there is no such freestanding "I." There are only slightly different ways to be (i.e., to Be) what one always already concretely *is* as some historical Dasein; there are only marginally different social (linguistic, behavioral) practices that constitute *us* as some specific "they." The difference between authenticity and inauthenticity—real as it is—is a marginal difference between "they-selves," between ways in which (in speech and behavior) we (i.e., some historical Dasein) "own up to" who we are. (One could almost say: authenticity and inauthenticity are just slightly different ways one has discovered one can talk about oneself. Except one then wonders what the "just" is supposed to indicate. Or what "about" means.) Authentic Dasein is a (verbal, behavioral) modification *at the margins* of those social practices we always already are "all the way down." And those marginal changes disclose further "factical" possibilities that can, over much time, bend the practice into almost unrecognizable forms. (Would Heraclitus see Carnap as a colleague?)

malized actions and reactions—projects, techniques, vocabularies—shared with others as ways of coping with the situation into which one has (along with them) been "thrown." Dasein's world is not fundamentally a world of its "objects," whether of cognition or desire; it is a world of *things,* things that are what they are because of their holistic relation to one another as "gear" (*Zeug*) in one or more of the social practices that constitute the existence of some historical Dasein.

What would it be for Dasein to be religious? At first glance the Heideggerian answer seems clear: a religion (Christianity, say) is but one social (linguistic, behavioral) practice among many that might constitute the Being of some historical Dasein. "Being a Christian" will be one of the projects into which (some) Dasein has been "thrown," and such pieces of gear as the Bible, the priest, the Eucharist, the Creed, and the confessional will gain their particular significance (their "Being," to use Heidegger's jargon) from their holistic relationships to one another in the context of that project as it elaborates itself into the future of its particular past. This project of Dasein, like any such project, will most of the time be carried on without any particular distinction or reflexivity; it will be a part of Dasein's normal (and normalized) coping with the "factical" situation into which it finds itself thrown. In its average everydayness Christian Dasein will be a Christian as "they" require and recognize and reward. (In Kierkegaard's terms, everyday Dasein will be an ordinary citizen of Christendom.) But as with any historical Dasein, there is always the chance for authenticity or inauthenticity. Confronted at some point with its "lostness in the [Christian] 'they,'" Christian Dasein has the chance either to resolutely admit the "groundlessness" of its religious identity and practice (and thus reveal to itself [*qua* social practice] hitherto undisclosed factual possibilities for being a Christian) or to seek metaphysical warrant for its faith (and thus condemn itself [*qua* social practice] to the received wisdom about what it means to be the religious being it is).

But perhaps by construing Dasein's capacity for religiousness as just the factical possibility of its being "thrown" into some particular historical religion—as I have construed it in the preceding paragraph—I am taking too short a way with the question of what it might mean for Dasein to be religious. Impressed by all the obviously Kierkegaardian vocabulary used by Heidegger to set out his existential phenomenology of Dasein (falling, fleeing, anxiety, guilt, the call of conscience), it is tempting to think that Heidegger's authentic Dasein is intended to be something of a secular replacement for—or at least a secular reinterpretation of—Kierkegaard's knight of faith.[24] Authentic, resolute Dasein might almost be taken as a nonmetaphysical double for genuinely religious human being. Perhaps authentic existence à la Heidegger is all that is left to us of religious faith, once its unacceptable philosophical elements have been purged. After all, in Dasein's drive toward authenticity, as in Kierkegaard's absurd heroes, there is the *Pathos* of an attempt to escape one's stultifying ordinary life into something hale and whole, something that—in the moment at least—appears to one as the truth that saves. In both there is an attempt at self-transformation by reference to something yet unrealized, and in both that self-transformation is the full (or at least fuller) realization of "what one really is." Most important, in both that fuller realization is supposed to restore savor to a life that has gone flat and insipid. Obviously there are huge philosophical differences between the author of *Being and Time* and the author of the *Postscript*, but a great deal of the ethical structure of their thought neatly overlaps. (How could it not, both of them being Western philosophical intellectuals, and one of them having avidly read the other?) Is Dasein's authenticity a kind of religiousness—or, if that word seems too old-fashioned to apply to Heidegger, is authenticity the kind of idealized human life—that, by escaping the Western philosophical tradition's account of human being as transcendental subjectivity, also escapes the normal nihilism that seems inevitably to accompany it? Does authentic, resolute Dasein—whether Christian or not, whether in any traditional way "religious" or not—escape from the mall?

I don't think so. While it certainly may be that authentic Dasein is privy to new factical possibilities for being whatever sort of Dasein it is (teacher, Christian, lover, African-American), possibilities that remain invisible either in average everydayness or in inauthenticity, those specific innovations do not reliably protect Dasein from the mood of devaluation that defines normal nihilism, and us as normal nihilists. The problem as originally set was this: the self-devaluation of our highest values proceeds so compellingly because a Nietzschean genealogy of those values—a genealogy unavoidable for us to undertake, as its impulse and form are rooted in the very same values we are thereby querying—seems to demonstrate their brute contingency, a contingency at odds with their own most fundamental claims for themselves. Consider, for example, truth, the very highest value for us end-of-century, Western intellectuals. By inquiring, as a concern

24. Something like this interpretation can be found in Hubert Dreyfus's and Jane Rubin's appendix to *Being-in-the-World*.

for truth requires us to do, into the nature and value of truth itself—for example, by pursuing the question of truth and its value through the philosophical and religious history I have sketched from the Yahwist and Plato to Descartes and Nietzsche—we have come to see (as it seems to us) the radical and irremediable contingency, not only of what we now cannot help taking as true, but also of the very value of truth itself. Under the spell of truth and its requirements, we have come to see that truth—the very idea of truth—is *itself* just a value: a contingent structure of interpretation; a particular way of reckoning used by human beings to survive and flourish in a dangerous world. Yet truth, as the reality it presents itself to be, and presents itself to be even (perhaps especially) in our search for the truth about truth, denigrates all such contingency. Truth, conceived as *we* (with our history) must conceive it, conceived as some sort of epistemic trump card, as something that answers to our need for "peace and rest," presents itself, even in its Nietzschean genealogy, in *its* inevitable claim to truth, as the *absolute alternative* to all convention and accident. Truth is (in its own account of itself to us) the way we hook ourselves into something steady and immovable beneath the restless flux of time and experience.

Thus the genealogical representation of truth pioneered by Nietzsche—the apparently truthful presentation of a historical account of truth as a value—devaluates the value it reveals truth to be. The very idea of a noncontingent relation to reality has been shown by that genealogy to be a contingent coping-mechanism: truth is (nothing more than, nothing less than) a value—a structure of interpretation—now normal to be employed by human beings like us. The devaluation of that value originates in the distance between the way that genealogy presents itself to us—as *true*—and what that genealogy (*if* true) shows us about the nature of truth itself (namely, that truth just is a value). Through that gap—the gap between (promised, absolute) truth and (actual, contingent) value—the supreme pathos of truth leaks away, leaving us with less than we were always (and even *now,* in the genealogy, and in these our truthful reflections upon its implications) being promised; that is, leaving us not with truth (with Truth) but with only a value, now of course somewhat devaluated. Following out this Nietzschean line of thought, we have come to see that all our values, and indeed the very notion of value itself, likewise finally present themselves as normal and normalized ways of human coping; and with each of these values the gap between promise (absoluteness) and result (contingency) again reappears, allowing the force of the value—now clearly seen as such—to diminish. Values are conceived *causally* by Nietzsche, as mechanisms to be understood and cherished only in terms of what they do for us; not in terms of what they "represent." We even have come to see that seeing our values as ways of coping is itself just a way of coping that has now, for good or for ill, become normal for us post-Nietzscheans. (The very notion of a value is itself [for us] a value.) In this way even the notion of "seeing," as used in these last few paragraphs (and in the next one), has lost (some of) its power to convict our attention. What we "see" to be so is what we have, by history and need, been accustomed to "see." "Seeing" is itself just a handy way of talking about complex chains of cause and effect in service to the will to power.

So, as a result of Nietzsche's causal conception of values, we have come to see ourselves—or to "see" ourselves—as (in Rorty's evocative words) "just another species doing its best," a contingent form of life doing its damnedest to maintain, against strong competition, its ecological niche in the welter of other life-forms. Our most cherished practices—things like languages, religions, philosophies, political parties—have begun to look like the flowers of the wild orchids or the prominent incisors of the beavers. They have begun to look, that is, like contingently evolved ways of helping us get along, causal mechanisms preserved (so far) by natural selection and making it easier (or, in some perverse cases, more difficult) for us to survive in the short and medium term. (Keynes has already spoken for the long term, of course.) Just as we don't expect the blossoms of the orchids to be "about" anything—a flower doesn't, in spite of our adolescent yearnings, "represent" the world in which it blooms: the story we tell of the blossom's evolutionary efficacy and of its relations to other things is entirely a causal one—it now occurs to us that our practices and their defining values may not be (certainly don't have to be) "about" anything either. Can't values and practices be understood just as orchid blossoms are: as mechanisms whose whole Being is explicable in terms of the causal roles they play in preserving and enhancing a particular form of life? It occurs to us that our traditional philosophical interpretations of their efficacy—that those practices are "in accord with" or "tell us about" an independent and determinate reality—are perhaps just that: our (perhaps for a time useful) interpretations of our evolutionary success (so far). And with that realization (or "realization") some of their wonted power seeps away.

What is at issue here is the *Pathos*—the "impressiveness," the power—of our constitutive practices.[25] A part of that power, some-

---

25. I use *"Pathos"* as it is used by Ludwig Wittgenstein in sec. 110 of the *Philosophi-*

times the largest part of it, has lain in the claim, whether explicit or not, that these practices are more than just the contingent behaviors of some historical being: that they rest on the very fabric of reality itself; that they necessarily are what they are, just as they are, or as they are so slowly becoming; and that we too, as formed by those practices, are necessarily what we are, or are becoming. Normal nihilism is our recognition, or "recognition," granted to us by a particular course of philosophical reflection, that the claim of our practices to that sort of absolute status cannot be warranted by the standards those practices have themselves taught us to honor. Thus our "highest values"—and in particular the value of truth, understood as a kind of necessity in what one sees and says—devaluate themselves.

I cannot see that Heidegger's existential phenomenology of Dasein goes any real distance toward reliably restoring the *Pathos* of our constitutive practices, whatever they are: Christianity, democracy, birding, or phenomenology. Indeed, it seems instead to offer a philosophical account of, and impulse to, our normal nihilism (in relation to those practices) that is even more powerful than Nietzsche's. Even as they are overturning the Cartesian epoch, Nietzsche's fundamental philosophical images—interpretation, perspective, and the like—remain derivatively Cartesian. The Nietzschean trope of interpretation is certainly not the same as the Cartesian trope of representation, but it retains (perhaps against Nietzsche's will) something of the latter's commitment to "aboutness." A given interpretation is always an interpretation *of* something; it is always "about" a text or an event or a person. The same is true for a perspective: it is always someone's perspective *on* something, something that stands there waiting to be seen. Notice, then, that both interpretation and perspective still belong to an image of the human that construes us as spectators trying to "see" something as it really is, and perhaps failing. Given the central role played in Nietzsche's work by images of interpretation and perspective, it is thus tempting to see that work as the logical extension of some standard skeptical-philosophical reflections: because we can't verify or falsify our "representations" of the world, we must give up the idea that they are representations at all and admit that they are only interpretations; we must admit that whatever we take as truth is always an interpretation (*of* something) relative to some per-

---

cal Investigations, trans. G. E. M. Anscombe (Oxford: Basil Blackwell, 1958). Miss Anscombe translates Wittgenstein's word as "impressiveness," which is excellent. *Pathos* is the impression of a profound and compelling importance, a seriousness that runs as deep as can be.

spective (*on* something), a perspective formed by a constellation of our contingent interests.[26] Notice that the spectator-stance of the Cartesian/Husserlian "transcendental subject" is not wholly absent from these Nietzschean philosophical reconstructions.

Heidegger's tropological distance from Descartes is greater than Nietzsche's. The phenomenology of Dasein in *Being and Time* offers a way of thinking of ourselves that takes us far from the spectator-self of the Cartesian tradition, farther even than the (residually Cartesian) self-interpreting, self-creating self of Nietzsche's Overman and of Kierkegaard's knight of faith. In Heidegger's work, as we have seen, Dasein is first and foremost the "they-self"; it is a set of overlapping social practices out of which some particular "selection" of linguistic and behavioral routines and responses has been precipitated ("thrown") for a time. To see oneself that way, if indeed one can hold the view steady for long enough, is to see oneself as even more radically contingent. One's very existence *as a self* is contingent; and not upon one's own superhuman will or upon one's own absurd choice, as it might be in Nietzsche or in Kierkegaard, but on a brute "thrownness" that is ultimately due to no particular thrower, not even "oneself." In *Being and Time* the Kierkegaardian vocabulary of spiritual ambivalence and decision ("anxiety," *der Augenblick*) is put to uses that undermine its fundamental assumptions, and the Nietzschean figure of the heroically self-creating Overman is reduced to authentic Dasein, characterized as "an existentiell modification of the 'they.'"

Reading *Being and Time* produces an extraordinary sense of *flattening*. One loses hold on oneself as in any real way separate from the ordinary run of things, and with that comes the loss of any intimation of spiritual depth. We have been accustomed to seeing ourselves as special, as free of the world because of our capacity to form accurate representations (or, at least, powerful interpretations) *of* it. And that space—the gap between the representation/interpretation and the reality, with us on one side of it—is the space not just of our freedom but of our spirituality. One could say without exaggeration that gap is the space of the soul itself. In *Being and Time* that space disappears, closed up by an account of us as social practices all the way down, as continually self-elaborating sets of normalized behaviors, as just another species doing its best. Our most cherished and careful utter-

26. Indeed, this is the way I presented the matter in Chapter 1. It is, I believe, the standard account of Nietzsche's work among us end-of-century, Western intellectuals. Again I make no claim that this ordinary account is the very best way to read Nietzsche. See Chapter 1, n. 23, for a suggestion that Nietzsche's tropes can (and should) be read against their own metaphorical grain.

ances—apparently "about" a world "over there," a world capable of being captured in our sly sketches of it—flatten out into useful (or not) signals adapting us to our environment. Philosophy itself—this book, or even (in an altogether different order of magnitude) *Being and Time*—comes to sound like the low of the cow or the whistle of the cardinal: just another way of marking territory or discharging anxiety or fending off an enemy or facilitating sex. Our distance from the world evaporates; we melt down into the rushing stream of life, one more ripple on the flood.

This cannot but be disheartening to us. Such an account cannot but bleed off some of the *Pathos* that our constitutive practices normally have for us, a *Pathos* that keeps us functioning efficiently and effectively within those practices. When Nietzsche inquires whether untruth might not be a condition of life, he is thinking about this sort of danger: when we lose our typical conviction that our constitutive practices are grounded in something necessary and firm, will we still be able to give them our best efforts?[27] Might we not need the "untruth" of our convictions about "lasting importance" or "final truth" (or some such phrase invoking the absolute) in order to pay out the large amounts of effort some of our practices demand? Will we still find ourselves so *interested* in law, or philosophy, or physics, or novel-writing, or saving souls for Jesus, when we realize the radical contingency, not just of *our* commitment to the practice, but also of the practice itself? And with the last turn of the screw, with the passing of the belief (or at least the hope) that our most central practices are in some more-than-causal way "about" something external to themselves, won't our commitment to them be even further diminished? Won't we suffer from this closing of the soul's space, a closing made more plausible to us by Heidegger's existential analytic of Dasein? I think so. Of course our interest in our constitutive practices will not disappear entirely, no matter how forcefully Heidegger's observations strike one. That would be to confuse normal nihilism with pathology. Soon we shall return to the normalized practices of everyday life: classes must be taught; cats must be fed. But things will not be quite what they were. One's mood will have darkened; one's grip on things becomes, at least at the margins, more tenuous. One will be more susceptible to the dangers either of depression or of bumptiousness recounted in Chapter 1.

So far as I can see, there is nothing in *Being and Time* that can

---

27. Friedrich Nietzsche, *Beyond Good and Evil*, in *Basic Writings of Nietzsche*, trans. and ed. Walter Kaufmann (New York: Modern Library, 1968), sec. 4.

remove, or even significantly diminish, those dangers. Authenticity, in religious practices or otherwise, offers no secure protection against the sense of loss that accompanies a recognition of the groundlessness of *all* one's practices. Only average everydayness or inauthenticity could do that, and the one is doomed to be periodically shattered and the other is (presumably) not available to the smart folks like us who have now read Nietzsche and Heidegger. And it does us normal nihilists little good to reflect, as we no doubt will, that our susceptibility to the dangers of normal nihilism is itself just a contingent fact about *us:* that it is only because we have been constituted by quite particular religious and philosophical practices that we now experience the contingency of those practices as loss. (If there had been no Plato, there could have been no Nietzsche. If there had not been last night's illusion of the permanently full glass, there would be no hangover this morning.) But that recognition would help only if it brought release from the dehydrated selves we now are, and it doesn't. Heidegger insists that Dasein's authenticity, which is predicated on a recognition of the contingency of everything, including our own sense of loss at the recognition of such contingency, is nothing more than "an existentiell modification of the 'they.'" It does not spring us from the selves we are; it merely shows us some new "factical" possibilities for being what we will be.

Is one of those newly disclosed "factical" possibilities the possibility of being a Christian, or a Democrat, or a philosopher, or a physicist, without any hankering for a "ground" for being what one is? It is hard to imagine that sort of freedom within the framework of *Being and Time*. In Heidegger's book the notions of anxiety, falling, the call of conscience, and so forth, are presented as necessary features of Dasein's existence, as what Heidegger there calls *existentialia.* Although he is strongly averse to using the philosophically standard (and inappropriately metaphysical) term "category" in this connection (*BT,* 70), it is clear that his phenomenology of Dasein is supposed to reveal (what one might call) *structural* features of the existence of the entity you and I are. If it is a structural feature of Dasein's existence that it is always falling into the "they," and then periodically being awakened to that "lostness" by the call of conscience, and then reacting to that call with either authenticity or inauthenticity, and then gradually subsiding once again into the "they," then it is difficult to see that Dasein will ever be free of the anxiety and the loss of *Pathos* characteristic of normal nihilism. In Dasein itself, as the "they-self" it first and foremost is, there is the need for the "untruth" of average everydayness and its (largely tacit) assurances of "meaning." And when that "untruth" is ruptured, to be replaced either with authenticity or its opposite, there is always a sense of dislocation and loss ("anxiety") that goes with the wake-up call. Heidegger's insistence that he is using such notions as *anxiety* and *the call of conscience* as ontological rather than as psychological terms is a way of enforcing his claim that the pattern he is describing is structural, not adventitious. Our periodic sense of estrangement from our lives is not to be done away with better therapy or better drugs. It is rooted in existence itself. To be Dasein is to be subject to the crisis of one's contingency, and the philosophical mood of normal nihilism—the mood of loss brought on by self-devaluating values, by practices that periodically reveal themselves as "groundless"—is our characteristic response to that crisis.

To this point, then, Heidegger's overcoming of Cartesian and Husserlian transcendental subjectivity by means of his existential phenomenology of Dasein has not undercut the normal nihilism that seems to be the outcome of our cultural history as end-of-century, Western intellectuals. Indeed, it seems to add a more nuanced and persuasive account of why such an outcome, along with its characteristic dangers, is inevitable. While it would of course be too simple to use this single impasse to explain the turn in Heidegger's thought in the middle 1930s, it does play an important role in that shift. For all its lack of references to the philosopher, *Being and Time* was a text in constant colloquy with Nietzsche. That conversation becomes more explicit in the lecture courses of 1936–40 in Freiburg, courses being given just as the turn was taking place. Part of the problem with the early work was its failure to deliver us from the normal nihilism Nietzsche had described and facilitated. It is time now to look at (some of) Heidegger's later work to see whether its try at such deliverance is more successful.

4

POETIC DWELLING ON THE EARTH AS A MORTAL

Being and Time offers an iconoclastic way of thinking about what it means to be a human being, a way that promises escape from the Western philosophical tradition of transcendental subjectivity. Dasein is not the mighty ego-subject that alone grants meaning to brute matter, and Dasein's world is not a collection of objects lying present-to-hand before such a godlike—godlike not least in its tendency to vanish upon close inspection—center of reflexive consciousness. Dasein and its world always already interpenetrate; we are all—persons and our things—holistic social practices all the way down. But for all its distance from the discarnate self ordained by our dominant philosophical tradition, and its equal distance from the more rugged self we typically and unreflectively take ourselves to be, Heidegger's Dasein is still recognizably *us* in a crucial respect: it remains subject to our mood of normal nihilism. The ordinary *Pathos* of our constitutive linguistic and behavioral practices, and thus the ordinary pathos of the selves and lives those practices make possible, is inevitably diminished by Dasein's philosophical reflection on the conditions of their origin: a reflection instantiated in *Being and Time* itself, of course.

Heidegger recognized this consequence of his work, I believe, and beginning in the middle 1930s he sought to avoid it. One important motive behind the turn in his thinking was to find a way to be true to his critique of transcendental subjectivity while at the same time escaping the diminished *Pathos* of Dasein's world and life.[1] Early and

---

1. I do not claim it to be the only motive. As I have already indicated, Heidegger's work is rich enough to support several illuminating readings of its underlying motivations; mine is only one of them.

late, Heidegger is struggling to give an account of human being that doesn't identify us as *res cogitans,* but in *Being and Time* his account of Dasein ridicules Descartes only to find itself impersonating Nietzsche: the things of Dasein's world have their original Being as *Dasein's* things; they are what they are only as the products of—the expressions of—Dasein's "will to power"; that is, its attempt to preserve and enhance itself within the life into which it has been thrown. Things are *Zeug* ("gear"), and their significance—their Being—is granted them by their place as such equipment within some ongoing public project(s) of Dasein.

Even Dasein itself is, proximally and for the most part, a kind of *Zeug:* as a teacher I stand alongside the lectern and the chalkboard and the textbooks and the students as part of an endlessly elaborating linguistic and behavioral practice we call *education.* Just as the lectern in my classroom is only one among many, with its marginal differences from other lecterns playing little if any role in the practices of teaching and learning, so too am I only one among many, with my differences from other philosophy teachers coming into play only at the margins. If I were suddenly to die in the middle of term, I would soon be replaced by a colleague: the remaining lectures would be delivered, more or less as I would have delivered them; the final papers would be marked, more or less as I would have marked them; and the course grades would be assigned, more or less as I would have assigned them. The ship sails on, whatever the changes in the crew. Dasein too is—is *only*—will to power: a set of linguistic and behavioral practices both older than anything distinctively "mine" and always already devoted to their own preservation and enhancement; a will to power utterly without centralized self-consciousness or genuine personality. No wonder we are diminished by such self-knowledge.

In the later work there is an attempt to be post-Cartesian in another key. Without reverting either to Idealism or to transcendental ego-subjectivity, Heidegger wants to find an account of being human that, as he says, *lets things be.* Just as *Being and Time* intended to replace the philosophical representation of the *res cogitans* with the more "original" existential phenomenology of Dasein, his later work too is devoted to revealing a particular and "more primordial" way of understanding what it means to be a human being: he wants to uncover what it means *to dwell poetically on the earth as a mortal.*[2] That

---

2. It is important to note that one doesn't need to buy into Heidegger's assumption that the way of being human (i.e., the particular set of social practices) he wants to

is his summary phrase—or the most important one of them—intended to direct our attention to the kind of human life he wants to celebrate and to foster, the kind of life that escapes (so he believes) the dangers consequent upon our normal nihilism. In this chapter we shall look closely at each element of that life, a life described most fully in four essays published in the early 1950s, "Building Dwelling Thinking," "The Thing," "'. . . Poetically Man Dwells . . .'," and "The Question Concerning Technology."[3] Our approach to poetic dwelling will make its way by examining Heidegger's account of *the thing,* as it is in the character of the thing that the character of the life which produced that thing becomes visible. We shall begin by returning briefly to the thing as it is understood in *Being and Time.*

Things as Gear

An understanding of the self and an understanding of the self's world are always given together. The transcendental ego-subject, for example, cannot be without its various objects of representation; philosophical subjectivity and philosophical objectivity are notions precisely

---

plump for here is somehow "more original" or "deeper" than the one advocated by Descartes or by Plato, or that its claim on our attention is somehow justified by that alleged depth or originality. The point is a general one: in order to find value in (some of) what Heidegger says, one doesn't need to accept the implausible and totalitarian myths to which his most interesting claims are usually joined. The most pervasive, and perhaps most dangerous, of those myths is a myth of origins: that there was a pure and primordial state of grace from which we here in the West have gradually withdrawn, a state of grace somehow preserved in some Greek texts (and some poems of Hölderlin), and a state of grace to which we long to, or at least need to, return. This sort of story (and there's much more to it in Heidegger's version, of course) strikes me as both unwholesome and hugely implausible. At any rate, I think the most important of Heidegger's claims—those about "technology," "standing-reserve," "poetic dwelling," "the clearing," and so forth—can be detached from any such mythical trappings. As this chapter progresses, I shall be trying to thresh the philosophical wheat from the mythical chaff.

3. "Building Dwelling Thinking" (hereafter cited as "BDT," followed by a page number), "The Thing" (hereafter cited by "T," followed by a page number), and "'. . . Poetically Man Dwells . . .'" (hereafter cited as "PMD," followed by a page number) are all to be found in Martin Heidegger, *Poetry, Language, Thought,* trans. Albert Hofstader (New York: Harper and Row, 1971. Page numbers in my text refer to this volume. "The Question Concerning Technology" (hereafter cited as "QT," followed by a page number) is found in Martin Heidegger, *The Question Concerning Technology and Other Essays,* trans. William Lovitt (New York: Harper and Row, 1977). Page references in my text will be to this volume.

made for one another. So it is in *Being and Time* as well: the account of Dasein and the account of Dasein's world are correlative. As we have seen, part of the burden of *Being and Time* was to give an account of Dasein's world as a world of *things,* where things were understood not as the Cartesian *res* but as Greek *pragmata.* "The Greeks had an appropriate term for 'Things': *pragmata*—that is to say, that with which one has to do in one's concernful dealings (*praxis*)" (*BT,* 96f.). But in spite of the truth of their initial linguistic insight, the Greeks left the character of such things essentially unthought: "[T]hey thought of these 'proximally' as 'mere Things'" (*BT,* 97). This essentially thoughtless understanding of the thing was taken up into the Latin *res* and eventually became the representational object set over against the transcendental ego-subject of Cartesianism. *Being and Time* offered an account of the thing that moved it past Cartesian objectivity in two major respects. First, in Heidegger's account the Being of a thing is always already holistic: Things are the things they are only in terms of a set of back-and-forth references to lots of other things, things that also depend upon such references for their Being. The Being of my pen—its sense, its meaning, its significance as the particular kind of thing it is—is given by its place within such a holistic network, a network constantly humming with simultaneous back-and-forth references among the things that compose it. The *pen* writes with *ink,* on a piece of *paper,* bound in a *notebook,* placed on a *desk,* taking down words from the *chalkboard,* words written there by the *teacher,* for the use of the *student.* . . . To understand the Being of any one of these things is necessarily to understand the Being of some indefinite number of the others.

Second, this holistic network of back-and-forth references that grant Being to things has a particular character. To see, as the Greeks dimly did, that things are *pragmata* is to see that they are what they are in relation to our "concernful dealings." The network of things is a network of *praxis.* Thus things are, as Heidegger famously put it, equipment: *das Zeug,* "gear" to be used in the various projects of Dasein. The pen, the paper, the ink are (i.e., have their Being as) Dasein's writing gear, and Dasein's writing gear has (part of) its Being as (part of) Dasein's educational gear, and so on. If particular things are granted their Being as particular things by their holistic references to other particular things, then it is the various projects of Dasein that provide the context—that provide, to use a later Heideggerian word, the "clearing"—within which those back-and-forth references between things are possible. For things understood as *Zeug,* Dasein—understood always and only as the "they-self," as self-elaborating social practices "all the way down"—is the condition of their Being, of their sense, of their significance as the things they are. Thus in a notorious passage in *Being and Time* Heidegger seems to reduce all of "Nature" to equipment for Dasein: "The wood is a forest of timber, the mountain a quarry of rock; the river is water-power, the wind is wind 'in the sails.' As the 'environment' [i.e., as Dasein's *Umwelt*] is discovered, the 'Nature' thus discovered is encountered too" (*BT,* 100).

Later in that same paragraph, even Nature characterized as Romantic grandeur and pathos ("the flowers of the hedgerow," "the springhead in the dale") is described as what "assails *us* and enthralls *us* as *landscape*" (*BT,* 100; my emphasis). As "landscape," as a tableau set there for us to see and to enjoy (and perhaps ultimately to be enshrined in a *Kurort* brochure or made the destination of a tourist bus), the flowers and the spring fundamentally "belong to" Dasein for their Being.⁴ They remain, in the broadest sense, a kind of *Zeug* (recreation gear, refreshment gear, *Naturreligion* gear, at the limit even absolute otherness gear). One way or another, and even if only by way of privation, they take their Being from our "concernful dealings" with our world.

So in *Being and Time* Heidegger has moved our understanding of things (and thus of the world, understood there as a world of things) past the understanding of them as Cartesian *res,* as objects of representation set before a transcendental subject. But for Heidegger after the turn, this movement does not go nearly far enough. Even *Being and Time*'s "pragmatic" understanding of things makes them a sort of "object," in this case an object of Dasein's use in its various "dealings" with the world. Flowers, trees, and clear running water are always somehow there *for us,* and this sense of their being conditioned by Dasein's needs and purposes saps some (though not, of course, all) of their *Pathos.* A "landscape," however pristine and beautiful, is not the grandeur of Yosemite or the holy silence of Paestum. No piece of our "gear," however impressive, intricate, and effective it may be, has the modest and pregnant gravity of the Greek urn or of Cézanne's earthenware bowl holding apples. In the "pragmatic" account of them in *Being and Time,* things are devalued, stripped of some of their customary pathos, as is the life within which those things have their original Being.

Thus even in its deft evasion of Cartesianism, *Being and Time* re-

---

4. It is important to see that this is not metaphysical and epistemological idealism of the Berkeleyan sort. It's not the "brute actuality" of things that depends on Dasein; it's their Being, understood as sense, as significance.

mains unaware (according to Heidegger) of its captivity to something more insidious, something older and more powerful, something of which Cartesianism was—for all its genius—only a particular and incomplete expression. It is this older and craftier understanding of things that condemns even the Dasein of *Being and Time* to the destiny of normal nihilism as foretold by Nietzsche; and it is this understanding of things that Heidegger is trying to replace in the later work. He calls this nihilistic understanding *die Technik:* technology. It is technology that stands in the way of our full "poetic dwelling on the earth as mortals."

Technology and *Bestand*

For most of us the word "technology" calls to mind the use of machines and tools, especially machines and tools powered by nonhuman sources of energy, to attain and to further human interests. This familiar idea is what Heidegger calls "the instrumental and anthropological definition" of technology ("QT," 5), and of course it is correct so far as it goes. But there is, he thinks, a deeper, more revealing, "truer" way to characterize technology; a way to characterize its "essence." The key is to see that technology is itself a way of revealing things, a way of letting something come to presence. The world for Heidegger, early and late, is always a world of things, and the world of technology we all inhabit is distinguished by the particular way in which in that world things are revealed as the kind of things they are: "Technology is therefore no mere means. Technology is a way of revealing. If we give heed to this, another whole realm for the essence of technology will open itself up to us. It is the realm of revealing, i.e., of truth" ("QT," 12).

For Heidegger, truth is not fundamentally the correspondence of some representation with the reality it represents; truth is the coming into presence of something in such a way that it can be seen for what it is.[5] Truth is dis-closure, un-covering, un-concealment. Technology bring things into presence—lets them be seen—in a particular way; it reveals them as having a particular character, a particular Being. In that way technology belongs to the realm of *aletheia;* it is, one might say, a kind of truth. Thus technology is not, for Heidegger,

5. See Martin Heidegger, "On the Essence of Truth," reprinted in Martin Heidegger, *Basic Writings,* ed. David F. Krell (New York: Harper and Row, 1977). He takes back the identification of truth and *aletheia;* see below, this chapter.

primarily the machines and the power-tools we usually associate with the term: it is not just the hydroelectric plant on the banks of the Rhine or the superconducting supercollider half-buried in the Texas plains. Technology is a way—according to Heidegger, it is now the *fundamental* way—in which the world of human beings is constituted and populated; it is an overarching set of linguistic and behavioral practices that allow our things to appear around us in a particular way, that give to the things that appear in our world a particular Being, a particular significance, a particular sense. The machines and tools we think of as distinctively "technological," such as power plants and particle accelerators, are just the most obvious instances of the Being of *all* (or at least almost[6] all) our things as they are constituted by our most basic social practices.

And what is that characteristically technological Being of things?

> The revealing that rules throughout modern technology has the character of a setting-upon, in the sense of a challenging-forth. Such challenging happens in that the energy concealed in nature is unlocked, what is unlocked is transformed, what is transformed is stored up, what is stored up is in turn distributed, and what is distributed is switched about ever anew. Unlocking, transforming, storing, distributing, and switching about are ways of revealing. . . .
>
> What kind of unconcealment is it, then, that is peculiar to that which results from this setting-upon that challenges? Everywhere everything is ordered to stand by, to be immediately on hand, indeed to stand there just so that it may be on call for a further ordering. Whatever is ordered about in this way has its own standing. We call it the standing-reserve [*Bestand*]. . . . [The word *Bestand*] designates nothing less than the way in which everything presences that is wrought upon by the challenging revealing. Whatever stands by in the sense of standing-reserve no longer stands over against us as object. ("QT," 16f.)

The characteristic kind of thing brought to light by the practices of technology is *Bestand*, "standing-reserve": that which in an orderly way awaits our use of it for the further ordering of things. When I walk down to my study in the morning and glance at the computer on the desk, the computer, as the thing it is, is *Bestand*. It reveals itself to me as waiting patiently for me to turn it on, to "get its things in order," so I can use it to order and reorder those things and others.

---

6. The qualification will become important later on.

The data stored there—words, sentences, thoughts, bank balances—
await my command so they can be transformed, distributed, and
switched about: they too are *Bestand*. And it's not just the glass-and-
plastic machines that reveal themselves to me as standing-reserve.
As I glance out the window onto the leaves I have not yet raked, they
too are *Bestand:* they patiently await my collection of them so they
can be put on the compost heap ("stored up" so the energy in them
can later be "unlocked") or bagged for the garbage collection ("switched
about"). The very house I inhabit is, as we have famously been told, "a
machine for living in," with the window out of which I gaze a device
for the orderly collection of light (and the orderly retention of heat).
The house patiently awaits its tenants for their use of it in ordering
their lives; the land on which the house sits reveals itself through the
window as garden and as landscape, waiting for the orderly touch
that shapes and preserves and cultivates. The mugs on the kitchen
shelf, the television in the loft, the cereal in the pantry, the toothbrush on the bathroom sink: all "stand by" ("QT," 17) in the manner of
"stock," as resources awaiting their call to orderly use in the ordering
of things.

For us (almost) everything reveals itself as *Bestand*. Most of the
time, of course, we are not explicitly aware that our things have that
sort of Being. Our consciousness of them as "standing-reserve" shows
itself not in anything we say or think about them; rather, it shows
itself in how we comport ourselves to them in unself-conscious everyday action and reaction. How I "see" my television set or my coffee
mug or my toothbrush shows itself in the way I carelessly handle
them, in the way my eye passes over them without a pause, in
the way I irritably react when they don't perform as expected, in the
thoughtless way I dispose of them when they are no longer useful,
and so forth. When I press the remote-control button that turns on
the television set, I don't punch it with the same delicacy of movement that a father might use in playfully poking his child in the ribs
to tickle him; when I pick up my mug at the breakfast table there is
no tactile attention to its surface in the way there might be when I
am handling a piece of sculpture or stroking my cat's fur; when my
toothbrush is worn out I don't burn or bury it (as Scouts are taught to
do with the country's flag)—I pitch it into the garbage and hurriedly
rip another from its package. In all these unreflective ways (and
others) I show what these things are for me: "standing-reserve."

And the things just named wonderfully conspire in our treatment of
them as *Bestand*. The deftly shaped buttons on the television's remote
control are made to be punched again and again (by anyone) with no

delicacy or attention, just as the white ceramic coffee mug is intended to offer to my hand (and to any hand) no resistance or interest.[7] These things, like the toothbrush and innumerable others, are supposed to "disappear" into our use of them; they are supposed to be there for us only insofar as they are useful without impediment and without our careful scrutiny. "In themselves" they are, one wants to say, anonymous and interchangeable; they have no reality for us as particular things. My television set looks and performs much like every other one, and certainly my coffee mug and my toothbrush are virtually indistinguishable from an indefinitely large number of similar objects. Today's breakfast Grape-Nuts taste exactly like yesterday's—and (this is the crucial point) *that's what makes them what they are.* That anonymous interchangeability is what makes all these things the kind of thing they are; that's what gives them their Being as *Bestand.* Their nature, one might say, is to have only a general nature, a nature exhausted by their impersonal usefulness to us. All these things suppress their reality as particular things. Or, to put it more precisely (but in a way that will demand further exposition), all these things are things the Being of which covers over the manifold conditions of their coming to presence.

So the things that appear in a technological world appear as some kind of *Bestand.* But why should this be so? Why should technology reveal things in that particular way, as having that particular kind of Being? Here we are asking after the essence of technology: "We now name that challenging claim which gathers man thither to order the self-revealing as standing-reserve: *Ge-stell* [Enframing]" ("QT," 19).

The appearance of things as *Bestand* is the inevitable result of those social practices that have as their nature and point what Heidegger calls *ordering.* In his highly wrought idiom (an idiom certainly not "anonymous and interchangeable"), technology is a "challenging-forth" ("QT," 16), and "that challenging gathers man into ordering. This gathering concentrates man on ordering the real into standing-reserve" ("QT," 19).

What is this ordering? The dominant social practices constituting our world are practices that "enframe": they are practices that put things in their proper places in such a way that they are readily available to be put to use by us with a maximum of efficiency and a minimum of attention to the conditions of their appearing. Such practices impose a "grid" (*Gestell,* frame) upon things so that within that

---

7. Here there is no necessary implication that anyone in particular consciously said or thought, "Let's make the mug this way."

grid—within the completely and immediately surveyable space created by that grid—those things are completely and immediately loca-
table and thus are completely and immediately available for whatever use we find it appropriate to put them to. In this way things are
made *orderly*. They are located within a frame that transparently ori-
ents us to them and them to us; as a result of that perspicuous orien-
tation within the frame they are ours to use and reuse easily and
quickly and essentially thoughtlessly. And the point of our use of our
orderly things is further ordering. Under the spell of technology, we
come to order things primarily for the sake of ordering itself.

Of course the "frames" Heidegger has in mind here are *conceptual*
frames; following Rorty we might call them *vocabularies*. Technological practices are first of all practices of careful and precise linguistic
categorization. They are practices that "enframe" by way of assigning
clear senses to the things they constitute: the more clearly and completely we can say what kind of thing it is we are talking about, the
more available that thing for what we want to do with it. In the world
of technology there should be no linguistic surplus value. Meaning
and use should exactly coincide. That way of putting the matter is a
bit misleading, however, since it makes it seem that (1) knowing what
something is and means and (2) being able to do something with it
are two different matters, and that the first is the best path to the
second. In the world of technology, however, the two are precisely the
same; they are simultaneously given in the notion of *Bestand*. Things
are what they are only insofar as they patiently await our orderly use
of them in our ordering of things.

Three techniques of erasure help secure the dominance of these
technological practices. First, there is the erasure of the particular
frame itself. Our dominant social practices seek—usually successfully—to obscure the fact that they are just our dominant social practices. They are practices that, through a shrewd combination of oppor-
tunistic rhetoric and institutional power, present themselves as not
just the truth about things but as obvious common sense. Think how
often one hears it said (or at least implied): "Only a fool would deny
that . . ." What replaces the ellipsis varies from platform to platform,
but each such appeal to our "obvious common sense"—"Obviously
that is a toothbrush"; "Obviously Yosemite Valley is there for us to
enjoy"; "Obviously the spotted owl is not worth thousands of jobs";
"Obviously there are some moral absolutes"—is a way of disguising
the particular conceptual and institutional "frames" that make the
appeals effective (or not) in the first place. Each is a way, perhaps
decisive in certain instances, of causing us to forget that our particu-

lar way of placing things in relation to one another and to ourselves is itself a particular historical construction. Technology is a frame that blinds us to itself as a frame. It is a way of revealing that makes us forget that it is *a* way of revealing.

Second, technological practices obscure not just their own character as particular ways of revealing things; they more generally blind us to the necessity of there being "ways of revealing" at all. Operating within such practices we forget not just that *this* particular account of things is contingent; we forget that such contingency is the condition of *any* account of what a thing is. "Thus the challenging Enframing . . . conceals revealing itself and with it that wherein unconcealment, i.e., truth, comes to pass" ("QT," 27). Under the spell of characteristically technological practices we forget "revealing itself"; that is, we forget history, and ourselves as historical beings. We forget that—to use a Nietzschean image—perspective is not just an accident of this or that particular vocabulary or social practice; perspective is the necessary condition of any seeing at all. We are not gods, and our lack of a divine standpoint is not an unfortunate accident perhaps at some point to be remedied. All our seeing is, and always will be, a perspectival seeing; all our seeing will come as the result of a "revealing"; that is, as the result of some contingent concatenation of opportunities and abilities, conceptual and otherwise. Engaged in certain practices—the ones Heidegger calls *technological*—we forget this necessary contingency, this necessary historical condition of all our thinking and acting.

Third, technological practices erase the particular conditions of the particular things they bring to presence. Here it is useful to think again about coffee mugs, toothbrushes, and Post Grape-Nuts. Specific instances of these things are, as I put it above, largely anonymous and interchangeable. This coffee mug looks and feels no different from that one; this bowl of Grape-Nuts tastes just like the one I had yesterday; any Oral-B 60 is much the same as any other.[8] What is crucial to see is that this anonymity and this interchangeability are not just accidents, and not just unfortunate features of living in a society rich enough to mass-produce breakfast foods and implements of personal hygiene; they are essential to our need for these things readily to "disappear" into our use of them. In practices given over (as Heidegger thinks almost our whole life is) to ordering for the sake of ordering, the more easily and quickly an entity can be thoughtlessly

---

8. Of course there are differences at the margins. The point is that those differences, to the extent they can't be suppressed, are not supposed to matter.

taken up into its particular task of ordering, the better. Explicit attention to the tool one is using distracts one from the job the tool is being used to accomplish and in that way makes the successful completion of the job less likely. If I notice the texture of the handle of my coffee mug, and then begin to wonder how it was made, and maybe even to wonder who made it, and under what conditions, I may be led into a train of thought that disrupts my normal and efficient progress from breakfast to newspaper to car to classroom, thus introducing a bit of disorder into my quite ordinary life. And—to push the matter in a more sentimental and unlikely direction—if I become aware of the fact that my mug was made in China (as indeed it was), and then begin to think about the economic and political conditions of the workers who made it, and then am moved to write a letter to my congressional representative protesting the continuance of most-favored-nation trade status for China in light of its atrocious disregard of human rights, and so on, my attention to my coffee mug might actually cause an even larger disorder. The more "unconditional" and "smoother" the appearance of the thing, the more readily it disappears into our use of it. The less we pay attention to particular things *qua* things, the more efficiently we carry on with the tasks we have inherited from the social practices that have constituted us.[9] An impetus to ordering for the sake of ordering—Heidegger's characterization of the essence of technology—will seek to efface anything that impedes such ordering. Thus it will seek to produce things that efface their own conditions of production. No wonder things like coffee mugs and television sets are so anonymous and interchangeable.

Thus it is also no wonder that our life—the life of end-of-century, Western intellectuals—is a life of normal nihilism. Such a devaluation of everything, even of the highest values that direct our lives as steady and efficient technocrats, is an inevitable consequence of our recognizing—perhaps only intermittently, of course—that the things that presence before us (including those cherished "highest values" of ours) are no more and no less than *Bestand*. To see ourselves as ordered by ordering to order things for the sake of ordering—late Heidegger's gloss on seeing ourselves as "social practices all the way down," which was itself a gloss on Nietzsche's claim that we are all finally "will to power"—is to see ourselves as something less impressive than we might have thought. The customary *Pathos* of our things and practices must be compromised by our awareness of their technological character.

9. The connection to what he says in *BT* about *Zeug* is obvious.

But why should the recognition of all our things as *Bestand* lead to their (and our) devaluation? Why should we not be able happily to accept that account of their Being? Conceived in late Heideggerian terms, our mood of normal nihilism originates in the conflict between (1) the apparent unconditionality of our things as they function within our ordinary practices of ordering and (2) the particular conditionality they exhibit when revealed by philosophical reflection as *Bestand*. Caught up in our everyday world of technological practices, and availing ourselves of the "standing-reserve" of things we bring to presence and use within those practices, we proceed as if our lives were unconditional. Neither our practices nor our things announce themselves as dependent for their Being on the marriage of several contingencies, both material and conceptual. My successful employment of my toothbrush or my television set requires that, to some extent or other, I be able to forget about them and the "frames" that make them what they are. My ability to give myself over fully to the practices within which they function depends upon my ability to see through my implements, and therefore finally to see through the practices themselves. To be *in* the practices; not to reflect upon them: that is the mark of their full pathos for us. We—we technocrats— value above all else that sort of unimpeded access to our continuing activity of ordering for the sake of ordering. The full pathos of our practices is in their ability to consume us, to obliterate any hint of their conditionality, to take us up into them without remainder: to make *us* an orderly part of our ordering.

This obliteration of contingency is never—or not yet—complete, however. Not only do accidents happen (e.g., the broken hammer of *Being and Time*), there yet survive other practices alongside our ordinary technological ones. These practices—Heidegger's deliberately recalcitrant philosophical writing is itself a good example—remind us, not only of their own conditionality, but of the conditionality of everything else as well. Once Heidegger has reminded us that a toothbrush (or an academic essay) is *Bestand,* some of its transparency is clouded. It obtrudes itself upon our notice in a way it heretofore did not. This phenomenon of obtrusion becomes even more marked the higher one goes in one's progress of self-reflection. When one turns one's attention to the values, not just to the specific material implements, that presence within one's practices as *Bestand,* the recognition of their conditionality is of quite powerful moment. The new visibility of those values *as values,* that is, as a "standing-reserve" of higher-order implements of interpretation employed for the sake of ordering, renders them less fully available to our efficient use of them. The more attention we have to give to our structures of interpretation, the less are we given over to our activity of interpretation itself. As the technological activity itself becomes the visible object of our attention, and thus comes to be seen *as* such technological activity, the *Pathos*—the impressiveness, the power—of that activity is diminished.[10]

So it is—thus far, at least—that the dominion of technology is not complete. As yet we still are sometimes made aware of the conditionality of our lives; in particular, we are still, even if dimly, aware of the character of most of our things (including our values) as *Bestand*. And with that awareness, which of course may show itself more in our everyday unreflective comportment to things rather than in any explicit assertions, comes that mood of nagging loss and incompletion—the loss of power—I have been calling normal nihilism. It isn't merely the recognition of contingency or conditionality that produces such enervation; it is that recognition occurring within a life that in its dominant practices must deny it. Normal nihilism is thus (to use a Nietzschean image for it) "the ghost at the feast": the return of the repressed, a return that disconcerts the practices, and thus the persons, that repressed it. Normal nihilism is in that way a symptom, a distressing indication of our (typically hidden) normal existence as orderly, ordering technological beings. If we were to respond to it thoughtfully, our symptomatic distress could be the first step in a cure. That is why Heidegger can say, in Hölderlin's voice: "But where the danger is, grows / The saving power also" ("QT," 28). But a painful symptom can call up another, and much more dangerous sort of response. It may provoke the sufferer merely to suppress the occasion of the suffering, rather than to eliminate its cause. The danger of our normal nihilism—a danger embodied either as unbridled addiction to

10. By speaking in this paragraph (and in other places in this chapter) of what "one" does or what "we" do, I make it sound as if we were discrete selves who willfully associate ourselves with various social practices and who take up particular psychological attitudes (e.g., despair, boredom, joy) to our lives. From Heidegger's point of view, of course, such quasi-Cartesian locutions are merely shorthand ways of talking about the particular elaborations—linguistic and otherwise—of the particular social practices constituting some form of human life. We are, he believes, "social practices all the way down"; there are no Cartesian or Husserlian egos to adopt particular practices or to have particular attitudes toward them. Thus the "loss of pathos" defining our mood of normal nihilism is not an ego's "psychological attitude" to its life. Rather, it is a public mood, understood as a particular linguistic or behavioral elaboration of a practice (or set of practices), an elaboration that to some extent clogs the smooth flow of that practice in its attempt to efficiently order things for the sake of ordering. For ease of composition and comprehension I shall sometimes use the familiar quasi-Cartesian linguistic forms, but the reader should at every such point be able to substitute the Heideggerian translations of them.

novelty or as total submission to the normal—is the danger that our need to suppress the disorder consequent upon the recognition of contingency will rebound with redoubled force upon our things and upon ourselves, that one way or another we shall be able to remove all barriers to the efficient ordering of things for the sake of ordering; that there will be no life for us outside the mall.

Gathering the Fourfold

Having described *die Technik* as its nihilistic alternative, it is now time to return to the description of the kind of life Heidegger calls "poetic dwelling on the earth as a mortal." In "Building Dwelling Thinking" Heidegger unambiguously identifies *dwelling* as the basic form of human life: "The way in which you are and I am, the manner in which we humans *are* on the earth, is *Buan*, dwelling. To be a human being means to be on the earth as a mortal. It means to dwell" ("BDT," 147).

By calling to mind here the Old High German word *buan* (which originally meant "to remain, to stay in a place") Heidegger is trying to forge a link between dwelling and the modern German word *Bauen*, which means "to build." Dwelling is building; building is dwelling. To be a human being "is always a staying with things" ("BDT," 151); the *things* one has *built* through one's *dwelling*. To be a human being is to bring things to presence before oneself and others, either through practices of cultivation (Latin: colere, cultura) or through practices of construction (Latin: aedificare). Dwelling is, therefore, always building things. Yes, but what are the things that human dwelling builds? In those practices we have been calling technological ones, the things brought to presence before us are there as *Bestand*, as the "standing-reserve" that awaits and makes possible our ordering for the sake of ordering. Heidegger is groping for a different notion of the thing, a notion that—in his typically mythical way—he thinks of as older and truer. In "The Thing" he focuses our attention on a simple earthen jug, presumably the kind of thing one might have found on any Black Forest farmstead a couple of centuries ago, and thus presumably also a thing (largely) uncorrupted by *die Technik*. What does it mean, he asks, to say that such a jug is a *thing?*

As is typical for Heidegger, he finds a key in the history of the word.[11]

11. The Heideggerian reliance on etymology one sees here is itself typically mythical:

In his account, the Old High German word for "thing" (*dinc*) means a gathering, "and specifically a gathering to deliberate on a matter under discussion, a contested matter" ("T," 174). From this (alleged) etymological insight he draws the conclusion that the thing is something that *gathers:* "This manifold-simple gathering is the jug's presencing. Our language denotes what a gathering *is* by an ancient word. That word is: thing" ("T," 174).

At first glance, this emphasis on gathering seems just a florid way of calling attention to the sort of meaning-holism we saw so clearly in *Being and Time*. Just as "there 'is' no such thing as an equipment" (*BT,* 97), there 'is' no such thing as a thing. Just as any one piece of Dasein's gear necessarily "refers to" other pieces of that gear (a *pen* is to be filled with *ink* for writing on *paper,* and so forth), so it is that any thing (such as a jug) is the thing it is only insofar as it presences in a social practice alongside other things (such as wine, plates, bread, cups, and so forth). A thing always "gathers" the other things that belong together with it. Its Being—its significance, its meaning, its sense—is always given in relation to those other things, just as their Being is always given in relation to it. But by calling a thing something that gathers, Heidegger has in mind more than this simple meaning-holism borrowed from *Being and Time*. A thing does not merely gather other things; *a thing gathers the fourfold* ("BDT," 153). Here are some crucial passages:

> *The fundamental character of dwelling is . . . sparing and preserving.* It pervades dwelling in its whole range. That whole range reveals itself to us as soon as we reflect that human being consists in dwelling and, indeed, dwelling in the sense of the stay of mortals on the earth.
>
> But "on the earth" already means "under the sky." Both of these *also* mean "remaining before the divinities" and include "belonging to men's being with one another." By a *primal* oneness the four—earth and sky, divinities and mortals—belong together in one.

---

it depends on the mythical idea that each of the "elemental words" had some pure and distinct meaning (a meaning from the Golden Age before we knew philosophical sin) and that saving remnants of that original meaning are retained in the great philosophical languages like German and Greek, where they can be unearthed by insightful Heideggerian etymology. As I have said, it is possible and (I think) desirable to separate Heidegger's insights from their mythical wrappings.

> This simple oneness of the four we call *the fourfold*. Mortals *are* in the fourfold by *dwelling*. But the character of dwelling is to spare, to preserve. Mortals dwell in the way they preserve the fourfold in its essential being, its presencing. Accordingly, the preserving that dwells is fourfold.
>
> Dwelling preserves the fourfold by bringing the presencing of the fourfold into things. But things themselves secure the fourfold *only when* they themselves *as* things are let be in their presencing. ("BDT," 149, 150, 151)

Think of the fourfold as the intersection of two axes. At the head of each of the four semi-axes is one of "the four": earth, sky, mortals, divinities. One axis is formed at either end by earth and sky; the other is formed at either end by divinities and mortals. At the center, at the intersection of the axes, is *the thing*.

What does Heidegger intend "the four" to be? His description of them is typically overblown and cryptic.

> Earth is the serving bearer, blossoming and fruiting, spreading out in rock and water, rising up into plant and animal. . . . The sky is the vaulting path of the sun, the course of the changing moon, the wandering glitter of the stars, the year's seasons and their changes, the light and dusk of day, the gloom and glow of night, the clemency and inclemency of the weather, the drifting clouds and blue depth of the ether. . . . The divinities are the beckoning messengers of the godhead. Out of the holy sway of the godhead, the god appears in his presence or withdraws into his concealment. . . . The mortals are the human beings. They are called mortals because they can die. ("BDT," 149f.)

Each of the four is, I think, intended to put us in mind of some one of the particular conditions that make possible ("grant") the life that brought to presence the actual thing before us; each of the four is what one might call a particular *dimension* of that conditionality.[12]

---

12. It will be clear to the philosophical reader that here I am reading Heidegger as a transcendental philosopher in the tradition of Kant, the father of all those thinkers who conceive the philosopher as calling attention to the necessary conditions for the possibility of various phenomena. (In this way Kant is the first philosopher to have thematized *indebtedness* as the fundamental philosophical category.) Heidegger is Kantian as well in his insistence, discussed below, that the conditions discovered by philo-

Conditionality is indebtedness. The conditions of a life, and thus the conditions of the particular things—poems, jugs, antibiotics—which that life brings forth, are what make that life (and those things) possible as such. Any actual and determinate life is possible only in virtue of something not itself, something "prior" (both temporally and logically), to which that life, and all its good and ills, is indebted. To live, therefore, is to owe one's life; to be human is to be always already in debt. The point may seem banal, but in our ordinary technological practices of production every effort is made to obscure those conditions, and thus our indebtedness. The coffee mug, the toothbrush, the television set—all these present to us a smooth and untroubled surface; they offer no impediment to our use of them. In that use they easily and helpfully disappear without calling any attention to themselves and to the life of which they are expressions. It is as if these things appear before us without human intervention at all: when things are going well in their use, there are certainly no indications of the presence of the particular human beings who made them and for whom they were made. Here is a homely example to illustrate the point. Last night there was a television news story about stubbornly harsh economic conditions in southern California; the story featured a couple of manufacturing plants that were considering leaving the state in search of cheaper labor, lower taxes, and less stringent regulation. One of these businesses made suitcases of a kind I happen to own, and I was shocked to see from the videotape that much of the assembly of the product is done by hand. I was taken aback as I saw my suitcase being put together—somewhat awkwardly, and at no small expense of energy—by a middle-aged woman in a sort of mobcap, wielding a large and apparently heavy high-speed drill. Nothing in the suitcase itself, so sleek and high-tech in its appearance, gives any indication of that woman or of her effort: buying and using my suitcase, I had not thought of her at all.[13] Nothing gives any indication of the materials—in every sense of the term—out of which it is made, and to which it is indebted. It is as if the suitcase appeared in the luggage-shop by magic: from nowhere in particular; for the use of

---

sophical reflection are ultimately ahistorical. In his view, *the fourfold* names dimensions of indebtedness common to every human life in every time and place.

13. And from Heidegger's point of view, it would be a mistake to moralize that failure, that is, to blame it on my own insensitivity or carelessness. The obscurity of the conditions of the suitcase (the woman and her effort among them) is rooted in the suitcase itself, in its sleek surfaces and in the practices of travel in which it is incorporated; not (only) in the blindness of its user.

no-one in particular. It appears to our use unconditionally so that it can disappear in that use completely. It is *Bestand.*

By contrast, each of "the four" calls our attention to a specific condition of the life that produced the thing presencing there before us. To call attention to the *earth,* to start with that dimension of the fourfold, is to call attention to the thing as conditioned by that which is ultimately "material," that is, by that which is finally beyond our power to make or to name. Earth is the stuff out of which a thing is made. At a first pass, one may think of that "material" as something concrete and namable, like ore or soil or bark; but those "raw materials" (as we end-of-century technocrats like to call them) are instances of something more abstract and original. Earth is not simply that which is (in our sense) "physical"; it is Heidegger's way of talking about that which is *an sich.* To speak of the Earth is to speak of the *substance* of things. Earth is the dark *physis,* that which rises up out of itself to confront us with its brute reality; it is that mystery which challenges us to respond to it by trying to draw it out into the light of our common understanding. Earth is that condition of human life that confronts us with the adamant "thereness" of certain unnamable but unignorable powers. It is a grasp out of the darkness; a seizing that shakes us into awareness of itself, demanding to be named. But earth has no final name. To speak of the earth is to be reminded of that always unilluminated darkness from which arises whatever we can see and thus learn to give words to. But to speak of the earth is also to speak of the "serving bearer." It is to recognize that the dark mystery of those powers that can never be finally named is also that out of which all that we make is made. If there were no darkness that surges and rises out of itself, no earth, then there would be nothing to emerge into the light of our conceptions, nothing to demand that light, however flickering. Our life of enlightened things is sheltered by that darkness.

Any life is a life lived "on the earth." Any life is, first of all, a life the illuminating conceptions of which are always conceptions of something that transcends those conceptions even as it makes them possible. The steady and reliable illuminations furnished by our constitutive linguistic and behavioral practices are always the lighting-up of something "in itself" dark, in the sense that in one way or another in its brute "materiality" it will challenge and defeat our attempts to constrain it only to our enlightened uses. Sooner or later the ceramic coffee mug will decisively "assert its materiality"; sooner or later it will, perhaps through breakage or prolonged disuse, withdraw from the shadowless light of our thoughtless use of it into the darkness of

its brute "stuff." It will fall out of our practices and become nothing at
all. Or, to use a different sort of example, consider a painting that
emerges from a host of academic daubs to challenge the scholastic
artworld certainties of its time. The painting's mystery, its power to
affect us and to render void all our previous assumptions of what a
painting might be, its demand that we find a new name for what it is
and what it aspires to—all that is an exhibition of the earth from
which that painting has been quarried. And here the mug or the
painting are just images for a condition of *all* intelligibility: that
which is now intelligible was not so, at some point, and at some point
will not be so again. Before there was a world of illuminated things,
there was the earth; and after this (or any) world of particular things,
particular practices, has passed away, the "earth" will remain. In
Heidegger's idiom, *earth* is a metaphor for the dark and unnamable
substance of all things. And that substance, dark as it is, is the necessary condition of any thing that is.

But a life lived "on the earth" is also a life lived "under the sky." In
Heidegger's usage, the metaphor has two resonances. First, the sky is
the source of light; it is only "under the sky" and its varying degrees
of luminance that anything can be seen as the thing it is. In this way,
to speak of the sky is to speak of those ongoing social practices—in
full flower or in decline; bright as day or dim as the dusk—within
which things come to presence as the things they are. A pen is a pen
only because (along with ink, paper, desks, teachers, and so forth) it is
a part of a coherent and ramified set of social practices that involve it
in writing. It is those writing-practices that "grant" the pen its Being
as a pen; it is only in the light of those writing-practices that the pen
can be seen for—can BE—what it is. Out of the "darkness" of earth,
something—some particular (kind of) thing—proceeds into the "light"
of our common understanding and use. In this way, a thing is the
thing it is "under the sky" of those illuminating linguistic and behavioral practices that constitute us and our common world. Those practices, whatever they are, are the conditions for whatever presences
within their shelter.

But to speak of the sky is to speak of more that just those practices
that light up things. The sky is "the vaulting path of the sun, the
course of the changing moon," and thus to speak of the sky is Heidegger's way of talking about the fit (or, more likely, the lack of fit) of the
human and its purposes into the inhuman and its impersonal cycles
and necessities. Our constitutive social practices—patterns of normalized and normalizing behaviors—are not the only regularities
that appear to our reflection. Our projected rounds and congruencies

are conditioned on patterns we can come to see are prior to them. Our lives, we might say (using an effective nominalization), always already answer to Nature. Under the spell of technology, human beings take themselves to be the center and the point of all things; there is little awareness, and even less overt acknowledgment, that our activities and projects are set within—and must ultimately accommodate themselves to—the inhuman, uncaring cycles of the "natural" world. The *Bestand* of technology appears to offer itself up to our use, and thus to offer *us* up to our technological practices, without reference to anything beyond ourselves. Our sky—our horizon—becomes *the* sky.

Again an example can serve as an image for Heidegger's philosophical point. Consider the normal way an American suburb is developed. The land is plotted and shaped so that maximum economic value can be realized in its sale—roads are laid out and paved, flows of water are diverted or enclosed, trees are cut down or planted, and so forth—and then houses are built on the lots that have been divided and sold. In a typical suburb, there may be no attention paid either to the natural features of the countryside being developed or to the climate—physical or cultural—within which the house will live. For example, the houses will typically not be designed or sited so as to take maximum advantage of the path of the sun in winter and summer; likewise the roads will be graded to facilitate ease of traffic flow (or to ensure an economically valuable personal privacy), not in accordance with the natural occurrence of rocks, streams, or trees. The style of the houses—New England saltbox, Old South mansion, Tuscan villa, Swiss chalet—will be determined by the whim (and the pocketbook) of the builder or by the "design concept" of the developer, rather than by the climate or the land. What matter that the summer sun floods the living room: just add more capacity to the air conditioner. What matter that this is a pencil-pine forest in Piedmont, South Carolina: if you want a French château, you can get it. Such houses forget, or perhaps actually deny, that they live "under the sky," and so do the people who live in them. That is, such houses are designed and built so as to conceal the conditions of both their building and their occupancy. They deliberately reflect neither the culture out of which they come nor the climate within which they will be used. Such things as these conceal the ways that the inhuman with its inflexible demands is prior to—is a granting condition of—the human with its temporary projects.

So the first axis on which the thing is situated is the axis formed by earth and sky: the thing is set "on the earth" and "under the sky." The second axis also reveals conditions of the life that produced the thing;

it is the axis formed by the divinities and the mortals. The divinities, says Heidegger, are "the beckoning messengers of the godhead." They are presences from another world, annunciators of a place of haleness and wholeness. The divinities are the reality both of human need for such weal and of our hope that it will someday be vouchsafed to us. "Mortals dwell in that they await the divinities as divinities. In hope they hold up to the divinities what is unhoped for" ("BDT," 150). Need and eschatological hope are (according to Heidegger) *conditions* of human life. To recognize one's fundamental neediness, to acknowledge that one is not the healthy and complete being one can imagine—if only inchoately—oneself to be, to look to the future for the gift of one's completion brought on the wings of a presence from another world—these are not just psychological tics or cultural quirks. They are, according to Heidegger, part of the matter of what it is to be us.

The things produced by technology conceal both the need and the hope. By holding out the promise of transparent availability to our current projects, and even more by frequently making good on that promise, these things hide from us our irremediable lack of wholeness; they also obscure the need to look forward to the apocalyptic future in readiness for the advent of the presence that will heal us. By making themselves and their practices invisible in our active immersion in them, our everyday things expertly fold us into the present they create, or into the future seamlessly extrapolated from that present. And by successfully meeting needs they have themselves largely created, they blind us to our need for something radically new and whole.

In spite of using the trope of theological language, it is clear that Heidegger is not identifying the divinities with the personified supernatural presences of vulgar religious belief. His presences from another world may be poems, paintings, works of philosophy, revolutionary political practices, new vocabularies of self-description: in short, whatever holds the promise of our healing self-transformation. To "await the divinities" is to solicit from the future—presumably by living a certain way here and now—the advent of some new "god" and its dispensation. And to live with this sort of attitude toward the future is at the same time to live in past and present in a particular fashion. Present and past are both wrapped up in one's eschatological hope. The apocalyptic future, though impossible to force, must be prepared for; and present and past are the story in which the traces of the god—traces both of absence and of coming presence—must be discerned: "The turning of the age does not take place by some new god, or the old one renewed, bursting into the world from ambush at some time or other. Where would he turn on his return if men had not first prepared an abode for him? How could there ever be for the god an abode fit for a god, if a divine radiance did not first begin to shine in everything that is?"[14]

The second constituent of the second axis is the mortals. "The mortals are the human beings. They are called mortals because they can die. To die means to be capable of death as death" ("BDT," 150). Everything at some point ceases to exist, but only human beings die. Only human beings live in awareness of their inevitable end: that is to be capable of death as death. "Mortals dwell in that they initiate their own nature—their being capable of death as death—into the use and practice of this capacity, so that there may be a good death" ("BDT," 151). Death is not an accident of human life; it is its very condition. The presence of death—of insuperable limitation, of our world's contingency, of inevitable failure at the last—is what makes a human life distinctively human: "Only man dies, and indeed continually, as long as he remains on earth, under the sky, before the divinities" ("BDT," 150). To be a human being is to be mortal and, in some way or another, to acknowledge (even if only by frantic denial) that mortality. To dwell is to dwell as a mortal, and to dwell is to build; so the things one builds are things that—either by way of fullness or by way of privation—show the conditions of the dwelling that produced them. Death is Heidegger's trope in this essay for conditionality itself. To know oneself to be mortal is not (merely) to know that one will oneself die; it is to know that all one knows and most cares about— everything: every thing—is contingent upon a constellation of circumstances that will someday no longer hold together. To acknowledge one's mortality is to acknowledge that abyss over which everything precariously juts, which is the abyss of pure, pointless time: time which is not history. Most of the things brought to light by our ordinary technological practices do not show the condition of our mortality in that sense. They are not things that acknowledge "death as death." Quite the opposite: things like my coffee mug and my television set conceal not just their ends but my own. With their ready availability and their featureless surfaces, they ease me into my everyday practices; in the normal case they offer me no friction, no im-

---

14. Martin Heidegger, "What Are Poets For?" (hereafter cited as "WPF" followed by a page number). The essay can be found in Martin Heidegger, *Poetry, Language, Thought.* There is here, as in many places in Heidegger, an unwholesome political resonance, a yearning to be ravished by some new and powerful presence, one that does not answer to anything but itself. I do not think Heidegger's work is vitiated by such ugly and antidemocratic resonances, real as they are.

pediment, nothing to remind me of my incapacities and of my final inability to sustain myself. These days even the things intimately concerned with the fact of our physical death obscure what they serve: a contemporary coffin has the metallic sheen and boxy strength of a Lexus; in neither thing is there any intimation of the junkyard crusher or of the inevitable depredations of adipocere. The conditions of the life that produced the thing are covered over in the thing itself.

Measuring Oneself Against the Godhead

To dwell is to build, to build is to build things, and things gather the fourfold. All human life is, one way or another, a dwelling and a building life, even the kind of life Heidegger calls technology. But the practices of technology produce things that only privatively gather the fourfold. The things of technology are things that (largely successfully) cover over the most general conditions of the life out of which they come.

As a paradigmatic alternative to the things of technology, Heidegger offers the Black Forest farmhouse:

> Let us think for a while of a farmhouse in the Black Forest, which was built some two hundred years ago by the dwelling of peasants. Here the self-sufficiency of the power to let earth and heaven, divinities and mortals enter *in simple oneness* into things, ordered the house. It placed the farm on the wind-sheltered mountain slope looking south, among the meadows close to the spring. It gave it the wide overhanging shingle roof whose proper slope bears up under the burden of snow, and which, reaching deep down, shields the chambers against the storms of the long winter nights. It did not forget the altar corner behind the community table; it made room in its chamber for the hallowed places of childbed and the "tree of the dead"—for that is what they call a coffin there: the *Totenbaum*—and in this way it designed for the different generations under one roof the character of their journey through time. A craft which, itself sprung from dwelling, still uses its tools and frames as things, built the farmhouse. ("BDT," 160)

Notice how this house, as a thing, "gathers the fourfold"; that is, makes clear in the thing itself the conditions of the life out of which the thing comes. The house is set "on the earth" and "under the sky." Its materials—wood and stone that will always bear the physical marks of their working—show the recalcitrance to human purpose of the dark *physis* from which they have been extricated by human labor and to which they will someday return. Its placement in relation to light, wind, and water acknowledges both the "bright sky" of the practices (of farming, of cooking, of childrearing) within which it comes to presence and the priority of the inhuman cycles of the seasons and of pure bodily need to any plans and projects we may voluntarily undertake. The presence of childbed and coffin corner are reminders of the specifically temporal character of human existence, and in particular of the death that awaits us all. The altar with its crucifix is a way of showing the openness to the future as the site of apocalyptic transformation for which the family hungers; it symbolizes the way in which the divinities, as messengers from another world to come, are always already being made present in our waiting for them. And notice how this house, as a thing, gathers all the conditions of its life "in simple oneness." No one of the features we have mentioned is an *ornament* (as they would be, if one were to imagine this house transported bodily to an end-of-century American suburb). All these features of the thing play off one another in an organic whole. The life within which the house comes to presence contains all four dimensions of our condition, and acknowledges both them and their necessary interpenetration. The thing exists at the intersection of the two axes, and none of "the four" is separable from the others. "The united four are already strangled in their essential nature when we think of them only as separate realities, which are to be grounded in and explained by one another" ("T," 180). That is, these conditions—the conditions that make the thing the thing it is—are not themselves *things*. They are not *super*things that "ground" the Being of the things there are. In this way the fourfold is in no way metaphysical; it escapes the Platonic paradigm, in which the Being of beings is itself identified as a being. The fourfold cannot be presenced as such. It is the "dimension" within which all presencing happens.

So the dwelling life is a life that brings to presence things that carry on their faces the conditions—both particular conditions and the overall conditionality—of the life out of which they come. All human lives are lives of dwelling, but not all such lives dwell *fully*. Not all our practices are practices that bring forth things that are radiant with the conditions of the life that brought them into being. (Technological practices do not.) Those practices that do, Heidegger calls *poetic* dwelling, taking the phrase from some lines by Hölderlin.

> Full of merit, yet poetically, man
> Dwells on this earth.[15]

"Making is, in Greek, *poiesis*" ("PMD," 214). And the making talked about in that word is different from the kind of making that produces the *Bestand* of technology.

> This producing that brings forth [namely, *poiesis*], e.g., erecting a statue in the temple precinct, and the ordering that challenges [*die Technik*] . . . are indeed fundamentally different, and yet they remain related in their essence. Both are ways of revealing, of *aletheia*. ("QT," 21)

Both *poiesis* and technology are ways of bringing things forth into presence, but the things they bring forth are very different. The things brought forth by the practices of technology are *Bestand;* but the things built by the practices of poetic dwelling "gather the four-fold." They make explicit the holistic concatenation (the "appropriating mirror-play" ["T," 179]) of the fundamental conditions of the life that produced them. In this way, and since both *die Technik* and *poiesis* belong to the realm of *aletheia,* one can say that the things and practices of poetic dwelling are truer than the things and practices of technology. These things and practices reveal more; they conceal less. In particular, and most important, they tell the truth about us as the conditional beings we are: "Thinking in this way, we are called by the thing as the thing. In the strict sense of the German word *bedingt,* we are the be-thinged, the conditioned ones. We have left behind us the presupposition of all unconditionedness" ("T," 181).

"We have left behind us the presupposition of all unconditionedness." One might say: to live in practices that bring forth things that gather the fourfold is to acknowledge one's *autochthony.* It is to have given up the illusion of oneself as a radically individual center of pure self-awareness, or pure will, that floats free of any particular history. By acknowledging that one is "be-thinged," one has acknowledged that one is not the transcendental subject held forth by the Western philosophical tradition since Descartes. And yet one is not merely the *Zeug*-using Dasein of *Being and Time,* either. One is a builder of things; one is, in the deepest sense, a poet. By *letting things be* one is cooperating with the earth in the bringing forth of *truthful* things, things that bear on themselves the marks of what brought them forth. In this way, one is living, we might say, a truthful life. One is

---

15. The provenance of the poem is given in "PMD," 213.

living a life true to its own autochthonous conditions, a truth bodied forth in the things it brings to presence. Such a life is the life of poetic dwelling:

> When Hölderlin speaks of dwelling, he has before his eyes the basic character of human existence. He sees the "poetic," moreover, by way of relation to this dwelling, thus understood essentially.

> Poetry is what really lets us dwell. But through what do we attain to a dwelling place? Through building. Poetic creation, which lets us dwell, is a kind of building. ("PMD," 215)

But there is one more important element in poetic dwelling we have not yet touched on. It is what Heidegger calls *measuring oneself against the godhead,* and here too he relies on some lines of Hölderlin's poem as the source of his imagery:

> As long as Kindness,
> The Pure, still stays with his heart, man
> Not unhappily measures himself
> Against the godhead. Is God unknown?
> Is he manifest like the sky? I'd sooner
> Believe the latter. It's the measure of man.
> ("PMD," 219)

Heidegger believes that fully poetic dwelling must include this reference to "the godhead," a reference that apparently moves one some distance past making things that gather the fourfold: "Only insofar as man takes the measure of his dwelling in this way [namely, by measuring himself against the godhead] is he able to *be* commensurately with his nature. Man's dwelling depends on an upward-looking measure-taking of the dimension, in which the sky belongs just as much as the earth" ("PMD," 221). Naturally, this "measuring" takes place through the poetic bringing forth of things: "The taking of measure is what is poetic in dwelling. Poetry is a measuring" ("PMD," 221).

What is at issue here? We must first be clear that the godhead is not, in spite of the supernatural imagery Heidegger uses, a notion that properly belongs to theology. To speak of "God" or "the godhead" is not to speak of Yahweh, Allah, or some other mythical divine being. We must also be clear that Heidegger is trying hard to keep the notion free of any distinctively philosophical inflection; he does not want

it to become a concept within a metaphysical representation of what
there is. Heidegger wants his words here—"the godhead," "the sky"—
to have a resonance beyond our familiar structures of "ontotheology."
He wants them to belong to that unprecedented sort of *thinking* (as
he calls it) that will succeed Western philosophy at its end, a thinking
that will give attention to just what all such philosophy from its beginning has concealed.[16] Thus it will not be easy for us to follow him
confidently. A beginning may be made, however, by returning to the
notion that the thing "gathers the fourfold." I have glossed that as
saying that some linguistic and behavioral practices (e.g., the farming
life of Black Forest peasants in the eighteenth century) bring into
presence things (e.g., their houses) that themselves call attention to
the most general conditions of their presencing; and the fourfold is
Heidegger's imagery for those conditions attendant (he believes) on
any human life. (We shall return to the question of whether such a
claim on Heidegger's part is insufficiently historicist.) In this way
these things make it possible for us to give attention to the things
themselves, and thus to ourselves too, as autochthonous beings, as
always already conditional (*bedingt*). Is that as far as such revelation—such truthful making of things—can go? No, thinks Heidegger,
since there is also (what one might call) the *meta*condition of the presencing of any conditional thing. That metacondition is what he tropes
as *die Lichtung*—the clearing, the lighting—and it is that metacondition he is imaging in his references to the godhead against which we
measure ourselves.

   The notion of the clearing is a central theme of Heidegger's essay
"The End of Philosophy and the Task of Thinking," first published in
1966. The central ambition of that essay is to gesture at a kind of
thinking that goes decisively beyond the *vorstellendes Denken* (representational thinking) characteristic of all metaphysics, and thus of all
philosophy. "What characterizes metaphysical thinking which grounds
the ground for beings is the fact that metaphysical thinking, starting
from what is present, represents it in its presence and thus exhibits it
as grounded by its ground" ("EP," 374). From that very rich sentence
let us extract only a couple of points. First, metaphysical philosophy
starts from what is present. It begins its speculation from the things
("beings") already brought to presence in our sight and in our use. It
asks: how did those things come to be—to Be—the things they are?

---

16. Martin Heidegger, "The End of Philosophy and the Task of Thinking," trans.
Joan Stambaugh, reprinted in Martin Heidegger, *Basic Writings*. The essay will be
cited by "EP," followed by the page number of *Basic Writings*.

Second, in asking its question about the Being of things, metaphysical philosophy is asking the question of Being by asking for the *ground* of those present things. That is, in asking about (in the widest sense) the determining conditions of the things that are present, Western philosophy always seeks to uncover those conditions as *themselves something present*. Metaphysical philosophy—nourished by its Platonic root—always seeks to explain the Being of beings by reference to some "higher" being, a *ground*, an avatar of the Form. Thus representational thinking (the kind of thinking definitive for all philosophy) is the kind of thinking that tries to presence the determining conditions of all presencing; it tries to represent (i.e., re-present; present as another present being) what makes any determinate representation possible.

As an example of what is at stake here, think of a simple and familiar Gestalt image, such as the one that can be seen either as a large urn or as two faces in profile staring at one another. Which way the image gets seen depends on which color gets seen as the figure and which gets seen as the ground. (It's either a white urn seen against a black ground or two black faces seen against a white ground.) Notice that it is a condition of any determinate figure's being seen at all that something furnish a ground for that figure. To try to presence that ground as *itself* a determinate figure (which in the case of this ambiguous image one can certainly do) is necessarily to make something else the ground: it is impossible to presence both colors as figure at exactly the same moment. Yet that is just the sort of thing metaphysical philosophy tries to do. In asking about Being as the ground of beings, and in trying to represent that ground as something itself directly representable, it is trying to presence, as something fully present, the conditions of all presencing. It is trying to turn the conditions of what beings there are into *itself* a being. In this way metaphysical philosophy is obscuring the "ontological difference," the difference between Being and beings. Questions about how meaning happens—about Being—cannot be answered by exhibiting things ("beings") that always already possess some meaning. Questions about ultimate conditions cannot be answered by exhibiting something that is always already conditioned by those very conditions.

Heidegger is trying for a kind of thinking that attends in a different way to the conditions of things. Part of that thinking we have already seen in his discussion of making things that "gather the fourfold," but the conditions imaged there as "the four" are not the, so to speak, *final* condition of the things brought to presence. Each of the four is still tied closely to the *human;* these are images for the most general conditions of human life, whatever its particular cultural forms, whether fifth-century Athenian or eighteenth-century Swabian. They are deliberately antiphilosophical images for "the basic features of human existence," features that can be visibly present in the things (e.g., the Black Forest farmhouse) brought forth within a life of fully poetic dwelling, and features that can be deliberately concealed in the things (e.g., the ceramic coffee mug) produced by technology. But there is, one might say, a further level of conditionality, the metacondition of human dwelling/building/thinking. (One might call it the conditioning condition of conditionality itself.) It is the condition of presencing in terms of which our human presencing of things like farmhouses and coffee mugs is but a particular instance. That is what Heidegger calls *die Lichtung*.

> But what remains unthought in the matter of philosophy as well as in its method? Speculative dialectic is a mode in which the matter of philosophy comes to appear of itself and for itself, and thus becomes present. Such appearance necessarily occurs in some light [*Licht*]. Only by virtue of light, i.e., through brightness, can what shines show itself, that is, radiate. But brightness in its turn rests upon something open, something free, which it might illuminate here and there, now and then. Brightness plays in the open and wars there with darkness.
>
> We call this openness that grants a possible letting-appear and show "opening" [*die Lichtung*].
>
> Light can stream into the clearing, into its openness, and let brightness play with darkness in it. But light never first creates openness. Rather, light presupposes openness [*Lichtung*]. . . . The clearing [*die Lichtung*] is the open region for everything that becomes present and absent. ("EP," 384–85; translation slightly altered)

It is difficult to say plainly what Heidegger is trying to get at here. He is trying to think about how it happens that anything, and especially something genuinely new, comes to pass. Why is there something—some new thing, something radiant with new Being—rather than blank nothing or humdrum sameness? How does Being (meaning, significance, sense) originate? And that is to ask not only how does this specific thing come to have the specific Being it has (a question that might be answered by an intellectual historian describing various human practices and their vicissitudes); it is also to ask after the ultimate condition of Being itself. How does anything come to be? That is the question (the one he called *die Seinsfrage*) Heidegger was asking in *Being and Time;* but he stopped too soon, with the determining condition of Dasein's "concernful dealings." He did not ask where *those* "came from." Nor did he ask about the source of the light he believed *Being and Time* itself to shed on those conditions. After the "turn," Heidegger is trying to give attention to the fundamental condition of *all* presence and originality, including his own: whence comes the new word, the new philosophical vocabulary, the new god, the new form of life, the new politics, the new artwork? What is the ultimate "ground" upon which any genuinely new "figure" appears? Whence come the words that allow us to ask these very questions— and then to begin to answer them with such words as "conditionality" and "the fourfold"? And he is trying to think about this matter in a way that does not fall into metaphysics. He is trying not to identify the "ground" of what comes unexpectedly to be present with anything that can be represented as *itself* some sort of presence (namely, as a ground in the sense typical to philosophy). He does not want to forget, as Western philosophy has, the "ontological difference" between Being and beings.

The image of the clearing is his way of attending to the unpresenceable final condition of any presence and its specific conditions. Think, as the German word *Lichtung* happily encourages, of a bright and open space in the evergreen forest. Into that clearing the light pours, and in that gathered light one can see emerge the animals and plants that are at home there. "But light never first creates openness. Rather, light presupposes openness." Without the light there could be no seeing, but without first the clearing there could be no confluence of light to make that seeing possible. And now think of that clearing as an event rather than as an enduring feature of the landscape; hear the word "clearing" as a gerund rather than as a noun. In that clearing-event whatever appears, appears. The clearing (clear-*ing*) gathers the light in virtue of which whatever is seen—the thing—can be seen for what it is.

Certainly it is Freud's vocabulary that lets me see—that lights up—my quirks and pathologies as my Oedipal residues, just as it is Rorty's vocabulary that lets me see Freud as the maker of an extraordinary vocabulary. These folks are the light-bringers, the ones we— rightly—sing as our heroes. But look closely enough at them and one must throw up one's hands, no matter how powerful the art of the biographer. It's not so much that one can't figure out where the bright

sparks originated: Freud read Sophocles and Schopenhauer and talked
to Fliess; Rorty studied Aristotle and Whitehead and Dewey before he
read Heidegger and Davidson. No, it's that one can't understand how
those scattered sparks actually coalesced into the particular flow of
light that now illuminates us and what we see. To begin to think
about that confluence, and to realize that no merely causal story (or
any other story we can tell) will do to explain it, is to have begun to
think about the clearing, albeit still at too concrete a level. Push, now,
one's questions about the origins of these particular linguistic and
behavioral practices—Freud's psychoanalytic therapy, Rorty's pragmatic readings—to the point of asking about how *any* such gathering
of light (including this one: Heidegger's) is possible. Why is there
steady illumination at all? Why is there not just darkness, or at best
stroboscopic flashes that add up to nothing? (And no Just-So stories
about the Big Bang, or Yahweh, or natural selection, or evolutionary
epistemology, or "social practices all the way down"—stories which
are themselves wonderfully illuminating, of course—can get at *that*
question, as they themselves are just instances of the illuminating
practices the question is asking about.) One is now asking about the
continuous, essential, and mysterious event of the clearing.

Notice further that the event of the clearing is not of human making. The human being is not the self-supporting "subject" upon which
all the presencing of things is erected. Even the appearance of the
human to itself *as* human is granted within a clearing. The clearing
(clear-*ing*) is something necessarily *given* to us; we cannot deliberately create the opening space into which the light of revealing rushes
and gathers and holds. To make this point Heidegger again relies on a
feature of the German language. Whereas in English we say "There is
a book," in German one says "Es gibt [it gives] ein Buch." The presence of the book before us is something *given*. The clearing within
which the light pools to show us the book is a clearing granted to us,
not a clearing we have made: "But where does the opening come from
and how is it given? What speaks in the 'There is/It gives'? ("EP,"
392).

The point is not to answer that question. The point is to keep the
question open, to live in its light, to forestall any (necessarily) premature answers to it. To speak of *die Lichtung* is not to traffic in
an answer to any recognizable inquiry, philosophical or otherwise.
Rather, the word is itself just shorthand for the question of what (if
anything) speaks in the "There is." But what is the point of a question
without an answer? Is the question of *die Lichtung* even a real question at all? Shouldn't we stick to questions of "origin" that can be

answered by physicists or biologists or intellectual historians? Such pragmatic skepticism, which is certainly ours, is just what one should expect, according to Heidegger. It is no wonder that the fundamentally repressed question of our history—"How does Being happen at all?"—doesn't even look to us like a genuine question. Shouldn't we expect that such a question—if there really is one—would at first skirt very close to nonsense?

Die Lichtung is for Heidegger the most fundamental expression of *aletheia,* understood as the event of unconcealing. The clearing is that "place" or "event" (the scare-quotes are intended to mark these words as tropes) within which every particular event of revelation transpires: "The opening grants first of all the possibility of the path to presence, and grants the possible presencing of that presence itself. We must think *aletheia,* unconcealment, as the opening which first grants Being and thinking and their presencing to and for each other. The quiet heart of the opening is the place of stillness from which alone the possibility of the belonging together of Being and thinking, that is, presence and apprehending, can arise at all" ("EP," 387).

But this absolute priority of the clearing (understood as *aletheia*) means that *aletheia* itself is not to be understood as truth. "The natural concept of truth does not mean unconcealment, not in the philosophy of the Greeks either" ("EP," 389f.)[17] Truth may be characterized as (to use Heidegger's words) "the belonging together of Being and thinking," and that concordance can only take place within an opening already granted. *Die Lichtung* is prior to anything that may disclose itself within it; indeed, it is the undisclosable—unrepresentable—condition of disclosure itself.

Let us take stock of where we have come so far in our exposition of Heidegger. The human life is a life of building/dwelling/thinking, a life of linguistic and behavioral practices that bring things to presence; and a life of fully poetic dwelling is a life in which, in that building, one "measures oneself against the godhead." I have taken the image of the godhead to be the same as the image of the clearing. To measure oneself against the godhead is to give attention to the unrepresentable and ultimate condition of all our (conditional) presentation of things. In "'. . . Poetically Man Dwells . . .'" Heidegger reminds us of Hölderlin's lines: "Is God unknown? / Is he manifest like the sky? I'd sooner / Believe the latter." God—the godhead—cannot be entirely unknown. If it were, how could it be the measure against

---

17. This is a rare admission of error on Heidegger's part, as he himself had earlier claimed both these things.

which we are constantly measuring ourselves? God is manifest, hints Hölderlin, "like the sky." And what is the sky? The sky is the blank but luminous background against which we see whatever we see.[18] The sky is the "lighting" (*die Lichtung*) in the shelter of which every thing appears: "The measure consists in the way in which the god who remains unknown, is revealed to us *as* such by the sky. God's appearance through the sky consists in a disclosing that lets us see what conceals itself, but lets us see it not by seeking to wrest what is concealed out of its concealedness, but only by guarding the concealed in its self-concealment. Thus the unknown God appears as the unknown by way of the sky's manifestness. This appearance is the measure against which man measures himself" ("PMD," 223).

To dwell poetically on the earth as a mortal is to live in awareness of the godhead, the clearing, the blank but lightening sky. It is to live so as to measure oneself against that Nothing—that No-thing—that grants the possibility of the presence of and the Being of the things that there are. Within that clearing, as Heidegger puts it, brightness wars with darkness. There we struggle against particular ignorances and incapacities to bring forth truth.

Conditionality and Pathos

So far in this chapter I have taken Heidegger's idiom pretty much for granted, but the notion of poetic dwelling on the earth as a mortal can usefully be separated both from his peculiar vocabulary and from his mythical (and perhaps ultimately political) ambitions to recast the history of the West as the inexorable progress of *Seinsvergessenheit* (forgetfulness of Being). The key to such separations is to see that each of the forms of life Heidegger discusses in his essays after the turn—*die Technik,* poetic dwelling—is itself just a particular set of linguistic and behavioral practices, a way of talking and acting, a way within which things come to Being before us. As such practices, and as the things brought into our awareness within such practices, they can be classified in terms of the kind of attention they foster.

In the first place, there are those linguistic and behavioral practices that let things appear unconditionally for our use. The coffee mug,

18. Here the trope of the sky is functioning differently from the way it did in the fourfold. Here the sky—a way of talking about the clearing—is not just social practices, which can be brought to presence before us as such. In Heidegger's reading of Hölderlin here, the sky can never be brought to presence as an entity.

the television set, the toothbrush—all these things refer no sustained attention to themselves. In fact, these things are such as to disappear into our ordinarily successful use of them, all the better to fold us into the lives within which they (transiently) appear, and which they make possible. Such things are smooth and featureless; they have little if any reality as particular things, intended as they are merely to facilitate—as transparently as possible—our unimpeded activity toward more unimpeded activity. These, of course, are the practices Heidegger calls *die Technik,* and the things that appear within them are *Bestand.* The Heideggerian labels are not important. What matters is our recognition that such practices and things actually do exist, that much of our present life is constituted by them, and that our awareness of that fact—an awareness that comes only intermittently—is the source of our mood of normal nihilism.

What is crucial is to see that these practices and things foster and support only a particular, and quite limited, kind of attention to the world they create. The things appearing within these practices appear, in the normal case, only so as to disappear. They encourage and support no enduring attention to themselves, nor to the practices that bring them to presence. It is not too much to say that these things and practices, because they offer no resistance, no foothold for our steady attention, cause our lives to disappear from us even as we are living them. By facilitating our unimpeded activity, by rushing us ever further and faster into the future, they cause the present to vanish; they make our lives—the lives we are actually living here and now—all but invisible to us. Aided by such things, we are continually sped toward a future that never fully appears.

But such things and practices are not the only ones there are. There are also practices that bring to presence things that carry on their faces the various conditions of their own presencing. In the first instance such things may call our attention to the particular conditions of the life that made them. These are things that celebrate their own autochthony, that brazenly call attention to their own style. With such self-consciousness comes the acknowledgment that their particular style is one among many possibilities, that the life out of which they come is only one life among many. Such a thing announces its own conditionality. It did not just mysteriously appear (in order to disappear); it was made *by* someone in particular—perhaps by an identifiable individual—*for* someone in particular. Such things don't pretend to be for everyone, or for all time; they come out of a certain life and are supposed to put one in mind of that life as one confronts them. In this way they make it possible for the character of a life to appear more fully to those whose life it is. They bring to presence, one might say, a particular present.

Think of the Easter eggs made by Peter Carl Fabergé for the Russian imperial family. (I choose this example specifically for the moral queasiness it may induce; not every truthful thing is as benign as Heidegger's Schwarzwald farmhouse.) These ornaments are perfect examples of things that exhibit the specific conditions of the life out of which they come and for which they are made. Their fantastic attention to detail and their extravagant design; the huge wealth necessary to underwrite their creation; the fact that they are Easter eggs, given to celebrate a Christian and a family holiday of particular significance to the Romanovs—all these features (and others besides) in the eggs require and reward a certain sort of attention. These features deliberately make one aware of the kind of life that produced the thing that has them. Fabergé's jeweled and golden treasures are not supposed to disappear smoothly into some use one might make of them. They are supposed to offer one—if, say, one were the recipient of this gift—a chance to reflect upon, to attend to, the particularly fortunate circumstances of one's life: wealth, leisure, a taste for beauty, the salvation of one's immortal soul, and so forth. The style of these Fabergé eggs is excessive and intentional; it is there to offer the resistance necessary to a particular sort of self-reflection and self-awareness. (That such self-awareness may be complacent and narrow is, of course, always a danger. Knowledge becomes virtue—if it ever does—only when sufficiently comprehensive.)

There is, however, a second level of attention a thing may insist upon, a level beyond that of the specific conditions of the particular life that produced it. The thing may in its features call explicit attention to (what one might call) the general and universal conditions of human life itself. This, I take it, is the kind of attention Heidegger was praising when he claimed that a thing "gathers the fourfold." The Black Forest farmhouse built two centuries ago exhibits not just the specific conditions of that sort of agricultural life (though it certainly does that); rather, "the four" are for Heidegger inescapable conditions of any human life whatsoever. Any human life, he thinks, is lived on the earth, under the sky, before the divinities, and among the mortals; to the extent that the things built by that life show—insist upon—those general and universal conditions directly and unambiguously, the more truthful a life it is. Not every life is the life the Romanovs had (thank goodness, one may say), and thus the Fabergé eggs—though in some ways remarkably true to the specific conditions of *that* life—do not call us to deep reflection on our own condition.

(They may do some of that, of course, perhaps by fostering a certain amount of resentment or, as with the collector Malcolm Forbes, making possible a hearty self-congratulation.) The farmhouse is more truthful than those treasures. It exhibits not only its own specific conditions of presencing but also—and quite perspicuously—the general and universal conditions under which any human thing comes to presence. It reminds us in a more general way that "[w]e have left behind us the presupposition of all unconditionedness" ("T," 181).

Here one may wonder whether Heidegger is insufficiently historicist. Is it really plausible to claim that "the four" are conditions of any and every human life whatsoever? And is Heidegger really claiming that? Neither question is easy to answer. It is certainly possible to read him there as making claims only about *us:* we end-of-century, Western intellectuals must recognize, either by way of fullness or by way of privation, "the four" as dimensions of any life *we* can see as human. And any attempt to approach the first question head-on ("Does every human life necessarily look to the future for apocalyptic transformation?") raises knotty epistemological problems. (How could we tell whether or not we are reading into alien form of life the very features we seem to find there, especially when the features are such general ones?) It is not necessary to think one has answers to such questions in order to see some point to what Heidegger is saying, however. Even if we were to be stringently historicist and deny the truth (or even the sense) of claims about "universal human conditions" or "the basic character of human existence" ("PMD," 215) we can still recognize that some of a life's conditions are more general than others. For all the differences between the Romanovs and the Russian serfs, there were some conditions of life they shared; and one can therefore judge the truth of their things in terms of how faithfully they instantiate that common life. The Fabergé eggs may wonderfully exhibit some of the conditions of the life of the ruling family for which they were made, but they do little to show—except perhaps by way of deliberate omission—the conditions of the life of the ruled. Indeed, those poor and exploited subjects are (almost) completely invisible in the eggs' enameled surfaces, although their harsh labor was essential to the wealth that produced such excess of style. In that way the eggs are, while more truthful than my toothbrush, less truthful than they might be. They reveal less than they might of the conditions of the life that brought them forth. One can imagine a progress of such truthfulness in things: from things that tell more and more of the truth about the specific form of life that brought them forth (e.g., late nineteenth-century imperial Russian) to things that tell more and more about wider and wider cross-sections of that life (e.g., late-nineteenth-century European, post-Enlightenment European, and so forth). The key is the *truthfulness*—the power of revelation—of the things. In what way do these things show in themselves the conditions, at whatever level of generality, of the life that produced them? Heidegger's idea, expressed in his talk about "gathering the fourfold," is that some things carry on their faces a way for us to see what they deterrminately are, in the sense that they exhibit and insist upon their own granting conditions, both specific and general. One can accept and value that idea without having to believe that at some level of generality all lives have the same set of such conditions, and that they are exactly four in number.

So far we have identified two sorts of linguistic and behavioral practices, and thus two sorts of things produced within such practices. There are those things, such as the coffee mug or the toothbrush, that (seek to) obscure or deny the conditions of their own production, and there are those things, such as the Fabergé egg or the Black Forest farmhouse, that insistently reveal (at some level of generality, and with some degree of success) the conditions of the life that brought them forth. There is also a third sort of practice, and therefore a third sort of thing. There are those practices which bring to presence things that exhibit not only the conditions—whether specific or general—of their own presencing but also call attention to the metacondition of that presencing. These are things that call attention to the conditioning condition of conditionality itself; they are things that direct us to consider what Heidegger calls "the clearing." In this way they remind us of the unrepresentable background of lighting against which anything that appears, appears. They remind us that whatever we have is something given, given not by a god or by a mysterious cosmic event (since those notions are themselves just particular figures appearing on the lighting ground) but by something that cannot be represented as a "something" at all but which nevertheless is really and necessarily "there." *Es gibt:* "It gives/There is." To give attention to the event of *die Lichtung,* as these things (presumably) make it possible for us to do, is to indulge a kind of postphilosophical "thinking," as Heidegger calls it; a kind of thinking different from metaphysics, as the aim of metaphysics since Plato has always been to identify the ground of Being as a particular sort of (super)being. To be reminded of the clearing is to be made aware that Being—sense, significance, meaning, lighted presence—ultimately has no "ground," if by that one means something that can be identified as itself a "something." To speak of the clearing, the light-*ing,* is to speak of that which one can never close one's hand around, any more than one can grasp the luminescence that spills from the lamp onto the table. The lighting is an "event" (and even that is a metaphor, of course), not a "thing." It can be attended to, considered, "thought," but not represented. We cannot bring it before ourselves, any more than we can bring before ourselves the ground of a Gestalt figure *as ground*.

Of course one will be asking for some examples of these remarkable things that exhibit not only their own conditions of appearance but also exhibit attention to *die Lichtung,* and to give those examples will be the burden of my next chapter. But before doing so I want to say a bit about the way in which such things, and in particular the practices that bring them to presence, can serve as a counterweight to our mood of normal nihilism. In this book's progress we have gradually become clearer about how our normal nihilism comes to be. In Nietzsche's originating account, sketched in Chapter 1, normal nihilism seems to spring directly from the explicit, intellectual recognition of the radical contingency of just those features of my life that seemed (and always already claim to be) proof against it. Once I recognize that my life is a life of "value"—that it is constituted by structures of interpretation that are themselves radically conditional causal mechanisms posited by will to power in its own service—then a diminution of that life's *Pathos* is inevitable. How can I give myself fully and joyfully to a life that is being imposed upon me, a life into which I have been thrown; and moreover a life that is only one among many possible forms of life, a life that lacks Reality's imprimatur? Contingency means a loss of power. A club I just happened to wake up a member of is not a club that can command my fervent loyalty. And with the recognition of that contingency can come a rabid insistence on *oneself* (conceived either as individual or as group) as the ultimate condition of everything: if God is dead, then everything falls back upon me. This is the point of Nietzsche's famous *mot* about changing the "thus it must be" to a "so I have willed it." Once my values have been recognized to be (only) values, the only way I can restore their full *Pathos* is by making them specifically and explicitly conditional upon *me;* that is, upon my self-grounding, transvaluating *will.* Thus the Overman: our normal nihilism is overcome only when the self-grounding will explicitly affirms itself as the originating condition of all value, which is to say for Nietzsche, the originating condition of all Being.

Heidegger's account of technology has shown that it's not (as Nietzsche thought) simply the intellectual/philosophical recognition of contingency or conditionality that provokes our normal nihilist mood. Rather, the loss of our life's ordinary *Pathos* occurs when such recognition takes place within a practical life that denies contingency altogether. As a life ruled by *die Technik,* our practices produce anonymous and interchangeable things intended to facilitate our unimpeded, orderly activity within those practices; much of our ability to give ourselves over to such activity depends upon the invisibility of the practices themselves. Our lives flow along smoothly in their normal channels only so long as those channels are not noticed as such. Self-consciousness increases viscosity. Attention to the channels tends to clog the flow. The practices of technology produce things that function as invisible, self-lubricating funnels of our activity, helping us to easily move forward toward more such forward movement, toward more such forward movement, toward more such forward movement. The unconditionality we normally experience in our lives of *die Technik* is a practical (not a theoretical) unconditionality; our practices and our things appear and disappear in our use of them to facilitate our unimpeded, orderly movement into the future. They call no attention to themselves or to the particular conditions of their hold on us. We flow from place to place, from activity to activity, as if the containers of our flow were not (conventionally cut) channels at all but were reality's own headwaters. When that sense of unconditionality is interrupted, either by accident or by the intrusion upon our attention of a different kind of thing or practice, we are brought to a stand, and our ordinary immersion in our ordinary practices is suspended. In that way their ordinary power over us, their ordinary pathos for us, is diminished. For later Heidegger, it is the noticeable appearance of our ordinary, technological lives before us, their visibility to us as our particular lives, that produces the mood of loss and lack one may call normal nihilism, a mood that will (normally) be quickly covered over (though not wholly obliterated) by one's swift reimmersion in one's routines.

In Nietzsche's original representation of it, our normal nihilism seems to spring from an insight into the deep and bitter nature of things, to be the result of our having seen something we had heretofore—gulled by philosophy or theology—been blind to. For Heidegger, however, normal nihilism is less a sustained philosophical insight than a mood, a mood predicated on an interruption in the steady progress of our orderly movement toward ever more orderly movement. Like Nietzsche, Heidegger too would count our nihilism as a truth; but it is not a philosophical truth that penetrates to the alleged heart of things. ("Now I see it: the final truth is that there is no final truth.") Rather, the truth of nihilism is the *practical* revelation of the self-concealing, technological character of our ordinary practices. It is the *fact* that when they become fully visible for us in all their conditionality (just that conditionality which they themselves have always so successfully hidden), then they no longer engage us in their normal way. The *Pathos* of our technological practices diminishes in direct proportion to our ability to see them as such, that is, to notice them at all.

"Poetic dwelling on the earth as a mortal" is a kind of life that accepts fully the contingency and conditionality of whatever there is. In fact, these linguistic and behavioral practices make a virtue of producing things—words, houses, jugs—that exhibit that conditionality in unmistakable ways. The things brought to presence by this sort of life are emphatically *not* anonymous and interchangeable. They wear on their faces the conditions, both specific and general, of the life that made them appear. Moreover, and in ways we have yet to discuss in detail, they exhibit in themselves the ultimate condition, what one might call the metacondition, of their appearance: *die Lichtung,* the clearing, the conditioning condition of conditionality itself. Thus in two ways these practices successfully resist the loss of *Pathos* we have been detailing above. First, since the life of poetic dwelling is a life that explicitly and continually acknowledges its conditionality— and does that by means of the things it brings to presence, things that refuse to disappear into our unimpeded use of them—there is no practical incongruity between the lives we are living (as such dwellers) and our recognition of the conditionality of those lives. In poetic dwelling we are always aware, aware in the ways we bodily and intellectually comport ourselves to our things, of that manifold conditionality; and thus in our practice we instantiate the truth—the conditionality—of that practice. Because "we have left behind us the presupposition of all unconditionedness" ("T," 181), and left it behind not just through possessing some new philosophical insight but through instantiating a new kind of practice, then the power of those practices is uncompromised by any inadvertent reminder of their contingency. There is no gap between the truth of the practice (as conditional) and the comportment of those of us constituted by the practice; thus there is no rift through which the *Pathos* of those practices can seep away. It is, one might say, the fully and continually acknowledged *truth* of our lives of poetic dwelling that safeguards their power for us.

Second, acknowledgment of *die Lichtung* preserves the *Pathos* of those practices that foster such attention; in particular this acknowledgment guards against the temptation to instantiate the human as the ultimate condition of whatever there is. To be reminded by one's things, and thus to enact in one's everyday comportment toward one's things, that the appearance of those things is always something "given" to one within a self-lighting space that cannot itself be understood as any particular thing or social practice, is to be brought up short before that which one cannot control or even negotiate with. It is to be made aware of one's dependence—not, of course, a dependence merely causal—on something (or, rather, no-thing) that cannot be inserted into the realm of onto-theology, and yet something to which attention, both practical and intellectual, can fruitfully be directed. The continuously renewed reality of that attention gives a particular quality to a life. To live in the light of the clearing is not to live as we ordinarily do. The truth of the life of fully poetic dwelling grants that life a particular *Pathos,* a peculiar power to safeguard itself against the corruptions we ordinarily endure. A fuller account of that *Pathos* must wait for the next chapter, where specific instances of such attention will be discussed; for now one can say that attention to the clearing restores to us something of the religious person's sense of being sheltered by the fully present and perfect realm of the "true world." Attention to the clearing (an attention, remember, that will show itself both in thought and in practice) returns one to a sense of one's finitude, to a sense of one's smallness before the ultimate condition of one's own self-appearance. And yet—this is crucial—the clearing is not something that can be worshiped, served, or appeased through any form of violence. It demands no sacrifices, neither of sons nor of words; and no stultifying theology can be erected within its precincts. To acknowledge oneself as having been "granted" the life one has, is to be able to recover, over and over again, the sense of the wonder of things that, according to Aristotle, is the original impulse to philosophy. "Why is there something and not nothing?" Asked in the right tone of voice—or, better, embodied in a particular kind of comportment toward things (the lover's touch, the poet's breath on a word, the farmer's care for her land)—that question is a thinking about the clearing, a thinking that over and over again enlivens the life of which it is a part.

One could think of it this way. Those practices Heidegger calls technological create and require a sense of their own unconditionality. In our normal technological activity with things, they and we appear and interact within invisible "frames" that (intend to) place us at one another's disposal for (relatively) effortless and thoughtless ordering. When those practices are well at work, we and our things are sped efficiently into the future, insulated from any sense of conditionality by the consolations of movement itself. But when those frames that hold and guide us are themselves made visible (e.g., through some sort of breakdown), the resulting sense of conditionality comes as a shock, and interferes (for a time) with our capacity to act as is normal for us. Expressed intellectually, that inhibition shows itself as *contingency,* a sense that our *Lebensformen* do not possess the absoluteness they implicitly claim. (Thus Nietzsche's talk of self-devaluating values: that could only happen when values become visible *as such,* and attention to them begins to clog our action with them.) Expressed in praxis, that inhibition shows itself as a particular *mood,* compounded both of bone-weariness and an inability to rest with what one has. It is the mood of the tired shopper who, running low on both cash and desire, has no more home to return to and can only push on to the next sale. I have called it the mood of normal nihilism.

In those practices that make things which "gather the fourfold," there is the explicit disavowal of unconditionality, but the resulting conditionality is conceived and experienced not as contingency but as autochthony or rootedness. No such practices claim for themselves the kind of absoluteness that sows the seeds of our normal nihilism; in the things made by those practices there is always explicit attention given to the conditions, particular and general, of the life that brought them forth. Hard as it is to express, one who has lived, even if for a time, outside the practices of technology knows there is a difference here. It is mainly a difference of rhythm, as if one habitually spoke one's native language slowly and deliberately enough to taste its particular flavor. What if one were now to *live* that slowly and deliberately, with that quality of attention to the particular and its conditions? It is possible, in some lives, to come to know of one's conditionedness without feeling that as diminishment; on the contrary, it can be an access of exhilaration, a source of heightened *Pathos.* "We are just who we are." "These little things—these streams, this soil, these books, these freedoms—have made us." Said in one way, these can be expressions of loss; in another, of curious joy.

But it is not as if there is no sense of absoluteness at all in such lives; to the extent to which they "measure themselves against the godhead" there is a perception of that which gives rise to what there is. One is rooted in something, *given* by something that is better—not truly—called an event (*das Ereignis:* "appropriation"; *die Lichtung:* "clearing") than a thing. The bright but blank sky against which all things appear is not itself a thing, but it can be noticed; and such notice is not (necessarily) trivial.

This sense of finitude, the sense that everything (even oneself as seen by oneself) appears against (or "from") the sky, prevents the recognition of one's conditionality from leading to the hypertrophy of the human that one sometimes sees in—or perhaps projects onto—a thinker like Nietzsche. Attention to the clearing forces one to recognize that even one's own appearance to oneself is something "granted" to one, not something one has done for oneself. It is impossible to believe oneself to be the "self-created creator of all values" (or whatever) when one realizes that the possibility of one's seeing oneself as that creator (or as anything at all) is a possibility given to one by a condition one can never know or name. Such a sense of having been "given" to oneself (as whatever one takes oneself to be)—but "given" by no-thing, by that which can in no way be comprehended or cajoled—is a reliable check on our temptation to set ourselves up as the replacement for the God that (to our happiness) went away.

To "dwell poetically on the earth as a mortal," then, is Heidegger's attempt to reconstitute what it might mean for us to be religious. It is to answer the *Seinsfrage* without indulging *Seinsvergessenheit*. Being—granted by and in "the clearing"—is in no way identified with a being, no matter how grand or mysterious. To live in the light of the clearing is to find practices of building, of making things, such that those things embody attention to both (1) the conditions of their own making and (2) the metacondition of all making, human and otherwise. Insofar as our lives are constituted by those sorts of linguistic and behavioral practices, those lives will be protected both from the loss of *Pathos* characteristic of our mood of normal nihilism and from the sense of limitless humanism that feeds our various addictions and simultaneously despoils the earth that shelters us. But what would such a life actually look like? It is now time to examine some concrete examples of what it might (even *should*) mean for us to be post-philosophically religious.

5

THE PLAIN SENSE
OF THINGS

On some philosophers religion hardly registers; on others (I am one of
them) it sits like a stone. It's a bit like having an abusive parent, I
suppose. Our lives depend upon getting free of its clutches, but down
the road we end up scratching around for something to take its place.
If we're not vigilant and lucky, we may even find ourselves passing on
to innocent others, as in a terrible dream, some of the same pains we
remember and resent. In this book I have been trying to find a way of
being religious that's still possible (or maybe the word is "decent") for
us. What would it be like to be religious without fudging our best
thoughts, without repressing anything we have learned, without tem-
pering the wind to the shorn lamb? What would it be like to be religious when we can't really believe any of that glorious stuff—creation
ex nihilo, virgin birth, bodily resurrection—we used to believe? It's
not decent, I think, to pretend to believe it, or to do a fancy philosophical number on "belief" or on "truth" so that religion ends up relying
on epistemic standards that would be laughed out of any good classroom or courtroom or laboratory. Nor is it decent to refuse to think
about one's religiousness, to shove it into a locked drawer sweetened
by sachets of tradition and *Sittlichkeit*. All that's dishonest, and it's a
kind of dishonesty too easily explained by weakness: some folks just
need to stay in touch with daddy, no matter that they've seen him
with his nasty pants down.

I have been trying to think about religion by thinking about its fate
in a culture in which the standard intellectual mood is profoundly
ironic—a culture of what, adapting a phrase of Nietzsche's, I have

been calling normal nihilism. For us, religion is—at most—a set of values, a set of structures of interpretation employed in the hope of preserving and enhancing what we most care about. Religion is, to use the illuminating image from *Being and Time,* a part of the (conceptual) gear some of us use to try to get what we are determined to want and need. Thoreau puts the point with characteristic pungency: "We"—we normal nihilists, he means—"have adopted Christianity merely as an improved method of *agri*-culture."[1] Seen in that way, as we must see them, religious values, like the other "highest values" of our civilization, have devaluated themselves. Under their own tutelage ("You shall know the truth and the truth shall make you free"), we have come to learn that our religious convictions cannot live up to their own largest claims for themselves. Their authority—which they claimed to be absolute—has been compromised by the scrupulous application of those techniques of reflection in which they claimed that authority to rest. In spite of the best efforts of press-agents of genius, Yahweh and Allah finally on close inspection turn out to be values, words, tools: not actual gods or even their philosophical avatars. "The

---

1. Here is Cornel West, a man whose moral witness I much admire, exemplifying an agricultural Christianity:

> My acceptance of the prophetic Christian tradition is rational in that it rests upon good reasons. These reasons are good ones not because they result from logical necessity or conform to transcendental criteria. Rather they are good in that they flow from rational deliberation which perennially scrutinizes my particular tradition in relation to specific problems of dogmatic thought, existential anguish, and societal oppression.
>
> My reasons may become bad ones. For example, I would give up my allegiance to the prophetic Christian tradition if life-denying forces so fully saturated a situation that all possibility, potentiality and alternatives were exhausted, or *if I became convinced that another tradition provides a more acceptable and enabling moral vision, set of ethical norms and synoptic worldview.* I need neither metaphysical criteria nor transcendental standards to be convinced, only historically constituted and situated reasons. (Cornel West, "The Historicist Turn in Philosophy of Religion," in his *Keeping Faith* [New York: Routledge, 1993], 134; my emphasis)

If the old system of crop rotation and planting by the moon doesn't continue to produce good yields, then I'll invest in a new tractor and some up-to-the-minute chemical fertilizers. The point, after all, is to get a good crop in the barn at season's end. The pragmatism here is philosophically unimpeachable, but one wonders what—to take a couple of figures from West's own tradition—Job or Jeremiah would say about it. Or Jesus, who at Luke 9:62 is reported to have warned: "No one who puts his hand to the plow and then looks back, is worthy of the kingdom of God." Pragmatists spend their lives looking back, or forward, or at least around.

trail of the human serpent is over all," said William James, staining even our divinities with our contingency and our need. Thus our irony: we cannot help having "radical and continuing doubts about [our] final vocabulary," religious or otherwise.[2] If religion is a set of values, conceptual *Zeug,* then there might be a better mousetrap being built right around the corner; there's no reason to get sentimental or bloodthirsty about this particular machine.

I have also thought there were some serious dangers connected to this loss of religion's ultimate *Pathos,* particularly two dangers apparently antagonistic: first, the danger of engrossing, limitless humanism; second, the danger of crushing submission to the conventional. I have been fearful of being lost in the mall, which for me represents a place where our addiction to individual self-enhancement, our collusive blindness to the true cost of things, and our susceptibility to the power of crowds, all come together in an intoxicating elixir. While traditional supernatural religion is no longer possible for us, we still need something: something to bound our temptation to eat up the earth and ourselves in pursuit of ever new, and ever more reckless, forms of self-fashioning; and—simultaneously—something to loosen our captivity to whatever particular form of life is commonsensically dominant here and now. For that is what traditional religion has sometimes been able to do with its sacraments: to combine, on the one hand, a sense that human will—the will to the will's own splendor—is limited by something greater, by something to which it must finally answer, with, on the other hand, a call away from the ordinary pieties of "the world" toward a life that is deeper and truer and richer. We need—without the dishonesties of traditional religiousness—access to something both encompassing and prophetic. We need a reliable way to keep alive the dialectic between a recognition of what is proper to us and a readiness to indulge "experiments of living" in the hope of better things.[3]

I have hoped to find that way in philosophy; and, if that is not laughable enough, I have even hoped to find it in an eccentric, selective (but not I think utterly wild) reading of Martin Heidegger, professor and National Socialist.[4] That reading, relying as it does mostly

2. Richard Rorty, *Contingency, Irony, and Solidarity* (New York: Cambridge University Press, 1989), 73. I owe the quotation from William James to Rorty, who several times cites it in his papers.

3. I have taken the quoted phrase from J. S. Mill, *On Liberty* (Indianapolis: Hackett, 1978), 54.

4. For the ugly and disheartening details about Heidegger's Nazism, see Richard Wolin, ed., *The Heidegger Controversy: A Critical Reader* (New York: Columbia University Press, 1991).

on texts from the early 1950s, is guided by my conviction (a conviction not, of course, original to me) that social practices shape subjectivity, not the other way round; and thus that the key to a decent religiousness for us is the description of some linguistic and social practices that can truthfully foster in us the dialectic of propriety and experiment adverted to in the last paragraph above. It is not a matter of our finding, as it was for Kierkegaard (and for Descartes, and for Plato, and for the Yahwist), a life always already "true to human nature"; rather, it is a matter of finding a life transparent to itself. That is not metaphysical realism; it is the requirement that a way of life reflect as fully as it can its own conditions of appearance.

I have thought that what Heidegger calls "poetic dwelling on the earth as a mortal" is a way of realizing such transparency while fostering such a dialectic; and so, looking first at *Being and Time* and then at some of his later essays, I have tried to lay out what I take to be the essentials of the practices he is there describing. In summary, I take those practices to be practices of making things, of bringing into presence before us things that allow us to, as he says, "measure ourselves against the godhead." I have taken that to mean that the things brought to presence within such practices, first, bear on their faces the manifold conditions of the life that made them (gathering the fourfold) and, second, simultaneously direct our attention to the unnamable metacondition of all such conditions (thinking *die Lichtung*). It has been my conviction that a life that foregrounds such practices will be a life that can thus preserve itself from self-devaluation, from the loss of *Pathos* characteristic of our ordinary intellectual mood, and can thus preserve the one who lives it from the dangers of our normal nihilism.

Separated from the incantatory rhetoric of Heidegger's prose, such a summary may seem comically thin, utterly unable to bear the weight I want to place on it. What does this have to do with being religious, with the huge and inspiring metaphysical and ethical claims and demands ("Thus saith the Lord. . . .") that have led to the founding of monasteries, the fighting of holy wars, the construction of intellectual systems of extraordinary beauty and power, the establishment of hospitals, orphanages, and universities, the enlivening of public conscience to our ordinary cruelties, and so forth? And what could these Heideggerian "things" look like, these things that, as he says, exhibit the "dimension" between earth and sky ("PMD," 220f.) within which "poetic dwelling" can go on? In this chapter I give some examples of the practices I have in mind. I shall start with Henry David Thoreau's *Walden*.

The Spectacle of the Familiar

Any great book has fed various appetites, and *Walden* is certainly no exception. It has made a meal for intellectual historians, for literary critics, for naturalists, for moralists, and lately even for philosophers.[5] Here I read the book philosophically and religiously; not for what fragments of (Kantian) philosophy or (Indian) theology it may contain, but as an instance of the practice of poetic dwelling on the earth as a mortal. *Walden* is, first and most literally, a book about dwelling: about thoughtfully building a dwelling, a small wooden house erected in 1845 on Emerson's land at the edge of Walden Pond near Concord, Massachusetts, and then about living there for two years. It is also a book about leaving that house and moving on, about becoming "a sojourner in civilized life again" (325).[6] *Walden* is about living at Walden Pond, certainly, but Thoreau's is a book written retrospectively, after having left the house he built and occupied. Thus it truly is, as it announces, the book of a sojourner, of one who comes and goes, and that sense of transience, of being just about to move on again, is not simply one of the features that makes it peculiarly American; it is also, as we shall see, one of the most important aspects of the kind of religious and philosophical practice the book exemplifies.

Walden, like *Fear and Trembling,* is a book written in cognizance of loss: "I long ago lost a hound, a bay horse, and a turtledove, and am still on their trail. Many are the travelers I have spoken concerning them, describing their tracks and what calls they answered to. I have met one or two who have heard the hound, and the tramp of the horse, and even seen the dove disappear behind a cloud, and they seemed as anxious to recover them as if they had lost them themselves" (336).

They *had.* The loss of this trinity is not Thoreau's alone. The disappearance of that dove behind the cloud is a withdrawal of divine approval not just for a personal mission, nor even for a national destiny; it is an absence that seems, and is, universal and philosophical. (Thoreau's language here bears fruitful comparison to Nietzsche's in *Thus Spake Zarathustra.* There is the same sense of a fundamental change in our condition, a change that has left us bereft of our familiar allies

---

5. The most important of these philosophers is of course Stanley Cavell; see his *The Senses of Walden: An Expanded Edition* (San Francisco: North Point, 1981).

6. Page references in my text are to the edition of *Walden* found in the Library of America volume of Thoreau's writing, *Henry David Thoreau* (New York: Library of America, 1985).

and assurances.) Our various baptisms and dedications—individual, communal, national—now go on without any reliable sign of divine sanction.[7] Our language, the place and medium of all those baptisms, is these days fit merely to be spoken, not read. It has been abandoned by its genius. It is no more the language of the "heroic books" carried by conquerors on their expeditions (403f.); it finds its proper place only in newspaper accounts of steamboat wrecks and in cheap novels like "Tittle-Tol-Tan" (407). We are left alone here, nostalgic for the time when our tutelary animals were beside us to confer authority and aid to our journey. Even when thoroughly immersed in civilized life, our sojourn is a lonely one; neither disciples nor forerunners can sweeten the road to our steps. We live in a time of reported encounters ("one or two who have heard the hound"), of decayed and ambiguous tracks, and of experimental calls to something now long gone. For all its good humor and its anticipation of the dawn, *Walden* is a book that proceeds from a keen sense of abandonment. One doesn't misplace one's companion animals as one might lose one's house-key; they run, or perhaps are chased, away. *Walden,* like *Fear and Trembling,* or like *Thus Spake Zarathustra,* is a book written for normal nihilists, for those of us left behind with our values after the disappearance of the divinities those values once seemed to be.

Walden's response to its originating loss is itself. The book—its writing and its reading—is offered as the cure of the malaise that provoked it. *Walden* is a particular kind of thinking about building and dwelling; the book exemplifies a specific linguistic and behavioral practice, of a sort one may as well call religious, or philosophical. It is first of all a practice of truth-telling, of confession and of explanation to those who have made "very particular inquiries" concerning its author's "mode of life" (325). But it is truth-telling of a quite distinctive sort, since its immediate object is the truth about the teller, and in particular the truth about the conditions of the life he shares with his neighbors in New England (326). That word "condition" should, as Stanley Cavell has pointed out, alert us to the fact that Thoreau sees his task as more than journalistic or naturalistic or autobiographical. It is a task properly understood as philosophical, as transcendental: the delineation of the conditions of the life we live. The Kantian resonance is obvious; but not determinative, since Thoreau is willing to ask whether these conditions are necessary (326), not to argue they must be. Thoreau's philosophical practice here is essentially historical and personal, not abstract and metaphysical. That is obvious from the

7. The dove is a clear allusion to Jesus' baptism by John. See Matthew 2:13–17.

very first page: "Moreover, I, on my side, require of every writer, first or last, a simple and sincere account of his own life, and not merely what he has heard of other men's lives; some such account as he would send to his kindred in a distant land; for if he has lived sincerely it must have been a distant land to me" (325).

Thoreau is putting great (perhaps *too* great) pressure on the notion of sincerity. What would "a simple and sincere account" of one's own life be? Sincerity is of course truthfulness, or at least the conviction and intention of truthfulness, since we very well know that some of the most sincere folks are also the most ignorant and deceived, and therefore the most dangerous. Thoreau's talk of sincerity here must be juxtaposed to his paean to reality at the end of "Where I Lived, and What I Lived For": "Be it life or death, we crave only reality." A cheap or comfortable sincerity is not enough. As we stand in the stream of time, there must always be the attempt to "settle ourselves, and work and wedge our feet downward through the mud and slush of opinion, and prejudice, and tradition, and delusion, and appearance" (400). Thoreau's insistence on sincerity is not a skeptical or weary dismissal of truth ("It really doesn't matter what you think, so long as you're sincere"); rather, it is an avowal of where and how truth is to be found. It's of little use to us to know a great deal "concerning the Chinese and Sandwich Islanders" (325f.). Truth happens when someone's life becomes transparent to itself. A "simple and sincere account" is one that reveals to the accountant—and then, perhaps, to others as well—the conditions of the life actually being lived. What one wants, first and last, from oneself and from others, is the identification of those structures that give one the life one has, the various structures that condition one's life into its particular contour. Sincerity, then, is transparency. Such an ambition does not give up the notion of truth, since there is still the necessity to shove aside the "mud and slush" in order to get at the reality, at the stream-bed that contains and directs the flow of the self through time. The fact that the stream's bottom itself can shift (that is a famous metaphor of Wittgenstein's, of course) does not mean that at any given instant it is not exactly *somewhere*.[8] The task of sincerity is to find it out and to mark it.

This is truth understood as *aletheia*, as dis-closure. That which was invisible—the bed of the stream, the conditions of the life flowing

---

there—now appears before one as fully real. One can now see how and why things go on as they do. In this image there is the familiar distinction (familiar to us from Western metaphysics, I mean) between what passes (Becoming) and what endures (Being). In Western religiousness it is the founding distinction between the Sacred and the Profane, and Thoreau himself invokes it as the conventional contrast between time and eternity: "Time is but the stream I go a-fishing in . . . but eternity remains" (400). But it would be a great mistake, I think, simply to take such philosophically loaded language at face value. For all his indebtedness to his intellectual tradition (the house by the pond is, after all, built on Emerson's property), Thoreau is not a standard Western (and certainly not an Eastern) metaphysician. Undoubtedly his aim is to discover the conditions of (his) experience and action, but unlike Kant he does not expect to find them in the universal and eternal structures of the intellect. Rather, they are to be found in the *imagination.* The key to the transparency Thoreau wants to make possible is to see one's life as fundamentally and necessarily given its shape by images, by "conceptions." A "sincere" account of one's life is an account that has disclosed the sources of that life in the imagination. Sincerity, one might say, is truth disciplined by the reality of imagination, and imagination disciplined by the necessity for truth.

> Men esteem truth remote, in the outskirts of the system, beyond the farthest star, before Adam and after the last man. In eternity there is indeed something true and sublime. But all these times and occasions are now and here. God himself culminates in the present moment, and will never be more divine in the lapse of all the ages. And we are enabled to apprehend at all what is sublime and noble only by the perpetual instilling and drenching of the reality which surrounds us. The universe constantly and obediently answers to our conceptions; whether we travel fast or slow, the track is laid for us. Let us spend our lives in conceiving then. (399)

"The universe constantly and obediently answers to our conceptions." Is that merely Thoreau's pious belief in some sort of epistemic Providence, his conviction that the Author of Nature wouldn't publish a book we couldn't eventually learn to read? Or is it merely the familiar Kantian claim that our experience of the universe is possible at all only because the mind is already furnished with categories, with "conceptions," that give a particular form and order to our sense-data?

Neither of those readings, plausible as they are, gets at what is most radical in Thoreau's revision of transcendentalism in this passage. His language here is under great pressure. Sentence follows sentence as if squeezed out in his rush to make everything clear at once; the resultant compression of his thought sets the expositor a hard task. In giving an account one must try to be as bold and as deliberate as Thoreau himself. (In that ambition, of course, one will almost certainly fail.) I prefer to connect the just-quoted sentence ("The universe constantly and obediently . . .") to the one that immediately precedes it, and to read the second sentence as the explanation of the first. Yes, there is something "sublime and noble" in the eternity—the unknowable past and future—that culminates in the present moment, in my ordinary life of "times and occasions." But we are able to apprehend that excellence, the sublimity and nobility of the familiar present, only by "instilling and drenching" the reality that surrounds us here and now.[9] (To *instill* here means "to pour a liquid drop by drop," as one might instill a medicine into a beaker.) We are, Thoreau is saying, the constant (if frequently unconscious) instillers of our local reality; we drench it again and again with our staining and revealing liquid. God culminates in the present moment only if we can see him there, only if we pour onto the "now and here" a reagent capable of bringing forth hidden patterns and colors. And with what liquid do we instill and drench reality, so as to reveal its otherwise undisclosed magnificence? With our *conceptions,* with our *imagination* of that reality.[10] "The universe constantly and obediently answers to our conceptions." Reality shows itself—"obediently"—in our continual imagination of it. In spite of our habitual estimation, truth is not remote, not "beyond the farthest star"; it is here and now, in the "perpetual instilling and drenching of the reality that surrounds us." Truth discloses itself in our "conceptions." "Let us spend our time in conceiving then." Let us make our lives transparent by locating (and then relocating) the tracks laid for them by the images we have inherited or created.

Odd as the conjunction sounds, Thoreau is a historicist transcendentalist. There are transcendental structures of experience that fix and make possible a particular life, structures that, as we might say,

9. Untraditionally, and perhaps to some ears tortuously, I hear the 'of' in that sentence as an objective genitive rather than a subjective one, so that it is we who are the agents, not the patients, of the instilling and drenching. My claim for this particular reading is justified, I hope, by the work it does for my reading of the book as a whole.

10. We shall see in a moment other instances of Thoreau's metaphorical connection of imagination to wetness, to water.

grant that life to the one who lives it ("the track is laid for us"); and it
is the task of philosophical self-reflection to identify those conditions,
and by identifying them also to ask whether they can be altered and
improved. But these structures, these transcendental conditions of
one's experience and life, are fundamentally given by the workings of
the imagination, by our faculty for "conception." They are not structures frozen for all time into the categories and relations of Aristotle's
logic and hard-wired into every intellect as exactly the same. The universe—always already *our* universe—readily answers (as Kant knew)
to our conceptions of it, but any particular set of those conceptions,
though it may be very general (perhaps even an alluvion of "shams
and appearances" that "covers the globe"), is not *necessary*. "Shams
and delusions are esteemed for soundest truths, while reality is fabulous. If men would steadily observe realities only, and not allow themselves to be deluded, life, to compare it with such things as we know,
would be like a fairy tale and the Arabian Nights' Entertainments"
(398). Yes, reality is fabulous: it is constituted in and by our fables; it
is formed into a parade of stories—images, tropes, myths, metaphors,
conceptions—in order to forestall the threatened death we all share
with Scheherazade. And the "shams and delusions" so constructed are
esteemed by some—both philosophers and farmers—to be necessities, taken by them to be the "soundest truths," as they push their
farms and houses before them down the road, or speculate in herds of
cattle in order to be able to buy shoestrings. It is, I take it, the assumption of a *particular* trope's necessity that makes it a sham and a
delusion. The reality that must be steadily observed is the reality of
fable—of imagination—as the necessary condition of all truth, as
that which makes any particular disclosure possible. To see *that* reality steadily—the constituting reality of the imagination—is a different kind of transcendentalism, and it leads one into a new and freer
relationship to one's constitutive conditions.

"By closing the eyes and slumbering, and consenting to be deceived
by shows, men establish and confirm their daily life of routine and
habit every where, which still is built on purely illusory foundations.
Children, who play life, discern its true law and relations more
clearly than men, who fail to live it worthily, but who think they are
wiser by experience, that is, by failure" (398).[11] For the playing child,
certainly, "reality is fabulous." She makes up her stories as she goes
along, inhabiting them effortlessly and temporarily, and miraculously
finding that things alongside the way confirm the tales she is telling

11. Almost certainly there is an allusion to Heraclitus here; look at fragment 52.

(this broom is a horse, this shiny stone is—lo and behold—the pearl of great price for which she has been seeking). Her universe answers "constantly and obediently" to her conceptions, conceptions she knows to be her play. Such a child understands the "true law" of life, and thus can rise every morning in joyful anticipation. "There is more day to dawn. The sun is but a morning star" (587). For slumbering adults, "consenting to be deceived by shows," there is only a daily life of routine and habit, "built on purely illusory foundations." To be deceived by a show is to fail to see an image as such; it is to "establish and confirm" the particular image as a necessity. "We predicate of the thing what lies in the method of representing it. Impressed by the possibility of a comparison, we think we are perceiving a state of affairs of the highest generality."[12] Self-deception is to forget the fables at the foundation of the world, and thus to convert them into illusions of necessity. It is to make oneself the prisoner of a trope.

The "law" of imagination's necessity is beautifully encompassed in an image that connects with the more famous images of water we have just been noting: "It is well to have some water in your neighborhood, to give buoyancy to and float the earth. One value even of the smallest well is, that when you look into it you see that the earth is not continent but insular. That is as important as that it keeps butter cool. When I looked across the pond from this peak toward the Sudbury meadows, which in time of flood I distinguished elevated perhaps by a mirage in their seething valley, like a coin in a basin, all the earth beyond the pond appeared like a thin crust insulated and floated by this small sheet of intervening water, and I was reminded that this on which I dwelt was but *dry land*" (390f.).

It is easy to remember the sense of giddiness one got looking down deep into a well and seeing at the bottom of that dark and musty cylinder a bright patch of light one suddenly realizes to be water. (Perhaps—and this is my own first memory of a well, come upon unexpectedly and dangerously one day during a holiday tramp in the woods—it's so deep or dark that one can't see the reflecting water at all; one only hears, after what seems an interminable interval, the faint and hollow splash of one's pebble.) The earth, which had seemed so solid and fixed beneath one's feet, now seems to have slipped its anchor; it floats on a sea one didn't even know was there. It is, as Thoreau wonderfully says, "not continent but insular." Its stability now appears as a kind of illusion, fostered by a lack of proper perspec-

---

12. Ludwig Wittgenstein, *Philosophical Investigations,* trans. G. E. M. Anscombe (Oxford: Basil Blackwell, 1958), sec. 104.

tive. But that's not quite the way to put it (despite Thoreau's ready use of the word), since the stability we walk on is not an illusion, exactly. Not being Jesus, after all, we do walk on dry land, not on the water. But it is a dry land that floats. Its stability turns on the fact that the water has subsided (for a time), leaving us with a solid place to put our feet. That on which we build our houses is, as Thoreau says with proper emphasis, "*dry land.*" It is land recovered for a time from those waters that, as we read in Genesis, at one time covered the whole face of the earth. Those waters have not ceased to be; they have just gone underground, leaving us buoyed and floating on what they left.

This is an image for the imagination itself. The land on which we dwell is *dry* land. It is land that, whatever its clear and distinct features ("this peak toward the Sudbury meadows"), floats on a feature-less sea, the sea from which it emerged and the sea which always threatens—hence the boon of Yahweh's rainbow promise to Noah—to take it back again. So it is with our lives: they are given their form and substance, their explicit topographical features, by particular images and conceptions; such are the dry lands on which we dwell. Living there, it is easy to forget the sea that floats them; it is easy to forget that blank and restless sheet of water from which the islands of our continents emerged. "It is well to have some water in your neighborhood. . . ." It is well to be reminded of the Nothing from which all our somethings emerged.

The metaphor of dryness works in another way as well; the water that buoys and floats the earth is an image not just of featureless support but also of fertility. Dry land is not only stable and determinate; it is arid. A rock's adamant solidity is purchased at the price of life. Nothing grows in the sandy desert or on the sheer cliff-face. The hidden water, the stream that can always arise to floodtide once again, is the ultimate nourishment for what is new and green. That is why there must be, on our part, "the perpetual instilling and drenching of the reality that surrounds us" (399). Reminded of their source by the water in our neighborhood, we ourselves must drench and instill our ordinary conceptions with new liquidity, just as the rising river floods the lowlands and nourishes the crops in the spring. We must invigorate the "*dry land*" on which we live with new water from the reservoir that supports and nourishes us all: "The life in us is like the water in the river. It may rise this year higher than man has ever known it, and flood the parched uplands; even this may be the eventful year, which will drown out all our muskrats. It was not always dry land where we dwell" (587).

I have linked that water to the imagination, and in the book one can see Thoreau drenching his life again and again, baptizing himself seven-times-seven in Walden Pond. Life is given us in the images we have of it, and Thoreau is always working to reimagine his life, to re-vision it through the irrigation of the images in which it comes to him. He is constantly working that life over in the imagination, flooding it again and again with fresh imagery, in order that something new about it be revealed. The image of the water that may (or may not) rise again this year makes an important point I have so far seemed to obscure. In one sense, of course, it is right for Thoreau to insist that the universe answers to *our* conceptions (399), but in another sense they are not ours at all. It's the *water* that does the work of unsettling and rearranging the landscape they inhabit. That water is not us, or even ours. It is Thoreau's image for what Heidegger thinks as *die Lichtung,* the event of opening, of spacing, of opening a space where the light can pool and shine and show. I have (weakly) called it imagination, and it is clear that as such it is not distinctly ours at all. I cannot survey the contents of my imagination as I can the contents of my sock-drawer. What appears in my imagination appears spontaneously, as unpredictably as a river floodtide in spring. I can ask for water, but I cannot make it rain. I can work and work on my lines, but I cannot add a cubit to the stature of even a single sentence. That, if it comes, is grace. The poet, as Heidegger says, is not the one who wills, but the one who is willing. Not the one who violently insists on pushing through her own way of seeing, but the one who is willing to be the necessary witness: the one willing to register, to be marked by (as with Thoreau's Nilometer), whatever flow of water may come.[13] They are *our* conceptions, those that come to us here and now, the ones to which *we* are the essential witnesses; but they are not conceptions we have at will made for ourselves. At most we can, through our willingness to be tested—to be those who are the measurers—give those conceptions a home: "We might try our lives by a thousand simple tests; as, for instance, that the same sun which ripens my beans illuminates at once a system of earths like ours. If I had remembered this it would have prevented some mistakes. This was not the light in which I hoed them. The stars are the apexes of what wonderful triangles!" (330f.).

To try one's life by these thousand simple tests is to try to uncover new images for one's ordinary tasks and requirements, images that

13. Martin Heidegger, "What Are Poets For," in his *Poetry, Language, Thought,* trans. Albert Hofstader (New York: Harper and Row, 1971), 140f.

will let them appear to one in new ways. As we hoe our beans in the light of the sun, we ordinarily don't consider that same light falling elsewhere. We think of the sun (if we think of it at all) as ours alone, as if it were our own particular source of warmth and illumination. But now to think of it, and thus of all our stars, as the apex of a triangle in which its relation to us is but one side, is to be put in mind of something quite important: the other two sides. First it is to be put in mind of the possibility (at least) of forms of life other than one's own; it is to become aware of the possibility (at least) of "other worlds"—perhaps just down the road—sharing one's light. "What distant and different beings in the various mansions of the universe are contemplating the same [star] at the same moment!" And it is also to be put in mind of the third side of the triangle: one's own relation to those others. "Who shall say what prospect life offers to another?" Yes, "if I had remembered this it would have prevented some mistakes."

Much of *Walden* is taken up with this sort of re-visioning. Some of the most familiar, and most powerful, instances have to do with reimagining the character of Thoreau's apparently wastrel life.

> If I should attempt to tell how I have desired to spend my life in years past, it would probably surprise those of my readers who are somewhat acquainted with its actual history; it would certainly astonish those who know nothing about it. I will only hint at some of the enterprises I have cherished.
>
> In any weather, at any hour of the day or night, I have been anxious to improve the nick of time, and notch it on my stick too; to stand on the meeting of two eternities, the past and future, which is the present moment; to toe that line. You will pardon some obscurities, for there are more secrets in my trade than in most men's, and yet not voluntarily kept, but inseparable from its very nature.
>
> To anticipate, not the sunrise and the dawn merely, but, if possible, Nature herself! How many mornings, summer and winter, before any neighbor was stirring about his business, have I been about mine! No doubt, many of my townsmen have met me returning from this enterprise, farmers starting for Boston in the twilight, or woodchoppers going to their work. It is true, I never assisted the sun materially in his rising, but, doubt not, it was of the last importance only to be present at it.
>
> So many autumn, ay, and winter days, spent outside the

town, trying to hear what was in the wind, to hear and carry it express! I well-nigh sunk all my capital in it, and lost my own breath into the bargain, running in the face of it. . . . At other times watching from the observatory of some cliff or tree, to telegraph any new arrival; or waiting at evening on the hill-tops for the sky to fall, that I might catch something, though I never caught much, and that, manna-wise, would dissolve again in the sun.

For a long time I was reporter to a journal, of no very wide circulation, whose editor has never yet seen fit to print the bulk of my contributions, and, as is all too common with writers, I got only my labor for my pains. However, in this case my pains were their own reward.

For many years I was self-appointed inspector of snow-storms and rain-storms, and did my duty faithfully; surveyor, if not of highways, then of forest paths and all across-lot routes, keeping them open, and ravines bridged and passable at all seasons, where the public heel had testified to their utility.

I have looked after the wild stock of the town, which gave a faithful herdsman a good deal of trouble by leaping fences; and I have had an eye to the unfrequented nooks and corners of the farm; though I did not always know whether Jonas or Solomon worked in a particular field to-day; that was none of my business. I have watered the red huckleberry, the sand cherry and the nettle tree, the red pine and the black ash, the white grape and the yellow violet, which might have withered else in dry seasons.

In short, I went on thus for a long time, I may say it without boasting, faithfully minding my business, till it became more and more evident that my townsmen would not after all admit me to the list of town officers, nor make my place a sinecure with a modest allowance. My accounts, which I can swear to have kept faithfully, I have, indeed, never got audited, still less accepted, still less paid and settled. However, I have not set my heart on that. (336f.)

What looks to those "somewhat acquainted with [his] actual history" like wasted time or lack of ambition, to Thoreau can be seen as his "business." The tramps through the woods, the keeping of odd hours, the obsessive and apparently pointless observations noted down in his journal, the playful concern for strayed animals, his haunting of the margins of field and town: all this is reimagined by

Thoreau as his *work*. He is an inspector of snowstorms, a surveyor of byways, an observer at the sun's levée, a correspondent for an obscure journal. In all these ways he is a faithful keeper of neglected accounts, disciplined by the need to do the job well, no matter that fees for his services will not be forthcoming. Everything, even the most humble of his bodily functions, can be imagined as an essential contribution to the community: pissing in the woods—another way of "drenching" reality—waters "the red huckleberry, the sand cherry and the nettle tree, the red pine and the black ash, the white grape and the yellow violet, which might have withered else in dry seasons." In this passage it is as if Thoreau sees himself as necessary to keeping the colors of the world alive, preventing through his imagination the world from bleaching into various shades of gray: "I got up early and bathed in the pond; that was a religious exercise, and one of the best things which I did. They say that characters were engraven on the bathing tub of king Tching-thang to this effect: 'Renew thyself completely each day; do it again, and again, and forever again.' I can understand that" (393). All of us take regular baths, but how many of us see them as a daily baptism, as a "religious exercise" from which we step renewed completely? For us, a bath is a personal and social necessity, a useful way to begin the day; it is not, as it was for Thoreau, an occasion of grace, consciously imagined as such.

Not all of Thoreau's imaginative re-visions of his life concern only himself. There is his famous passage on the railroad, one that turns on the word "sleeper," which is another term for "crosstie": "We do not ride on the railroad; it rides upon us. Did you ever think what those sleepers are that underlie the railroad? Each one is a man, an Irishman, or a Yankee man. The rails are laid on them and they are covered with sand, and the cars run smoothly over them. They are sound sleepers, I assure you. And every few years a new lot is laid down and run over; so that, if some have the pleasure of riding on a rail, others have the misfortune to be ridden on. . . . I am glad to know it takes a gang of men for every five miles to keep the sleepers down and level in their beds as it is, for this is a sign they may sometime get up again" (396).

These sentences exemplify the way the ethical momentum of the book derives from its play of images. The moral energy of Thoreau's critique is inseparable from his having found in the punning use of "sleeper" an image that reveals something about the railroad and its costs that had been hidden—or, if not wholly hidden, at least unappreciated—in our ordinary view of it as a method of fast and efficient transportation. So it also is with the image of one's house as a box

(346) or of the young farmer pushing his barn before him down the
road (326) or of Thoreau's own good behavior as a kind of demonic
possession (331). All these images reveal something not otherwise
able to be seen.

> The poet makes poetry only when he takes the measure, by
> saying the sights of heaven in such a way that he submits to its
> appearances as to the alien element to which the unknown god
> has "yielded." Our current name for the sight and appearance
> of something is "image." The nature of the image is to let some-
> thing be seen. By contrast, copies and imitations are already
> mere variations on the genuine image which, as a sight or spec-
> tacle, lets the invisible be seen and so imagines the invisible in
> something alien to it. Because poetry takes that mysterious
> measure, to wit, in the face of the sky, therefore it speaks in
> "images." This is why poetic images are imaginings in a dis-
> tinctive sense: not mere fancies and illusions but imaginings
> that are visible inclusions of the alien in the sight of the famil-
> iar. The poetic saying of images gathers the brightness and
> sound of the heavenly appearances into one with the darkness
> and silence of what is alien. By such sights the god surprises
> us.

That is Heidegger, of course, from "'. . . Poetically Man Dwells . . .'"
(225f.), but he could easily be writing about (or *for*) Thoreau. Thoreau
too sees the discipline of the poet as "imagin[ing] the invisible in
something alien to it." An image is a "visible [inclusion] of the alien in
the sight of the familiar." Many have seen the crossties on which the
rails are laid, and many have known them to be called "sleepers"; but
Thoreau includes in that familiar phenomenon, experiential and linguistic, a glimpse of something "alien," of something new and unfa-
miliar and uncanny. In his mouth the word "sleeper" is invested with
the power to reveal something not otherwise seen. "Did you ever
think what those sleepers are that underlie the railroad? Each one is
a man, an Irishman, or a Yankee man. The rails are laid on them and
they are covered with sand, and the cars run smoothly over them."
The image thus becomes—always already *is*—a "sight or spectacle"
that "lets the [ordinarily] invisible be seen," and lets it be seen right
there in the familiar. The ordinary is re-visioned, and thus becomes
an occasion of grace, and perhaps even of ethical witness. "By such
sights [i.e., by such sightings of the alien in the familiar] the god
surprises us," says Heidegger.

But we are thus surprised not only by, say, the inclusion into our world of the permanently sleeping Irish that our morning train to Boston runs upon; the poet brings something more alien than that into our familiar neighborhood. What is most uncanny about the work of the poet is its way of bringing one to see and feel the *continual* possibility of the familiar's sacramental transformation into the alien. The real power of an unexpected and revelatory image is not what it actually lets one see there and then (though in the case of a great poet like Thoreau that in itself may be powerful almost beyond all our words of praise); rather, it is the sense that there are innumerable other images where that one came from. The power of poetry is not only that it lets us see; it lets us see the seeing, and thus lets us see the possibility of even more surprises as the unknown god yields to its alien element, to the sights and sounds that appear against the bright background of the sky. One way to say this would be to say that great poetry reminds us, even in the apparent inevitability of its particular images, of the inexhaustible power and reach of the imagination, and thus of the transience and partiality of any particular manifestation of it: namely, this one. Without devaluing itself by the admission, great poetry proclaims its own conditionality; and it does so by letting one see poetry itself as the work of the imagination, of a particular imagination, one situated in a particular language and body and time. The images of a poet are *things:* they wear on their faces the conditions of the life within which they came to appearance. (That is why the words of a poet are so clearly her own: a line from Adrienne Rich won't be confused with one from A. R. Ammons.) But one of those conditions is a metacondition. Great poetry always invokes (what one might call, too weakly of course) the imagination itself. It always invokes (though not necessarily in an explicit trope) the nameless, featureless godhead: the bright sky out of which everything appears. It always gestures at the clearing, *die Lichtung,* at that open and opening space—the space between luminous sky and darkening earth—within which the act of poetic inclusion, of measuring, happens. Looking down into the well, or across at the pond, from the dry land on which one stands, one is conscious of that intervening space, and of the alternation of drenching and drying out that goes on there. Poetry proclaims, simultaneously, both its inevitability and its contingency: this line is *true,* a fixed star to light one's way; but there is more light to come. In *die Lichtung* necessity and contingency are one. "There is more day to dawn. The sun is but a morning star."

In *Walden* it is the *discipline* of re-visioning that becomes the sacrament, the occasion of grace. In the book one sees Thoreau bringing to bear on his life, in all its ramifications, a particular sort of imaginative attention. One of his most characteristic activities, his detailed naturalistic descriptions of his environment, serves as a metaphor (or perhaps as a scaffold) for the discipline required by his larger task of fronting the conditioning facts of his life. When painstakingly surveying the bottom of the pond "with compass and chain and sounding line," or discriminating the various colors of ice found in the ponds round about, or noting the habits of the whippoorwills, or carefully observing "the forms which thawing sand and clay assume in flowing down a deep cut," Thoreau is doing more than just filling a diary with curious facts. This is natural history of quite unusual distinction. This is a *discipline,* an activity of thinking that teaches one to (in Wittgenstein's famous injunction) "look and see," to pay attention to what is there. Most of the time, of course, we don't see what is there. Whether doing philosophy or walking in the woods, we mostly see what we expect to see, what we have been told and taught to see: "The universe constantly and obediently answers to our conceptions." (Wittgenstein in his philosophical remarks is especially concerned with those "conceptions" that are rooted in the "pictures" inherent in our grammar.) In order to "look and see," one must first learn to see those conceptions, to detach them—momentarily—from the world they constitute; and that is a hard discipline. It must be learned, and one way it is learned is *practically.* "Don't think, but look!" said Wittgenstein. The danger in thinking is that one will do nothing but trace round and round again the dimensions of one's comfortable cell, while all the time believing oneself to be striding through open fields. One needs a discipline, a way of training one's attention toward a particular sort of goal. For Thoreau, that discipline is variously practical: he surveys the pond's bottom, or tracks a fox, or builds a house with his own hands, or hoes beans, or writes. The point of those activities is not just themselves and their characteristic pleasures, nor even the "products" they lead to. They are ways to learn to pay a particular sort of attention. "If you stand right fronting and face to face to a fact, you will see the sun glimmer on both its surfaces, as if it were a cimeter, and feel its sweet edge dividing you through the heart and marrow, and so you will happily conclude your mortal career" (400). But such fronting of facts is not a simple matter of holding one's eyes open. It isn't a matter of keeping a journal or of merely wanting to get things right. It demands practices, disciplines, that reinforce the reality of the Wittgensteinian distinction between what we ordinarily *think* (about houses, or beans, or ponds, or persons) and what we can come to *see* about them. And once we have learned to make that distinction, it becomes possible to see them in a new way.

> There is some of the same fitness in a man's building his own house that there is in a bird's building its own nest. Who knows that if men constructed their dwellings with their own hands, and provided food for themselves and families simply and honestly enough, the poetic faculty would be universally developed, as birds universally sing when they are so engaged. But alas! we do like cowbirds and cuckoos, which lay their eggs in nests other birds have built, and cheer no traveler with their chattering and unmusical notes. . . . I never in all my walks came across a man engaged in so simple and natural an occupation as building his house. We belong to the community. (358f.)

The point of disciplining oneself in some practical task is not (*per impossibile*) decisively to free one's vision from the enabling constraints of imagination; it is to become aware of all the unnoticed ways that "we belong to the community" in what we see and think. An economically efficient division of labor (hiring carpenters to build one's house, buying one's food from the market rather than sowing and reaping in one's own field, reading books others have written) may actually have led one to subcontract to others the heart of one's life. "No doubt another *may* also think for me; but it is not therefore desirable that he should do so to the exclusion of my thinking for myself" (359). To learn to "look and see" is not to learn to dispense with all conceptions. It is, first, to learn to see the ordinarily invisible conceptions always already there in our seeing, to learn to see them by having them highlighted by the ways in which our concrete practices of, say, building, farming, and writing cast up phenomena (sagging rafters, poor yields, stillborn sentences) that put the lie to those conceptions. True, the universe reliably answers to our conceptions but, as Heidegger insisted, there is also a darkness in the earth that resists all our conceptual attempts to illuminate it. There is a constant struggle between lighted world and dark earth, a struggle to which our self-concealing technological practices normally blind us. We need to put ourselves into that space in between, where the struggle is going on and where we can become aware—through their failure—of the presence of those pictures that silently condition our experience. And that awareness can develop in us the "poetic faculty" of the singing birds, a faculty that can solicit *new* images to reveal to us our condition. We shall live in some house or other; we shall inhabit some world or other of tropes and images. But will the house be one we ourselves have built, or will it be one we have, like the cowbird and the cuckoo, merely taken over from some other maker? To live "sincerely" is to discipline oneself to self-reliance. It is to have paid attention to the ways in which one belongs to the community, to the ways in which one's thinking and living is common. Ordinarily, our condition is the common one; no wonder it is so poor. But one's steady attention to the common can transform it, setting the stage for new communities, built on new "conceptions" to which the universe will (for a time) "answer" (399). Discipline in self-reliance can awaken the "poetic faculty." The singing bird can thereby build its own nest, just as a man like Thoreau can build his own house (albeit on Emerson's land, borrowed for the occasion).

I have said that it is the discipline of re-visioning that becomes the sacrament, and it is (in Thoreau) the connection of this discipline with the more bodily practices of building, hoeing, walking, and surveying that establishes the regulative idea of reality at its heart. "Be it life or death, we crave only reality. If we are really dying let us hear the rattle in our throats and feel cold in the extremities; if we are alive, let us go about our business" (400). If the house is poorly built, the roof will sag and leak: that is reality. If the beans are poorly hoed, the weeds will choke them out: that is reality. If the sounding line is tangled, the water's depth will remain unknown: that is reality. And if the image one lives out is conventional or turbid or flatteringly grandiose, the life it conditions will suffer thereby: that too is reality. To re-vision one's life is not a matter of fancy or fantasy. It is not a matter of blithely taking what first comes, nor of just making up what one wants. One feels constrained—not just any image will do; not just anything goes. One struggles with the dark earth to bring something to light, just as one struggles with the maddening tendency of wet line to tangle and of bitter weeds to grow up among the beans. To pay this sort of imaginative attention to things is a practice of sincerity; it is a particular sort of truth-telling. As in prayer, one beseeches. Just as there is a way of hoeing beans in which every stroke of the hoe asks for grace and accuracy and strength, and just as there is a way of driving nails that with each blow begs the perfect combination of power and delicacy, so too there is a way of thinking and writing that hopefully submits itself to the space between earth and sky in search of just the right words to speak to and of our condition. "Be it life or

death, we crave only reality." In Thoreau's mouth, these words are not
the philosophical thesis of Realism; no, they are phenomenological
expressions of a certain kind of practice of imaginative attention.
They are indications of a subjectivity formed by a particular sort of
discipline, a discipline that (to use Heidegger's imagery) puts one in
the measureless space between earth and sky and sets one there the
task of measuring oneself against the godhead. One does that work of
measuring—notice the realism (but not the metaphysical Realism)
implied by that image—by fronting oneself to facts, by finding in
those facts (some of which are the facts of one's own conditioning
imagination) the alien substance to which the god has (for a time)
yielded. Such a measuring requires patience, scruple, sometimes
guile, and always a willingness to walk on into futurity, leaving the
enterprises of the old—the old self—"like stranded vessels" (331). It
is no wonder that Thoreau calls himself a sojourner.

By working over his life as he does—by making of it a sincere account: truth disciplined by imagination; imagination disciplined by
truth—Thoreau makes it a thing endowed with a particular kind of
Pathos. It is a thing that carries on its face the conditions of its own
making. It does not pretend to speak for and to everyone; it intends
only to show the conditions of the life it knows in New England. It
tries to be transparent to itself, to front its own constitutive facts, to
notch on its stick its own present moment. More, it is a thing—this
account, this life, the book *Walden*—that alludes to more than just
itself and its particular conditions. In it one encounters not just the
specific images through which Thoreau's life is at present flowing,
and not just the surprising and unpredictable appearances of new
images that will deepen and redirect that flow; one also comes to
front the unnamable source of those images. One comes in this book
to the edge of the forest's deepest clearing, where one must learn to
sit quietly in hope that the animals will show themselves by turns, or
one comes to feel the tidal pulse of the subterranean sea on which our
dry land at present floats and out of which it aboriginally came. The
facts that the book fronts through its various disciplines of imaginative attention are finally known as the familiar but alien element to
which the unknown god yields. There is only this world, no other; but
"God himself culminates in the present moment, and will never be
more divine in the lapse of all the ages" (399). This intimation of the
unknown god (as Heidegger imagines it), this possibility of seeing the
familiar invested with traces of revelatory numinosity, preserves
one's life against both complacency and impropriety. The recognition

that there is every hope of a new conception of one's conditions, that there is always the possibility that the water will rise to drench again the parched uplands in which we commonly dwell: such a recognition frees one, to a significant degree, from one's captivity to the conditions, and thus the life, one has hopelessly inherited and desperately is passing on. Having seen the act of seeing, one can now appropriately ask for—look for—other ways to see.

> With thinking we may be beside ourselves in a sane sense. By a conscious effort of the mind we can stand aloof from actions and their consequences; and all things, good and bad, go by us like a torrent. We are not wholly involved in Nature. . . . When the play, it may be the tragedy, of life is over, the spectator goes his way. It was a kind of fiction, a work of the imagination only, so far as he was concerned. This doubleness may make us poor neighbors and friends sometimes. (429f.)

That is not metaphysics, not—as many have thought—the affirmation of some spiritual substance one may call the Oversoul. It is ethical recognition of our condition as both constrained and freed by the imagination. It is the assertion that our present condition, constituted as it is by our conceptions, is both inevitable but contingent. We do not ourselves make our lives, but we can undertake to have them made different. We are not free to make them what we will, but what they will come to be made through our efforts is not something that can now already be known by us.

Thus in the writing of his life as a narrative conditioned by imagination, as "like a fairy tale and the Arabian Nights' Entertainments" (398), and yet as a life that in its writing seeks to offer "a simple and sincere account" of itself (325), a life that "crave[s] only reality" (400), Thoreau has made a thing—a book, a form of life, a subjectivity—that stands in the middle and looks two directions at once. It toes the line of the present moment, standing firmly on the earth and wedging its feet down through the muck to place them on "a hard bottom and rocks in place." And at the same time it puts itself "beside [itself] in a sane sense." It is aware of the present moment, of that *"dry land"* on which we live, as the meeting place of two eternities. It is aware that whatever we see we are conditioned to see, and aware as well that the source of that condition can be beseeched to yield itself again and anew to our disciplined attention to the spectacle of the familiar.

Good Games and True Stories

Walden is self-reflection turned into a particular kind of art. The thing Thoreau made—his "simple and sincere account" of his two years in the woods—takes himself, the conditions of his own life there in nineteenth-century New England, as the focus of its attention. But not every instance of poetic dwelling on the earth as a mortal needs to be so obviously autobiographical. As an example of another kind of writing that achieves some of the same specificity and resonance as Thoreau's, I look—more briefly—at Norman Maclean's *Young Men and Fire*.[14]

Walden is a young man's book;[15] *Young Men and Fire* is not. Maclean died in 1990, at the age of 87, leaving the book not quite in its final state; although for a long time he had hoped to write about the subject, he had begun to draft a manuscript only in his seventy-fourth year (vii). The book recounts a terrible event (a "catastrophe," he frequently calls it): the forest fire in Mann Gulch, Montana, on 5 August 1949 that took the lives of thirteen young U.S. Forest Service Smokejumpers. Maclean, who grew up in Montana and who all his life—even while earning his living as a professor of English at the University of Chicago—kept a cabin at Seely Lake in that state, had seen the Mann Gulch fire still burning a week or so after the blowup that killed the young men, and he had never been able to get the disaster out of his mind. As a young man Maclean fought fires himself, and thus knew firsthand the danger of the kind of frightful death those men suffered. This book of his old age pays a debt not just to those thirteen, but to Maclean's own youth, to the elite young men and women—"often troubled"—that he had taught through a long and distinguished career, and (perhaps most of all) to his wife, who had died of cancer of the esophagus. The book is, in many ways, a memorial.

Like *Walden*, Maclean's book is hard to characterize justly. It is about a particular event, and it struggles to tell the truth about that event, in that struggle even requiring its author to master technical material about mathematical models of fire-behavior and about fuel-types and moisture content; but it is not a work of journalism, or history, or science (any more than *Walden* is). It is, to use Maclean's

---

14. Page references in my text are to Norman Maclean, *Young Men and Fire* (Chicago: University of Chicago Press, 1992).

15. Although not published until 1854, the book was begun at Walden Pond in 1846, when Thoreau was twenty-nine.

own characterization, and one invested with a great deal of particular
meaning for him, a *story:*

> Although young men died like squirrels in Mann Gulch, the
> Mann Gulch fire should not end there, smoke drifting away
> and leaving terror without consolation of explanation, and con-
> troversy without lasting settlement. Probably most catastro-
> phes end this way without an ending, the dead not even know-
> ing how they died but still "alertly erect in fear and wonder,"
> those who loved them forever questioning "this unnecessary
> death," and the rest of us tiring of this inconsolable catastrophe
> and turning to the next one. This is a catastrophe we hope will
> not end where it began; it might go on and become a story. It
> will not have to be made up—that is all-important to us—but
> we do have to know in what odd places to look for missing parts
> of a story about a wildfire and of course have to know a story
> and a wildfire when we see one. So this story is a test of its own
> belief—that in this cockeyed world there are shapes and de-
> signs, if only we have some curiosity, training, and compassion
> and take care not to lie or to be sentimental. (37)

To render the Mann Gulch fire as a story is to fill in the "missing
parts." Some of those parts are things that can be contributed to the
account by history and science. Some of what are missing are some
facts: Why did the lightning-strike fire in Mann Gulch so quickly turn
from being a manageable blaze into an inferno moving up the ridge
faster than the men could run? Why did the party of firefighters first
move toward the fire and then turn back? Did the "escape fire" set by
the squad leader Wag Dodge contribute to the death of the young men
at the same time it was saving his own life? Why did Eldon Diettert,
who reached the top of the ridge just behind the survivors Sallee
and Rumsey, turn away from the opening in the rocks they passed
through, thus giving up his only hope of safety? These are questions
that require truthful and factual answers; even if some of the answers are not now possible for us to discover, because the facts are
unrecoverable, it is still our task to try to answer these questions in
that truthful and factual way, "tak[ing] care not to lie or to be sentimental." "Unless we are willing to escape into sentimentality or fantasy, often the best we can do with catastrophes, even our own, is to
find out exactly what happened and restore some of the missing
parts" (46f.).

But not all the "missing parts" are of this sort. There is also the responsibility of the storyteller to go further into the minds of his characters than is possible (or proper) for a historian: "If a storyteller thinks enough of storytelling to regard it as a calling, unlike a historian he cannot turn from the sufferings of his characters. A storyteller, unlike a historian, must follow compassion wherever it leads him. He must be able to accompany his characters, even into smoke and fire, and bear witness to what they thought and felt even when they themselves no longer knew. This story of the Mann Gulch fire will not end until it feels able to walk the final distance to the crosses with those who for the time being are blotted out by smoke. They were young and did not leave much behind them and need someone to remember them" (102).

The distinction of the storyteller is not just the requirement to enter imaginatively into the sufferings of his characters, however that may be managed. (And here the danger of sentimentality, noted at page 37, is acute.) The deepest task of the storyteller is to find "some shape, form, design as of artistry in this universe we are entering that is composed of catastrophes and missing parts" (46). To do history may be (for Maclean) merely to pile up fact upon fact, to answer those questions that scholarship and science can answer, to note the questions that can't be answered so, and then to cease, having done what one can do. But to tell a story is a matter of finding some shapeliness, some form, some artistry in the scrupulously reconstructed and reported events that concern us. That is the way a catastrophe like the Mann Gulch becomes a tragedy. The discipline of Maclean's kind of storyteller is to tell a *true story*. That is not just history, and it is certainly not sentimental or lying fantasy. It is to see that here "in this cockeyed world there are shapes and designs, if only we have some curiosity, training, and compassion" (37).

Notice that the "shapes and designs" Maclean is asserting to be the proper material of the storyteller are present "in this cockeyed world." I suspect the word is carefully chosen: to see the shapes and designs in the world (in *this* world: no other is in question) one has to cock one's eye; one has to squint, to peer sideways. And that is what the storyteller is doing, with her "curiosity, training, and compassion." She is learning how to squint, to look slant, in order to see the patterns she is needing. She cocks her eye as a way of beseeching things to reveal hidden designs and colors. It is only in "this cockeyed world," the world of one who knows that what one sees is always already conditioned by the slant of one's eye; it is only in the cockeyed world that "shapes and designs" begin to show themselves. This is connected, I think, to what Maclean says about the need for the storyteller to "follow compassion wherever it leads him." It is finally compassion—a "suffering-with"—that will allow us to understand what it was like "to walk the final distance to the crosses with those who for the time being are blotted out by smoke." And compassion is not, or not only, a function of the intellect or of the feelings; it requires of us that we call upon the imagination—upon the resources of figures, tropes, and metaphors—in order to suffer with those we are not. Such compassion is not the writing of sentimental interior monologue for those about to die, words that through the feelings they provoke may falsely console us with the ugly illusion that we now know what it was like for those young men to be "blotted out by smoke." Such literary empathy is only a fantastic simulacrum of what is wanted. Genuine compassion is a matter of connecting ourselves to them by finding in language some orderly and satisfying way ("shape, form, design as of artistry") for *us* to tell *their* story (always keeping in mind the all-important difference between the two). Our suffering with them is, partly at least, given in that gap between the honest memorial we wish to give and our recognition of its inevitable condition in our own language. Try as we might to conjure, only the living speak; never the dead. That is the storyteller's suffering, a recognition of mortality, of conditionality and finitude, that might—*might*—bridge some of the gap between the old man and the suffocating boys. But only if the suffering shows up in the storyteller's language itself. Here again the notion of truth is crucial for Maclean. Speaking of his own attempt to tell the story of the Mann Gulch fire he says:

> True, though, it must be. Far back in the impulses to find this story is a storyteller's belief that at times life takes on the shape of art and that the remembered remnants of these stories are largely what we come to mean by life. The short semi-humorous comedies we live, our long certain tragedies, and our springtime lyrics and limericks make up most of what we are. They become almost all of what we remember of ourselves. Although it would be too fancy to take these moments of our lives that seemingly have shape and design as proof we are inhabited by an impulse to art, yet deep within us is a counterimpulse to the id or whatever name is presently attached to the disorderly, the violent, the catastrophic both in and outside us. As a feeling, this counterimpulse to the id is a kind of craving for sanity, for things belonging to each other, and results in a comfortable feeling when the universe is seen to take a garment from the rack that seems to fit. (144)

But that "comfortable feeling" is dangerous; our need to find a story that the universe fits can lead us into the familiar and hackneyed territory exploited by popular art, which is sentimental and consoling. This happened with the Mann Gulch fire too, when it became the subject of "Red Skies of Montana," a 1952 movie starring Richard Widmark, Constance Smith, Jeffrey Hunter, and Richard Boone. The movie finds a story in the fire, to be sure, but it is "the old 'disgraced officer's plot,' the plot in which the military leader has disgraced himself before his men, either because his action has been misunderstood by them or because he displayed actual cowardice, and at the end the officer always meets the same situation again but this time heroically (usually as the result of the intervening influence of a good woman)" (155). In the film the foreman lights an "escape fire," just as did the foreman at Mann Gulch. In the first instance, as with Wag Dodge, his men ignore the fire, are killed, and the foreman is disgraced; in a second fire, however, "his crew heeds him, and everybody lives happily ever after" (155).

That may be a consoling story—if not, why is it so popular?—but it is not what happened at Mann Gulch. It is an "escape into sentimentality or fantasy" (46) and is therefore unworthy of the true storyteller. The storyteller is under the discipline of truth: "A story that honors the dead realistically partly atones for their sufferings, and so instead of leaving us in moral bewilderment, adds dimensions to our acuteness in watching the universe's four elements at work—sky, earth, fire, and young men" (144). Notice: the dead must be honored *realistically*. It is not enough to make up some story and claim it for them as their own; that would dishonor them and leave us even more morally bewildered. Only the truth will do. At the same time, finding a true story of the Mann Gulch fire (or of anything else) is not just a matter of finding out all the "facts" about it. Those are likely to be disorderly, violent, and catastrophic, whether inside us or outside (144). The impulse to storytelling is an impulse to sanity, to finding out *how things belong to one another* (144); and that is a task for the imagination, for that "counterimpulse to the id" (144) that puts things—words, sentences, lives—together as if they belong so. The storyteller is under the discipline of truth, but it is always already truth disciplined by imagination. There is no other way to make sense of things. Without the synthetic work of the imagination, connecting and illuminating by means of its tropes, nothing properly "belongs" to anything else. Our lives are conditioned by—given substance by—the stories we tell about them, and "the remembered remnants of these stories are largely what we come to mean by life. The short semi-

humorous comedies we live, our long certain tragedies, and our spring-
time lyrics and limericks make up most of what we are. They become
almost all of what we remember of ourselves" (144). What is left over
and above our stories are the free radicals, mere events (disorderly,
violent, catastrophic), the detritus of life that eventually drags us
down back again into the merely organic.

The storyteller is under the discipline of truth, and Maclean's nuanced understanding of our need (as storytellers) to retain the regulative idea of truth while simultaneously resisting the easy (and by now
familiar) antithesis of truth to imagination is illustrated in the story
he tells about the physicist A. A. Michelson.

> When I was a young teacher and still thought of myself as a
> billiards player, I had the pleasure of watching Albert Abra-
> ham Michelson play billiards nearly every noon. He was by
> then one of our national idols, having been the first American
> to win the Nobel Prize in science (for the measurement of the
> speed of light, among other things). To me, he took on added
> luster because he was the best amateur billiards player I had
> ever seen. One noon, while he was still shaking his head at
> himself for missing an easy shot after he had had a run of
> thirty-five or thirty-six, I said to him, "You are a fine billiards
> player, Mr. Michelson." He shook his head at himself and said,
> "No, I am getting old. I can still make the long three-cushion
> shots, but I'm losing my touch on the short ones." He chalked
> up, but instead of taking the next shot, he finished what he had
> to say. "Billiards, though, is a good game, but billiards is not as
> good a game as chess." Still chalking his cue, he said, "Chess,
> though, is not as good a game as painting." He made it final by
> saying, "But painting is not as good a game as physics." Then
> he hung up his cue and went home to spend the afternoon
> painting under the large tree on his front lawn.
>
> It is in the world of slow-time that truth and art are found as
> one. (145f.)

This story, though it may strike one as a bit too pat, as if Michelson
(and perhaps Maclean as well) had many times rehearsed the lines
for the benefit of younger and more impressionable colleagues, is nevertheless indicative of Maclean's conviction in writing *Young Men and
Fire*. In the slow-time of great age, Maclean is trying to tell a story in
which truth and art are one. Part of his ability to do that is his having
seen the point of Michelson's remarks that day at the faculty club. In

the final analysis, billiards and chess and painting and physics—and storytelling—are all good games. And what makes them good? In them there is a clear difference (clearly perceivable to the competent players, at least) between playing them well and playing them poorly. All these activities put one under a strenuous discipline: not just anything goes in chess or in physics or in painting. Playing the game, there is a clear sense of what counts as a legitimate move and of what doesn't, and of what counts as a brilliant stroke or as a blunder. Calling them *games,* as Michelson does, is a way of acknowledging that the source of the compulsion the player feels to meet the standards of the activity is not external to the play itself. It is to acknowledge that one doesn't have to be a metaphysical Realist in order to appreciate the difference (in billiards, chess, painting, or physics) between doing it right and doing it wrong. Playing billiards is certainly not about learning how the world *an sich* Really Is; yet the game is such that one can say things like, "Michelson is a true billiards player; he plays the game truly and well: the way it ought to be played." Even as the game it is, billiards is an activity to which the notion of truth is indispensable. Likewise, the notion of truth, certainly indispensable to a storyteller like Maclean, doesn't require to be spelled out in terms that would satisfy Descartes or Bernard Williams. It doesn't require an "absolute conception of reality." There is no doubt that a physicist or a painter feels herself under the discipline of truth: whatever she is doing, she must *get it right,* must *do it right.* She is not, in the first instance, in the business of satisfying herself, and she can't change the rules in order to make her attempts at whatever she is doing more successful. She must answer to something "over there." She is under discipline. (Michelson feels compelled to deflect Maclean's compliment: he knows he has lost his touch on the short shots. And he knows he can't do first-rate physics—the best game—any more; that's why he spends his afternoons on his front lawn with brush and canvas.) Yet what sort of account must we give of this discipline? Must we assume that in her need to get it right she is answering to something metaphysically "absolute," something truly and ultimately describable independent of the activity she is pursuing? In Michelson's voice Maclean is saying no. Physics is a very good game, perhaps the best we have so far learned to play; yet in it, finally, "truth and art are found as one." Physics—like storytelling—is a *game;* both are aspects of our "counterimpulse to the id," of our "craving for sanity, for things belonging to each other" (144). Both are ways of "measuring ourselves against the godhead," a measuring in which truth and art are found as one. That's what both Michelson and Maclean (and Heidegger, sometimes) learned in the slow-time of their old age.

It is not easy for us to learn this, and it certainly is not easy for us to say what we have learned when (and if) we do. One of the most impressive things about *Young Men and Fire* is its philosophical awkwardness, the way the old man out there on the steep and baking ridge keeps stumbling over his own old-man notions of story, history, truth, poetry, and art. He doesn't quite know how to bring them together—none of us do—in such a way that justice is done both to imagination and to intellect (a justice in which "truth and art are found as one"). (Those familiar terms of contrast—"truth" and "art"— are of course an indication of just the problem he faces; we cannot help resorting to such tired distinctions, even in our attempts to get out from under them.) A perfect example of the awkwardness I am talking about is found in a passage recounting Maclean's last visit to Mann Gulch:

> It frightened me that this was probably my last trip into Mann Gulch and my last chance to find out the truth of the tragedy. I kept myself going by reminding myself that the only poem I had a chance of writing about the Mann Gulch fire was the truth about it. I kept saying to myself, "Remember, you've got to keep thinking straight even if you're too dry to swallow." I added, "Or to recite poems." I added as a final truism for myself, "True poems are hard to find." (202)

The culmination of this thought comes a few pages later, when— exhausted, dehydrated, nearly incapacitated—he and his friend are about to leave the gulch, having figured out those things that were troubling him:

> Looking down on the worlds of the Mann Gulch fire for probably the last time, I said to myself, "Now we know, now we know." I kept repeating this line until I recognized that, in the wide world anywhere, "Now we know, now we know" is one of its most beautiful poems. For me, for this moment, anyway, the world was changed to this one-line poem. Finding it a poem, I hoped I could next complete it as a tragedy, more exactly still as the tragedy of this whole cockeyed world that probably always makes its own kind of sense and beauty but not always ours.

There was no water for the horses until we reached Willow
Creek. I was sorry for the horses, but I was no longer sorry for
us. Such can be the effect of the beauty of a very short poem.
(207f.)

It is awkward, perhaps even maudlin, for Maclean to identify an
avowal of knowledge—in this case knowledge of some quite specific
facts of Mann Gulch topography—with a poem, just as it is awkward
for him (and embarrassing to us) to indulge the kind of lyricism one
finds in his prose here (and elsewhere). But the awkwardness is deliberate, or at least unavoidable (for him), since he is trying to get
beyond the normal contrasts—fact versus imagination; truth versus
poetry; games versus real life—that shape both his material and our
appropriation of it. We don't yet know how to talk, to talk *well*, about
those linguistic and behavioral practices in which there is an absolute
sense of discipline—a full-fledged requirement of *truth*, of getting it
right and of doing it right—and, at the same time, an understanding
that this sense of absolute requirement in no way requires an "absolute conception of reality."[16] We don't know how to represent those
practices that ask us to "measure ourselves against the godhead," a
"measuring" as strenuous and as exhilarating as any we know of, and
yet a "measuring" that refuses to countenance any substantial characterization of that against which we measure. No wonder we fall
back on broken-backed terms such as imagination, poetry, game, *die
Lichtung,* the godhead.

Walden is undoubtedly a great book, an ornament of world literature; *Young Men and Fire* is, I suspect, not. But both books profit
from their comparison, Thoreau's by showing us how remarkable his
achievement really is, Maclean's by showing us the reach of his ambition. Both are books about the making of books: stories about storytelling; accounts that try to account for their own accounting. In that
way they gesture at the godhead, at the unrepresentable source of all
representation, and they measure themselves against it. But mostly
they are about something quite concrete and visible: what it is like to
live in New England, as a Yankee man or even as an Irishman, in the
middle of the nineteenth century; what it is like to chase a loon
around a pond; what it is like for an old man to try to climb a hot and
treacherous hillside trying to solve a thirty-year-old mystery; what it
is like to see your wife die with dignity and pain; what it is like for a

16. Bernard Williams develops the idea of an "absolute conception of reality" in his
Descartes: The Project of Pure Enquiry (Harmondsworth, England: Penguin Books,
1978), 65–67, 211–12, 245–49.

nineteen-year-old to see roiling smoke blot out his future. And both
are books that gather the fourfold; they are books that carry on their
faces the conditions of the life that brought them to appearance.
Partly they do that through the autobiographical testimony they contain; but they do it more through their spiky and arresting language.
Neither allows itself to recede into some easy use we might make of
it. In spite of its years of perdition as a school text, *Walden* is not just
Bestand. And *Young Men and Fire*, like (I suspect) the man who wrote
it, won't lie down and roll over the way we want it to. Both are books
redeemed for us by their particular kind of awkwardness: philosophical; linguistic; spiritual. Neither has the smooth surface and ready
availability that marks the anonymous products of *die Technik*, and
in both cases their refusal to submit is connected to a notion of truth
that doesn't separate itself from the workings of imagination. Such
recalcitrance is rare, in books or in people; and it is the best indication of the justice—I think—in claiming for them the status of Scrip-
ture in a way of being religious that escapes our normal nihilism.

As a Necessity Requires

The Plain Sense of Things

After the leaves have fallen, we return
To a plain sense of things. It is as if
We had come to an end of the imagination,
Inanimate in an inert savoir.

It is difficult even to choose the adjective
For this blank cold, this sadness without cause.
The great structure has become a minor house.
No turban walks across the lessened floors.

The greenhouse never so badly needed paint.
The chimney is fifty years old and slants to one side.
A fantastic effort has failed, a repetition
In a repetitiousness of men and flies.

Yet the absence of the imagination had
Itself to be imagined. The great pond,
The plain sense of it, without reflections, leaves,
Mud, water like dirty glass, expressing silence

> Of a sort, silence of a rat come out to see,
> The great pond and its waste of the lilies, all this
> Had to be imagined as an inevitable knowledge,
> Required, as a necessity requires.
>
> —Wallace Stevens

I should like to be able to think of this book as a footnote to that poem, as a kind of philosophical illustration of it—something, I fear, like a Classic Comics version of Proust.[17] We began our thinking about religion with a sense of having at last reached—after all the leaves, the pages, have fallen—the plain sense of things, a sense of having come to the only possible end of a great experiment of the imagination that started (for us) with someone like Hesiod or the Yahwist, was extended by Plato's mythopoeic genius, began to go fatally sour in the seventeenth century, and then finally concluded in some rented rooms in Sils Maria and Genoa in the 1880s. The gods have abandoned, or have been driven off, the old homeplace at last, leaving us— us end-of-century, Western intellectuals—here among the flaking columns, the muddy water, and the skeltering leaves. No wonder we feel that a "fantastic effort has failed, a repetition / In a repetitiousness of men and flies." Indeed it has been a fantastic effort, an effort we now can see as a kind of fantasizing, repeated again and again in different keys, and always unaware; but now we have come to see it for what it was (and still is), and to see that leaves us chilled. I have thought of our "blank cold" as the intellectual mood Nietzsche calls normal nihilism, and like Stevens I have thought that a proper attention to the imagination—and in particular to the imagination cultivated as a religious discipline—was the key to our being able somehow and sometime to pass through this mood and into our next.

Stevens's poem does us the great service of insisting that imagination lies both at the beginning and at the end of our efforts in this book. "Yet even the absence of the imagination had / Itself to be imagined." To the Yahwist or to Plato or to Descartes—at least in our normal philosophical representation of them—the exercise of the imagination was not a part of what they were about. They thought they were telling the flat truth about things, not fashioning new tropes for them. But from where we stand we can see these men imagining that very absence of imagination. They were inventing characters and telling stories—positing values, spinning vocabularies—all along, no

17. The poem can be found in Wallace Stevens, *The Collected Poems* (New York: Knopf, 1954), 502.

matter what they imagined to the contrary. We can (we think) see them plainly now; and see ourselves too, who are beyond such fantastic consolations. But even our normal nihilist view of "the plain sense of things"—the necessary absence for us of any credible theological or metaphysical imagination, the deflating triumph of the age of values and its pragmatism—is just as much imagined as is any practice or thing that might answer to our need for more than that plainness. One does not suddenly start (or stop) measuring oneself against the godhead; one has been doing that all along, if only one could have imagined it so. The philosophical and cultural movement from the Yahwist to Plato to Descartes to Nietzsche and then to us, which in its broad sweep now seems utterly unavoidable, "had to be imagined as an inevitable knowledge."

Three things are discovered in Stevens's remarkable line. First, our grasp of our own history is present only in the story we tell of it, that is, is necessarily an effort of our own historical imagination. Second, in that respect we are no different from Plato, Descartes, or the Yahwist, since they too cannot make sense of themselves without some form of storytelling about who they are and where they come from. And third, no-one is free to tell whatever stories about herself that she wishes. One's history, philosophical or personal, has to be scrupulously imagined "as an inevitable knowledge." It has to be imagined as "required, as a necessity requires."

That third is the crucial point, and must not be overlooked. In the normal run of things, as we all know, it is not possible for us to think or to believe whatever we wish: reality rarely gives us that free a hand. It is equally impossible that we should "[imagine] as an inevitable knowledge" whatever just happens to come to mind when we open ourselves to fantasy. Imagination contains its own hard discipline of truthfulness, of getting it right, as anyone who has tried to write a poem, or who has played make-believe with children, knows. The *Pathos* of our history—personal, political, cultural, philosophical, evolutionary, mythical—lies in its contour of inevitability. Event must be seen to follow event "as a necessity requires." Even good postmodernists like us, who have eschewed any hope of a theological or metaphysical metanarrative to give sense to our career through time, haven't given up the hope of showing how some specific tissue of contingencies inevitably led to this, and exactly this, particular outcome. In the right hands, and for the short term, genealogy can have all the traditional pathos of *Geistesgeschichte*. There may have been, for example, no cosmic destiny guiding my infantile traumas, no god who took a particular interest in my abusively rigorous toilet-training, say; but even so, those events, contingent and banal as they were, made me what I am. Here too there is the uncanny *Pathos* of inevitability: I am what I was made to be. To be known as a child of efficient causation can be just as impressive as to be known as a child of God, so long as the first characterization is argued in a sufficiently detailed and circumstantial way, and so long as it can be "imagined as an inevitable knowledge."

The *Pathos* of the Yahwist, or of Plato, or of Descartes, or even of Nietzsche, is contained in their claims to be telling us the inescapable and necessary truth (the "plain sense") about things, the truth about *us* and our ineluctable situation. They are effectively—brilliantly—imagining their assertions, imagining them for *us,* "as an inevitable knowledge." In their success we cannot but think what they do. In Nietzsche's imagination, of course, those claims of inevitability, formerly grounded in the full presence of some god or Form or *Ding-an-Sich,* are rendered philosophically problematic; but they are not thereby eliminated. They could not be. We all, including Nietzsche himself, live at any moment under the sway of truth; we all acknowledge the commanding power of what we now inevitably assent to. We—we end-of-century, Western intellectuals—find our normal nihilist understanding of "the plain sense of things" impressive because it impresses itself on us in a particular way: we *cannot help* seeing things the normal nihilist way we see them, once we have seen them that way. Even the post-Nietzschean recognition that we see things only as we are *conditioned* to see them, and conditioned not by hardwired Kantian categories but by tropes and images and grammatical pictures which themselves have a history and can in no way be checked for their "accuracy," is not—in itself—sufficient cause for us to abandon our hopes and claims of seeing. (Nietzsche still sees what he sees, and cannot help doing so—even if what he sees is the historicity of all his seeing.) But this post-Nietzschean recognition of contingency can and will on reflection diminish the *Pathos* of any particular thing seen, *itself included;* and that is because that recognition, like any such, can and will *itself* be recognized to be "just another way of seeing things."

Indeed, I have been arguing that such diminishment is the common inheritance of normal nihilists like us, who realize that the best we can hope for are contingent and transient "values"—structures of interpretation, ways of reckoning—to guide us on our way. We are in an odd bind, therefore. We cannot help thinking what we now think, if we have thought about it at all; yet in the next moment we recognize that whatever it is we now think, it's just one way of thinking among

many, one to which we are susceptible for causes—images, tropes—
we ourselves (perhaps) can actually recount, along with their history.
The *Pathos* of our thinking at present what actually we do think,
resides in our sense of its proper inevitability; yet that inevitability
now seems to us post-Nietzscheans to be of a quite particular kind: an
imagined necessity, a particular and contingent way of seeing that
has been "imagined as an inevitable knowledge"—and that insight
(the contingency of what I see and think) seems so to us in virtue of
another inevitability (crudely put, the inevitable replacement of Plato
by Nietzsche), itself equally imagined. In that iteration of imagined
necessity, in that alternation of the moment of truth and the moment
of *another* truth (a truth now about the *conditions* of that first truth:
and so on up the ladder to exhaustion), some of the *Pathos* of the
particular vision, of *any* particular vision, leaks away, leaving room (I
have argued) for some dangerous substitutes. Truth devalues itself in
our scrupulously truthful imagination of truth's conditions in the
imagination.

Dewey was right: in our time the problem with supernatural religion is belief.[18] However lovely and powerful the stories of the gods
and their minions are, there's just no way that for us they are "required, as a necessity requires." To say that we can't really believe in
them is just to say that we aren't now forced to; they are not any more
for us "an inevitable knowledge." There are plausible—more plausible—alternative accounts of the phenomena upon which the supernatural has based its claims on us: in the public square, or at least in
the college quad, genes now compete with gods, and win. For us, full
Pathos, full belief, comes only with an intellectual or artistic inevitability. Having put myself to the question with all the scruple I can
muster, it's only what I cannot help saying that seems genuinely true,
and therefore capable of being believed and acted upon with a clean
heart. That's what we admire (surely on the whole naively) as the
achievement of natural science. Those folks in the smelly buildings
across the campus, we fondly imagine, have figured out a way of putting the question to themselves in such a way that at the end of the
day—experiments done, data collected and analyzed—there's only
one possible answer for them to give. Science, we think, creates and
enforces intellectual techniques of a kind that, when they are fully
engaged, exact from our brains single and inevitable responses to our
queries. Thus scientists—in this popular representation of them—are
a species of ascetic visionary. By a kind of rigorous and sometimes

18. John Dewey, *A Common Faith* (New Haven: Yale University Press, 1934), 29.

painful self-discipline, they induce the universe to speak about itself through them. That's why we are justified in believing and doing what they say: the words proceed from the disciplined inquirers' mouths with an aura of inevitability; they cannot help saying them.

Surely, as I say, that is a naive picture of the way natural science actually works, or could work; but such necessity is nevertheless a central part of our common epistemic and ethical ideal. (That's why this representation of science is, for all its crudity, so powerful, and why cheerful debunkers like Feyerabend are so distrusted by those who in one way or another profit from the representation.) Probability may be the guide to life, as Bishop Butler thought, and even possibility has a certain cachet; but there's nothing like necessity— epistemic and ethical—for quieting the sharpest hungers of our sort of intellectual. "Here I stand; I can do no other." Both Kantian duty and Cartesian certainty—equally absolute—can take Luther's words as their motto. And like it or not, absolute duty and absolute certainty constitute our culture's most powerful and familiar and reliable sources of *Pathos*. Even the ironist intellectual can (and needs to) say, "Here *I* stand; *I* can do no other": ethnocentrism (Rorty) or voluntarism (Sartre) replaces Reason or Grace as the explanation of the necessity of one's inhabitation of one's particular form of life. The loss of a metaphysical ground does not mean the loss of the *Pathos* of inevitability. It just means something else has been substituted as the object of that *Pathos,* and as the source of that necessity.

But what for us has that *Pathos?* Certainly not supernatural religion: which of us *has* to believe in God?[19] My fear, expressed in this book several times already, is that for us normal nihilists the object of our ultimate *Pathos* will become either the self's addictive will to novel satisfactions or the existence of a particular historical form of life. Crudely put, we normal nihilists will end up either strung out or locked down: either eating up ourselves and the earth in our search for the next great high; or fully folded into, more or less happily, some specific manifestation of *das Man*. Dewey thought that science itself, natural or social, could take up the slack left by the gods' departure, and that the dedicated, tolerant, truthful, democratic scientist could become for us a moral paradigm comparable in impressiveness to the religious and metaphysical visionaries of our past. That hope now

19. At one point Cornel West claims that *he* does when he says that "the self-understanding and self-identity that flow from [the Christian] tradition's insights into the crises and traumas of life are necessary *for me* to remain sane." I don't know what to make of that claim, especially as it seems inconsistent with his words quoted in note 1 above.

seems as dated as those old predictions that by the end of the century we'd all be flying our own helicopters, wearing dorky-looking unisex clothing, and zipping off to Luna-Port for the weekend. Too much of science's claim on our attention was fostered by the metaphysical Realism that was its childhood companion. Take that away and science, like Christianity, becomes just another method of agriculture.

I have been arguing that for us the only thing capable of taking the place of supernatural religion is a life that takes as central to itself a particular kind of social practice. If Dewey wanted to erect the scientist as a figure proof against our cynicism or gluttony or abandon, I have (following Heidegger, of course) wanted to raise up instead a poet like Thoreau or Maclean. In their kind of writing, and that is to say in their kind of thinking and building, there is still the full *Pathos* of inevitability. Both know themselves to be working under the discipline of truth. Sentence must follow sentence, board must follow board, thought must follow thought, "as a necessity requires." Nothing in the thing is accidental or excessive or ornamental or invisible; everything—every word, every action, every stroke of the chisel shaping a farmhouse windowsill or every sweep of a scythe through a field of grass—*tells*. The work of writers like these shows a constant and overriding concern to "get it right," to "tell the truth," to offer "a simple and sincere account," to "stand right fronting and face to face to a fact"; so much so that it is not an exaggeration to see their lives, as recounted in their books and things, as something like prayer: beseeching the godhead to invest itself in "the alien," hoping to be surprised as the clearing opens before one and one is struck by seeing there the ordinarily invisible. *That* is the discipline of truth; that sort of questioning, that sort of continually renewed asking-for, is the piety of thinking.[20] What comes as the result of such petition must come "as an inevitable knowledge." It must come with the force of a revelation, the fact that splits us like a scimitar and happily ends our mortal career.

Yet for all its rigor, for all its recognition of being under the discipline of truth, the practice of thinkers like Thoreau or Maclean in no way requires a metaphysical Realism to support it. It is truth they seek, certainly, but truth disciplined by imagination. There is no hope in them of transcending the conditions of appearance; indeed, no *sense* for them in such a hope. Doing his natural history of the neighborhood, or playing with the loon, Thoreau knows that Nature answers to our conceptions of it; and Maclean, trudging around in Mann

20. Martin Heidegger, *Vorträge und Aufsätze* (Pfullingen: Neske, 1967), 1:36.

Gulch thirty years after the fire, knows too that it's a properly shaped story he's after. Yet in each of them that knowledge—which is knowledge of contingency, of genuine human mortality—is in no way in service of any philosophical skepticism, however mild. It would even be wrong to think of them as ironists. (They do not doubt their particular perspectives, although they do recognize them as such.) They do not anxiously fear or regret the imagination, and I think that's because each of them found in it all the inevitability, all the necessity, that metaphysics or religion had promised and failed to deliver. In the imagination and its requirements they have found a way to measure themselves against the godhead, a way that offers both the satisfactions of occasional achievement—"By such sights the god surprises us"—and the humility of more frequent failure. In this discipline there is the constant dialectic between the necessity of doing things as it is proper to do them (imagination's own discipline of truth, I have called it) and the freedom—the need—always to try again, to listen better, to front the fact more directly. However good and true a poem may be, there is always call for more such poems. Poetry is a practice that destroys both idolatry and anomie. There is, after all, the right word to speak, the one properly required for this sentence (if only I can hear it), but it is a word properly required *only* for this sentence, not for the next or the next. It is the right word, the only right word; but it is not the Word of the Lord, nor of any of the Philosophical Fathers.

But why call this practice of poetic dwelling a way of being *religious?* I keep that word for two reasons. First, I think each of the three structural features of Western religiousness deployed in Chapter 1 has its significant analogue in the practices of writing and living I have recounted. There is the binary division between *die Lichtung* and whatever appears in it: between, on the one hand, the imagination (that weak but inevitable word) as the ultimately conditioning source of whatever we see and, on the other, whatever in particular we *do* see, ourselves included. There is also a relation of ground here: the recognition that without the gift of a constituting image there would be nothing—no-thing—at all to be seen. The universe constantly and obediently answers to our conceptions, and only to them. ("The universe" is of course just a such conception too, as is "conception" itself.) That which Heidegger tropes as "the godhead" is necessary for the existence and the intelligibility (the two are inseparable, of course) of whatever else there is. And finally there is the sense that our proper relation to *die Lichtung* has been compromised, and that our health depends upon righting it. Both Thoreau and Maclean are moved to their writing by a sense of neediness. By working on the house, or by working on the book, they are in fact working on themselves. The account they give of things is finally an account of themselves, and in their disciplined submission to the necessities they discover in their imagination of their materials, they also discover (not once for all, of course) the haleness that marks a proper relation to things.

Of course in the practices I have been valorizing there is no mythical or metaphysical construal of these structural features. Neither Thoreau or Maclean feels any great need to construct a "true world" over and above this one in order to account for their need and ability to "measure themselves against the godhead," nor do they try to give a philosophical representation of the dialectic of necessity and freedom they discover within their practices of building/dwelling/thinking. They are, on the whole, content to take their practices as they come to know them, without reaching for any justification outside their own demands. How is that possible? How can they have not succumbed to the need, so familiar to us, to account in a particularly philosophical way for the lives we are living? I believe it is because the *Pathos* of inevitability they discovered in the imagination was great enough to displace any need for more than that. If one has felt the inevitable rightness of a sentence or a hoe-stroke, if one has known the inescapable demand for a "simple and sincere account" of one's own life, and if one has recognized the possibility of answering to that demand by the making of true things, then one does not need the (as it will then seem) secondary satisfaction of "justifying" all that. Thoreau was right: to be split in two by some fact one has fully fronted is to end one's mortal career. To *career* is to move at full speed, to rush. The rushing that is ended by the fully fronted fact is, among other things, the rush to metaphysical justification. Nothing is more mortal—more human, more deathly—than the career toward philosophical representation, toward discovery and worship (frequently resentful) of the "true world" that underwrites and explains. (And nothing is more mortal than our reaction of hurt and cynicism—or at least ironic anxiety—when we find it is not there.) What can stop this familiar career? Only the *Pathos* of inevitability; only our ability to imagine "as a necessity requires." It is in that imagined necessity—in the things one has made that show it forth—that one faces up to the conditioning facts that constitute one. In those things, the things themselves, there is *Pathos* sufficient to the day.

That brings me to a second reason for wanting to characterize thinkers like Thoreau and Maclean as religious figures. I have several times said that in our culture of normal nihilism we miss the sacraments traditional supernatural religion used to provide. In particular, we miss the *Pathos* of the god or of the Absolute that both gives us a sense of propriety—the discipline of a life that is properly our own to live—and yet pricks us with the necessity not to settle for any present form of it. "Be ye perfect, even as your Father in heaven is perfect." There is a way for you to be, there is a proper Form to which you answer in your attempts to do and be good; but its realization is forever beyond your grasp. One measures oneself against the godhead, but one can never identify oneself or one's present form of life with it. But for us, of course, the pantheons and the various philosophical Absolutes are gone, dissolved into a congeries of values; and good riddance too. There's no way any more that we can imagine Yahweh or the Form of the Good "as an inevitable knowledge." Other forms of imagination have supplanted those, forms of imagination that have caught themselves in their own conceptions. In the self-referential whirl of the life of values that knows itself, and knows its knowing, as itself a life of values, there is little if any defense against the complementary dangers of the runaway pursuit of addictive excitements or the hunkered-down escape into the comforts of reaction.

The practice of poetic dwelling on the earth as a mortal offers an antidote (I don't say the *only* antidote) to those dangers. It is a practice that, without any need for an "absolute conception of reality," puts one under a discipline as absolute as any that can be imagined. Thoreau's attempt to front his facts, to notch the conditions of the present moment on his stick in a "simple and sincere account," or Maclean's attempt to discover a story that realistically honors the dead young men of Mann Gulch, and at the same time justly memorializes both the patient courage of his dead wife and his own sense of the grave's close approach: these are efforts of working on oneself, of working oneself and one's situation over in the imagination, that demand from one a commitment to truthfulness, to propriety, that is absolute and overriding. Writing—and living—this way always puts one under the sway of truth, or (better) truthfulness; one cannot say or do whatever one wants, however one wants to do it. One knows there is a proper way to tell the story, or to construct the book, or to build the house, or to hoe the beans. One is aware of oneself as under discipline. The point is not one's various satisfactions, which may or may not come; the point is to *get it right*. One is measuring oneself against the godhead. One is continually asking for the right word or image or hammer-blow or hoe-stroke. Under such discipline, required to honor such propriety, one has access to a *Pathos* capable of standing against the blandishments of the mall.

In the same way, the practice of poetic dwelling—that is, the various practices of building/dwelling/thinking that can be collected under that rubric—offers effective defense against the temptation to identify oneself with some particular form of *das Man*. To recognize that whatever life one is living is conditioned by tropes and images given to one by the disciplined activity of measuring oneself against the godhead, and further to recognize that those tropes and images, no matter how truthful, no matter how "required, as a necessity requires," are capable of being supplanted by truer—more inevitable—ones, is to recognize the impossibility of being contented with what one has. It is to know oneself to be under the discipline of experiment; it is to know that the act of measuring is never done once for all. Such an inability to remain satisfied with the current state of play in one's life is quite different from the febrile hunger of the shopper rushing from place to place in hope of new thrills. It is not satisfaction or self-enhancement one is after; it is propriety. One wants truthfulness, sincerity; one wants to have found the story that realistically honors one's subject (which may be, but need not be, oneself). And that is never done. One starts the narrative where one is, of course, and one uses the materials ready to hand; but one always knows oneself to be under the prophetic demand to change one's life by a better account of its conditions. "Be ye perfect, even as your Father in heaven is perfect." It may even be, as Thoreau hoped, that the search for this sort of imaginative integrity can show us how to replace the demonic morality of our ordinary "good behavior"—whatever that is like—with a way of living that does more justice to ourselves and others.

The question that remains is the question that originally provoked this book: Is this a way of being religious that can withstand the devaluation of our normal nihilism? Can the *Pathos* of this particular sort of practice remain secure and undiminished in spite of everything we have learned about ourselves from Nietzsche and his heirs? In particular, can we resist the claim that poetic dwelling on the earth as a mortal is just another shop in the mall, soon to become passé? I think the answer is yes, so long as we remember to whom and about whom the question is asked. It is asked to and about *us,* us end-of-century, Western intellectuals, those who at an impressionable age read the Yahwist, Plato, Descartes, Nietzsche, and Rorty and whose history is therefore ineluctably that history. Indeed, it is the fact that that history is so inescapably *ours,* that it comes to us "as an

inevitable knowledge" (albeit now also recognized to be "imagined")
that is the key. It is *we*—you and I—who realize that we cannot just
think and live however we want. It is *we*—you and I—who know ourselves to be under the discipline of the conditioning imagination: we
cannot but think what we do. To recognize that part of what we cannot help think is that such thinking is always a beseeching, is always
a matter of measuring ourselves against something that exacts an
absolute discipline of truthfulness and yet refuses the consolation
of an absolute achievement of truth: to recognize that is to be who *we*
are. It is also to recognize that this discipline of truthfulness now
proceeds without the support of metaphysical or theological assurance. It is not because we know or hope for some "true world" outside
this one that we demand and work for the truthful word or action; it
is only because such truthfulness is for us *in fact* "required, as a necessity requires." No metanarrative is either necessary or sufficient to
account for that requirement, since for us any such metanarrative
would itself have to meet the very requirement it was invoked to explain; it would have to present itself, and to account for itself, "as an
inevitable knowledge." No metanarrative could explain such inevitability; none could account for it once for all. (Why? Because the question can and will arise at any level, including the level of the metanarrative itself: What requires of, and gives to, that account its
inevitability?) At best a proffered metanarrative can effectively exhibit inevitability anew, and thus (temporarily) quiet our need for it.
The point is decisive: at the demand for truthfulness, for inevitability,
for the *Pathos* of *aletheia,* our spade is turned. Nothing could, or need,
account for that demand or for its fulfillment; for us they are "proto-
phenomena."[21] Poetic dwelling on the earth as a mortal is the practice
of truthfulness, not a theory of truth, and for *us* therefore it is not a
practice alongside and equal to others; it is not just another shop in
the mall.

Could it become so? How could one confidently say no? Certainly it
seems possible to imagine (even if only faintly) people who were free
of any overriding discipline of truthfulness, who did not in any way
understand the requirement—except perhaps as a way to some temporary thrill or to some necessary accommodation with their peers—
that they "get it right." For them, perhaps, a regime of pleasure, not
truth, would matter most. Were such folks to become the norm, it
seems possible that our sense of propriety could entirely disappear.[22]

---

21. The word derives from Wittgenstein. See *Philosophical Investigations,* sec. 654.
22. In fact, it doesn't seem—to me—possible that such folks *could* become the norm.

But those people, perhaps dimly imaginable, would not be us, and one does not know exactly what sort of attitude to take to their alleged possibility. Does it make sense to fear the possibility that the things most dear to one might someday seem silly or even wicked? One disadvantage of such fear is that it might encourage one to try to ensure that such a circumstance never come to pass, thus presenting us with the all-too-familiar (and all-too-disheartening) spectacle of the intellectual who sees himself as the little boy with his finger in the dike, holding back the flood of unreason. On the other hand, I suppose it might be sensible to regret, rather than fear, the possibility of propriety's disappearance, just as one can regret that one has to die. But such a possibility is not a cause for despair in *us;* we are people who care about truthfulness, and who seem likely to continue to do so. The third founding question of this book is, What should it mean *for us* to be religious? I have answered it thus: to dwell poetically on the earth as a mortal. That the question and its proper answer might at some time be unintelligible or trivial is not to the point, so far as I can see. This is *our* life: Should we not live it as simply and sincerely and joyfully as we can?

I find it incredible that any human society could survive without shaping itself up into coherent normative practices, practices that enforce the difference between what is and what is not done, and point out one has the discipline of truth—whatever it might be called. Nevertheless, I am reluctant to identify my inability to believe something with its transcendental impossibility. That's why I am willing to consider in this paragraph the notion that our concern for truth and truthfulness might disappear.

INDEX

James C. Edwards is professor of philosophy at Furman University in Greenville, South Carolina. He is the author of *Ethics without Philosophy: Wittgenstein and the Moral Life* (1982) and *The Authority of Language: Heidegger, Wittgenstein, and the Threat of Philosophical Nihilism* (1990), both published by the University Press of Florida.